# China's National Innovation System

Adrian Băzăvan

# China's National Innovation System

## Industrial Policy, Funding Mechanisms and Foreign Investment

palgrave
macmillan

Adrian Băzăvan
Bucharest, Romania

ISBN 978-981-97-3264-7 ISBN 978-981-97-3266-1 (eBook)
https://doi.org/10.1007/978-981-97-3266-1



This Palgrave Macmillan imprint is published by the registered company Springer Nature Singapore Pte Ltd.
The registered company address is: 152 Beach Road, #21-01/04 Gateway East, Singapore 189721, Singapore

# Acknowledgements

I express my deepest gratitude to my advisor and mentor, Professor Ph.D. Cătălin-Emilian Huidumac-Petrescu, for his indispensable guidance and support throughout all the stages of this research. His outstanding academic knowledge, extraordinary passion for research and strong motivation to teach served as my highest inspiration during my research programme at the Bucharest University of Economic Studies, as well as throughout my life.

I would also like to thank the advisory committee that have always provided their time and crucial advice, allowing the improvement of this research. Moreover, I would like to thank the leadership and the administration of the Doctoral School of ASE Bucharest that have always been very helpful, understanding and responsive, with all the steps along this journey.

Not the least, I would like to thank the leadership, professors and administration professionals at Yenching Academy of Peking University, that has provided immense research support during my two years university programme between 2017 and 2019.

# About this Book

After four decades of sustained high-rate economic growth, China has become the world's second largest economy. Concurrently, the nation has also become the world's second largest R&D spender, outperforming the European Union as a whole, and it is expected to surpass the USA within the next decade. Moreover, China became both the first source and first destination of foreign direct investment in the world and is rapidly climbing global value chains in an increasing number of sectors. In this transition, China is openly aiming to become an innovation powerhouse with the edge in crucial technologies.

In its relationship to global markets, China positions itself in an asymmetric type of integration, aiming to be a leader and holding critical nods of the global supply chains, while also striving to achieve complete autonomy from foreign technology and becoming immune to global supply shocks. But beyond mainstream discussions about the roles China plays within global supply chains, the actual understanding of the real performance and future perspectives of its national innovation system is still limited.

This research aims to provide a deeper understanding of China's technological progress, thus contributing to a better-informed decision-making process. Based on a thorough qualitative and quantitative review of China's industrial policy documents and relevant commercial databases, adding to a set of focused interviews with relevant stakeholders in China, the study highlights the status and prospects of the nation's innovation system. It does so by examining in detail its key features, including the public policies, funding mechanisms for innovation, inbound and outbound foreign investment,IPR legislation and patents, public perception towards technology, priority industries and others. The study also identifies the main innovative actors including government, industry and academic or research institutions, highlighting the patterns of interaction among them. The findings are showcased in a focused case study on the artificial intelligence industry. On this basis, the conclusions section illustrates the main characteristics and trends of the national innovation system in China, as well as its strengths, challenges and prospects. Lastly, the findings will serve to advance several policy recommendations for the EU.

The key findings are the following:

- The role of the Chinese government in the national innovation system is evolving from being a central actor, to becoming a facilitator, enabler, partner and even customer to private-led technology companies. However, in the sectors deemed strategic that exceed market capacity or interest, the government is willing to intervene strongly with funding, subsidies, favourable policies, but also with market restrictions that go as far as complete bans against foreign companies.
- Policymaking should be seen through the lens of structured uncertainty. Governance in China, including in the field of innovation, is highly decentralised and varies significantly between regions and industries. While the central government establishes top-down policy targets, subnational authorities are competing to find the best policy methods for achieving the goals.
- Experimentation, pilot projecting and non-regulation are essential innovation policy instruments, allowing room for experimentation. However, after technologies reach maturity, the government can take abrupt regulatory measures to solve ongoing systemic risks.
- Overall, funding for innovation is fast increasing and is mainly driven by private actors, with little contribution from the state. As it is highly atomised across a large population of companies, funding is mainly inclined towards applied research and experimental development. Therefore, there are few Chinese companies that have the

capacity to engage in costly radical innovation and compete with American peers.

- Both inbound and outbound foreign direct investments contribute significantly to China's technology advancement through knowledge spillovers, technology acquisitions and access to talent. China used to be a destination for investment, but as it accumulated financial resources, it became a net investor abroad, especially through mergers and acquisitions in sectors relevant to technology.

Therefore, China's technological progress is based on a unique mix of limited liberalisation and opening, imitation and incremental innovation, FDI, technology spillover, strong R&D spending, pilot projecting and policy experimentation, competition between authorities at different levels of administration, emerging clusters specialised in particular technologies and burgeoning market scale, and others. During the last decade, China's leadership has raised innovation as a top national priority, with the 14th Five-Year Plan highlighting the country's ambitions towards achieving technology independence and global pre-eminence in key strategic sectors.

However, progress has been uneven, with some industries and administrative regions emerging as truly global leaders, while others falling short of their targets. While Chinese companies have shown increasing capacities across the board, they still face key bottlenecks and dependencies in priority technologies, such as semiconductors, software and operating systems, algorithms and even globalisation and discursive influence in relevant international contexts.

Overall, within the last decades, China has succeeded to transit from a labour-intensive and low-cost manufacturing base to a sophisticated, knowledge-based economy. Technology progress and resulting productivity gains were key to achieve this remarkable catching up and elements of this transition could serve as study cases for other developing economies that aim to achieve similar results. However, it is important to note that given the particularities of China's political, economic and social system, its solutions might be only fit for China.

Finally, in the context of rapid technological breakthroughs in China,the USA and the rest of the world, the paper puts forward a set of 10 policy recommendations to promote the technological innovation of the European Union. The EU should identify innovation as a top policy priority and act accordingly, fast, by deploying adequate resources, a variety of strategies and measures, at different levels but in an integrated approach, thus fostering domestic innovation. Domestic innovation is crucial to preserve the values of the EU, the governance system and economic prosperity.

# Contents


| | | |
|---|---|---|
| 1 | **Introduction** | 1 |
| | *1 The Transition from Industrialisation to Innovation* | 2 |
| | *2 China's Innovation Imperative* | 3 |
| | *3 Strategic Concerns and the Need to Understand China's Innovation System* | 5 |
| | *4 Scope and Aims of the Research* | 6 |
| | *References* | 12 |
| 2 | **Literature Review** | 15 |
| | *1 The Nature of Innovation* | 15 |
| | *1.1 Innovation as a Driver of Economic Growth and "Catching-Up"* | 18 |
| | *1.2 Theoretical Framework for Studying Innovation* | 19 |
| | *2 Foreign Direct Investment and Internationalisation* | 22 |
| | *3 Investment in Research & Development (R&D)* | 23 |
| | *3.1 Government Financial Incentives for Innovation Activities Performed by Private Companies* | 25 |
| | *4 Summary* | 26 |
| | *References* | 26 |

3 **Methodology** 35
*References* 38

4 **Government and Public Policies** 39
*1 Decentralisation* 42
*2 Policy Pilot Projecting and Experimentation* 43
*3 Priority Technology Areas* 46
*4 Technology Independency and Self-Sufficiency* 47
*5 The Scale of Government Intervention* 50
*6 Standardisation* 51
*7 Summary* 53
*References* 55

5 **Funding for Innovation** 59
*1 Funding for R&D* 59
*1.1 Gross Expenditure for R&D (GERD)* 59
*1.2 Basic vs. Applied Research* 60
*1.3 R&D Funding by Source (Public and Private)* 62
*1.4 Business Expenditure for R&D (BERD)* 65
*2 The Venture Capital and Start-Up Scene* 67
*3 Summary* 69
*References* 70

6 **Foreign Direct Investment and Internationalisation** 73
*1 Inbound FDI* 73
*1.1 From Process Innovation to Radical Innovation* 74
*1.2 Market Restrictions* 75
*1.3 International Concerns* 77
*2 Outbound FDI* 78
*2.1 Investment Outflows by Type and Destination* 80
*3 Summary* 83
*References* 84

7 **Other Systemic Factors** 87
*1 Introduction* 87
*2 Talent* 87
*3 Intellectual Property* 91
*4 Patents* 93
*5 Public Perception Towards Technology Adoption* 94
*6 Priority Industries* 95
*6.1 Semiconductors* 95

6.2 *ICT and the Digital Economy* 100
7 *Summary* 105
*References* 106

8 **Case Study on Artificial Intelligence** 109
1 *Government and Policy* 113
2 *Funding* 114
3 *Foreign Direct Investment and Internationalisation* 116
3.1 *Inbound Investments* 116
3.2 *Outbound Investments* 117
4 *Market Scale and Industrial Output* 119
5 *Data Availability* 120
6 *Clusters* 121
7 *Summary* 122
*References* 124

9 **Global Consequences of China's Rise in S&T and Recommendations for the European Union** 127
1 *Changes in the System of International Relations* 127
2 *Policy Recommendations for the European Union* 128
2.1 *Build a Truly Integrated European Approach to Research and Innovation* 129
2.2 *Increase R&D and Innovation Spending Significantly* 129
2.3 *Prioritise Key Strategic Domains* 130
2.4 *Nurture Domestic Tech Champions and Technological Independence* 131
2.5 *Promote the Global Reach of Domestic Companies* 133
2.6 *Enhance the Talent Pool* 133
2.7 *Encourage Experimentation and Public—Industry Cooperation* 134
2.8 *Increase University—Industry Cooperation* 135
2.9 *Power Military Research and Military-Civil Technology Flows* 135
2.10 *Build Innovation Clusters* 136
3 *Summary* 137
*Reference* 137

10 Conclusions 139

Annex I: National Talent Programmes in China 147

References 153

Index 171

# Abbreviations

| | |
|---|---|
| AI | Artificial Intelligence |
| BAT | Baidu, Alibaba and Tencent |
| BERD | Business Expenditure on Research and Development |
| CIS | Corporate Innovation System |
| CPC | Communist Party of China |
| CFIUS | Committee on Foreign Investment in the United States |
| EDA | Chip Design Software |
| EU | European Union |
| FDI | Foreign Direct Investment |
| FOF | Funds-Of-Funds |
| FTZ | Free Trade Zone |
| GDP | Gross Domestic Product |
| GERD | Gross Expenditure on Research and Development |
| GGF | Government Guidance Funds |
| GII | Global Innovation Index 2017 |
| HNTE | High- and New-Technology Enterprise |
| HSR | High-Speed Rail |
| HTDZ | High-Technology Development Zone |
| ICT | Information and Communication Technology |
| IFDI | Inbound Foreign Direct Investment |
| ILO | International Labour Organisation |
| IMF | International Monetary Fund |
| IoT | Internet-Of-Things |
| IP | Intellectual Property |
| JV | Joint Venture |
| M&A | Mergers and Acquisitions |

| | |
|---|---|
| MIIT | The Ministry of Industry and Information Technology |
| MLP | National Medium- and Long-term Program for Science and Technology Development (2006-2020) |
| MNC | Multinational Corporation |
| MOST | The Ministry of Science and Technology |
| MS | European Union Member States |
| NEV | New Energy Vehicles |
| NIS | National Innovation System |
| OECD | Organisation for Economic Co-operation and Development |
| OFDI | Outbound Foreign Direct Investment |
| PE | Private Equity |
| PCT | Patent Cooperation Treaty System |
| PPP | Purchasing Power Parity |
| SAR | Special Administrative Region |
| SEZ | Special Economic Zone |
| SOE | State-Owned Enterprise |
| S&T | Science and Technology |
| STI | Science, Technology and Innovation |
| ROW | Rest of the World |
| R&D | Research and Development |
| SDO | Standards Developing Organizations |
| SME | Semiconductors Manufacturing Equipment |
| S&T | Science & Technology |
| STEM | Science, Technology, Engineering and Mathematics |
| TMFT | Trading Market For Technology |
| TSMC | Taiwan Semiconductor Manufacturing Company |
| UK | United Kingdom of Great Britain and Northern Ireland |
| US | United States of America |
| VC | Venture Capital |
| WIPO | World Intellectual Property Organization |
| WTO | World Trade Organisation |
| Y-O-Y | Year-On-Year |

# List of Figures


**Chapter 4**

Fig. 1 Total value of industrial output by ownership types of firms (*Source* China S&T Statistical Yearbook 2007–2016, compiled by Li [2017]) 51

**Chapter 5**

Fig. 1 GERD in constant USD PPP, million (*Source* OECD Main Science and Technology Indicators 2022) 60

Fig. 2 R&D Intensity in several countries, GERD as % of GDP (*Source* OECD estimates based on the OECD Main Science and Technology Indicators Database, March 2022) 61

Fig. 3 R&D by Funding Source as a % of GERD, 2018 or latest available year (*Source* Author's compilation, based on data from OECD [2019]) 63

Fig. 4 Government direct funding and tax incentives for BERD, China, 2000–17 as a percentage of GDP, 2015 prices (right-hand scale) (*Source* OECD, R&D Tax Incentives Database, http://oe.cd/rdtax, December 2021) 63

Fig. 5 Direct government funding of business R&D and tax incentives for R&D, 2019 (latest available) as a percentage of GDP (*Source* OECD, R&D Tax Incentives Database, http://oe.cd/rdtax, December 2021) 64

Fig. 6 Main changes of presence (number of companies) of the main geographic regions between 2016 and 2021 (*Source* The 2021 EU Industrial R&D Investment Scoreboard, European Commission, JRC/DG RTD) 66

## Chapter 6

Fig. 1 China's flows and stocks of OFDI (billions USD) (*Source* China 2020 Statistical Bulletin of Outbound Direct Investment) 80

## Chapter 7

Fig. 1 Number of researchers per 1 000 employees, 2000–2020 (*Source* OECD [2021], "Researchers" [indicator], https://doi.org/10.1787/20ddfb0f-en, accessed on 29 May 2022) 88
Fig. 2 Biggest users of the PCT system, by country, 2021 (*Source* WIPO Statistics Database, February 2022, available at https://www.wipo.int/edocs/infogdocs/en/ipfactsandfigures/) 93
Fig. 3 China's integrated circuit market and domestic production, USD billion (*Source* IC Insights [2021] in Schneider [2021a]) 97
Fig. 4 China's imports of semiconductors by country of origin, 2018–2020 (*Source* China's general administration of customs in Bloomberg [2021b]) 98
Fig. 5 Share of global semiconductor manufacturing capacity by location (%) (*Source* Semiconductor industry association in Varas et al. [2020]) 99
Fig. 6 Largest internet companies by market capitalisation as of June 2022, US billion (*Source* www.companiesmarketcap.com, accessed on June 18, 2022) 101

## Chapter 8

Fig. 1 Private investment in AI by country, 2020, USD million (*Source* 2021 AI Index Report [Zhang et al.]) 115
Fig. 2 Private investment in AI by geographic area, 2015–2020, USD million (*Source* 2021 AI Index Report [Zhang et al.]) 116

CHAPTER 1

# Introduction

The shift from an industrial to a knowledge-based economy, accelerated by globalisation and the necessity for constant innovation, has reshaped the global economic landscape since the latter half of the twentieth century. This transformation has prompted governments worldwide to develop national innovation systems (NIS) in order to harness resources for fostering innovation. The chapter highlights the evolution of global innovation dynamics, with a particular focus on China's rapid ascent as a technological powerhouse. Despite traditionally relying on technology imports from developed economies, China has emerged as a leader in innovation, challenging the historical dominance of Europe, the USA and Japan. This change is attributed to China's effective utilisation of its demographic dividend, capital investment and significant economic growth, transitioning from a model based on low-value manufacturing to one driven by knowledge-intensive products and services. These efforts are contextualised within China's broader economic and industrial policy objectives, including the aspiration to lead in emerging technologies and to navigate the challenges of a middle-income trap. This course has significant global implications, in the economic, social and security realms. Through a detailed exploration of China's innovation ecosystem, the chapter sets the stage for understanding the complex interplay between economic growth, technological advancement and global competition in the twenty-first century.



A. Băzăvan, *China's National Innovation System*,
https://doi.org/10.1007/978-981-97-3266-1_1

## 1 The Transition from Industrialisation to Innovation

Beginning in the second half of the twentieth century, the world's economy began to undergo a steady shift from an industrial model to a knowledge-based one. As globalisation made the international markets increasingly competitive, constant innovation became the driving force for the sustainable development of economies, as well as the only option for companies to survive and thrive (Carraro & Galeotti, 1997; Gârleanu et al., 2012). However, innovation is a complex process, influenced by factors that vary greatly between different industries, regions and contexts (Zhang, 2021). This understanding led governments to actively develop national innovation systems (NIS) with the aim of better coordinating available resources in order to build the necessary soft and hard infrastructures, solve difficult externalities and develop policy mechanisms that facilitate innovation (Lin, 2017).

The knowledge required to achieve impactful innovation is concentrated, requiring prohibitive inputs and posing significant risks (Tambosi et al., 2019). Therefore, for a long time, the scope of technological innovation has been limited to companies in developed economies (Gong, 2021). However, over the course of the last two decades, the global technological environment has started to change, as the creation of novel, disruptive ideas and their commercial application has become increasingly multipolar. Some late-developing countries which traditionally used to rely predominantly on imports of technology from developed economies, have recently succeeded to progress and become leading actors on the global scene of innovation. Historically, it has been Europe, the United States of America (USA) and Japan leading global innovation, but currently actors such as India, Korea and China, in particular, have gradually emerged as new technology powerhouses.

During the last four decades after the reform and opening-up initiated by Chairman Deng Xiaoping, China has successfully made good use of its demographic dividend, attracted capital investment and achieved an outstanding economic growth (Gong, 2021). According to the World Bank, in 2020, China's GDP in purchasing power parity (PPP) reached USD 24.28 trillion, making it the largest market in the world, ahead of the United States and India (World Bank, 2022). This scale offers unique possibilities to both domestic and international companies, which can experiment and find market niches for their new products and ideas (Li, 2017).

## 2 China's Innovation Imperative

But China can no longer rely on unlimited capital and labour inputs to achieve its development goals (Development Solutions Europe Ltd., 2018). Times are changing and the low-hanging fruits of economic growth have already been depleted. Currently, China faces a multitude of macroeconomic bottlenecks, including the depletion of demographic dividends and cost advantages, environmental damages, energy constraints and resource shortages, as well as the lack of domestically developed core technologies (Zou et al., 2021). Therefore, a model based on low-value manufacturing is no longer sustainable, as China's economy enters the "new normal", in which extensive growth needs to be replaced by intensive growth (Zhang, 2021).

In order to avoid a middle-income trap and ensure long-term, sustainable growth, China is attempting to shift its growth fundamentals towards innovation, and actually declared its ambitions to become a global leader in the field (Chu et al., 2021). In other words, the country envisions to shift away from a resource-driven model towards a technology-driven and knowledge-intensive model. As such, landmark policies such as the *National Strategy of Innovation-Driven Development* (State Council, 2016) point out that innovation has become a key element for achieving economic growth, increasing internal consumption and reducing dependencies on external markets. At all governance levels, "innovation" has become a leitmotiv within policy documents and commercial outlooks, as a sacred mission acting as the key of progress from a backwards economy towards a prosperous one. Therefore, the Chinese government spares no effort to promote innovation and an important indicator of this is the massive increase in expenditure for research and development (R&D) during recent years, in both nominal value and as a share of GDP. In addition, the state supports an effervescent venture capital ecosystem, promotes national champions in strategic industries, and makes long-term bets on fundamental R&D (Ding, 2018).

In 1978, China launched the reform and open door policy, embracing a "spring of science" (Sun & Cao, 2020). The opening-up allowed foreign companies to come and invest in China, bring technology, capital and know-how and thus seed the early grains of a competitive industrial system. Gradually, Chinese domestic companies developed and became themselves the vehicles for the upgrade of China's industrial infrastructure (Wang & Zhu, 2021). Over time, with increased capital and accumulated knowledge, the industrial landscape became increasingly complex, with domestic companies climbing value chains and becoming competitive in sectors such as next-generation communication technologies, new energy vehicles (NEVs) and robots. After the launch of the landmark "Made in China 2025" plan and by the end of the Thirteenth Five-Year Plan (2016–2020), China also succeeded to lead the development of several emerging technologies such as high-speed railways and artificial intelligence (AI) (Zenglein & Holzmann, 2019). This coincided with the fact that China's economy became the second largest in the world in nominal value and the first in terms of PPP, a scale that supported an increase in prominence in global technology markets (Chu et al., 2021).

As far as innovation outputs are concerned, the country came to rank second in the world in terms of share of its total national value added created by the high-tech manufacturing, and third in commercial knowledge-intensive services such as business, financial and information and communication technologies (ICT). This is strongly reflected in international trade positions. China became the first exporter in the world by volume and its shares in global markets continue to rise. And that is not caused by larger quantities or by an expansion of low-cost manufacturing. On the contrary, it is caused by the fact that China's exports are shifting to higher-value-added products or from products to services whatsoever (Zhang & Zhou, 2015). Actually, China has also become the largest exporter of high-technology products in the world, with a global share of 24%. It is important to mention that the share of intermediate inputs from other countries accounts for an ever-increasing share of the value of China's exports (National Science Board, 2018). Therefore, to some extent, China is transitioning from 'Designed in California. Made in China' to 'Designed in China. Made in Southeast Asia'.

Other innovation outputs include total number of academic publications, publications in high-impact journals and citations, as well as the number and quality of patents and designs. In most of such metres, China achieved already undisputed global leadership.

In terms of innovation inputs, the nation's gross expenditure on research and development (constant USD PPP) exhibits impressive figures, as over the last two decades it has grown at an average rate of 20%

y-o-y, exceeded the EU as a whole in 2014, exceeded USD 500 billion in 2019 and is expected to exceed the US by 2030 as the world's largest spender on R&D. In terms of R&D funding intensity, China achieved 2.4% of GDP in 2020, surpassing the level of the EU—situated at 2.2%, but still behind OECD, USA, Japan and Korea.

Another important innovation input is the growth of a large talent pool whose quality has also been steadily improving. Within the last two decades, the number of university graduates in China grew tenfold, topping 7 million students per year, more than double the numbers in the USA (Lundvall & Rikap, 2022). Of these 7 million, 4.7 million are graduates of science, technology, engineering and mathematics (STEM), which is overwhelmingly more than India (2.6 million) and the US (568,000).

Overall, every year China rapidly climbs composite indexes that measure innovation, such as the *Global Innovation Index* 2021 (WIPO, 2021). According to the latest ranking, China[1] became the 12th most innovative country in the world, and the only upper middle-income nation in Top 30. It is also the first time that mainland China ranks above Japan (13th) and Hong Kong (14th). The composite ranking reflects vast improvements in indicators such as human capital and research, infrastructure, market sophistication, business sophistication, knowledge and technology outputs and creative outputs. The report shows that China has the institutional capacity, human and material resources required to achieve its objectives and close the gaps, but still it has a long way to go to achieve its full potential and reach the supply chain summits (Sun & Cao, 2020).

## 3 Strategic Concerns and the Need to Understand China's Innovation System

In recent years, China's achievements and ambitions in core technologies have raised considerable concerns in other countries about the risks posed to their interests and values. Therefore, trade tensions and technological competition have gradually become defining elements of the USA-China relations. The Director of the Central Intelligence Agency, Bill Burns, considers that technology will be 'the main arena for competition and rivalry' between China and the USA (Alisson & Schmidt, 2021).

[1] Mainland China, without Hong Kong

Eric Schmidt, former Google CEO and current security advisor in the US stated that "many Americans still have an outdated vision of China" and that "the United States now faces an economic and military competitor in China that is aggressively trying to close our lead in emerging technologies" (Schmidt, 2020) [..]: "Unless these trends change, in the 2030s we will be competing with a country that has a bigger economy, more research and development investments, better research, wider deployment of new technologies, and stronger computing infrastructure" (Schmidt, 2020).

Indeed, China's overall technology capacities have gradually grown in recent years, leading the country to become an influential actor in an increasing number of fields. On the other hand, China still has a long way to go to become THE leader across the board. It still remains behind in critical sectors, including operating systems and security software, essential semiconductors, globalisation of domestic companies and even discursive influence in relevant international organisations. The USA still leads in innovation strength, sometimes by a wide margin, on indicators such as the number of top research universities and attractiveness for talent, accountability of tech companies and the government to the public, global reach of domestic companies, and of course, core technology capacities across industries such as aerospace, semiconductors, defence, etc.

Given this background alongside the growing strategic concerns regarding technological interdependencies and polarisation, studying China's national innovation system has become essential to understand its competitiveness and innovation capabilities and thus make better decision-making in terms of international relations, trade policy and corporate plans (Sun & Cao, 2020). Traditionally, China has made more effort and has achieved better results in understanding and learning from 'the West'. It is now the time for other countries to better understand the evolution of China. China's NIS is large, heterogeneous and tremendously complex, and there has always been a tendency for over-simplification in our analysis (Lundvall & Rikap, 2022).

## 4 Scope and Aims of the Research

This research aims to bring a contribution to understanding China's technology landscape, taking stock of the state of the national innovation system and the progress made in key technology areas over the last decades. It will do so by identifying and describing the main policies, financial mechanisms, systemic causes and social institutions that drive or, by contrary, hinder, China's transition to an innovative economy. The main areas explored are: the roles of central and subnational authorities; the nature of public policies; funding for R&D and entrepreneurship; the role of foreign-invested companies; outbound investments; public perception towards technology; and other systemic factors, in an attempt to capture the entire NIS. It will explain which are the major actors and in what technology fields they operate, how they are distributed and how they interact, what is the role of private and public innovation investments, how innovation spills across the network, which technology areas are successful and which ones, on the contrary, are not. It will verify the information against a case study on artificial intelligence. Finally, the research will examine the shifts in the international relations system and will advance policy recommendations for the EU.

It is not in the scope of this research to measure the capacity, quality or level of innovation in China. The research will not answer the question "How innovative is China?"—an important topic which is due for further endeavours, requiring a different set of quantitative indicators. Instead, this research's overarching goal is to answer to the question: "How does China innovate?". It also attempts to address several long-pertaining misconceptions, revealing the arguments and contradictions of previous studies and casting light on frequently omitted elements.

The first chapter sets the theoretical background of innovation studies in general and of innovation studies in China in particular, discussing the nature of innovation, different perspectives regarding the relationship between innovation and economic growth, as well as the main schools of thought regarding foreign direct investment (FDI) and state funding for innovation.

The following chapter explains the methodology used to select and process indicators for data analysis, combining both qualitative and quantitative methods. Data collection relies on both publicly available documents and fieldwork in China. It draws on political documents and statements, commercial databases as well as on academic and policy commentaries, in addition to a series of structured, semi-structured and informal interviews that were conducted in order to validate data, collect deeper insights, clarify questions and avoid misunderstanding, with the aim to build an accurate representation of China's views.

Chapter 3 will review the complex roles played by the government within the innovation system, including an overview of the most relevant policies since 1980, with a focus on the latest major developments. It highlights China's strong commitment and growing ambitions to develop domestic capacities and independence from foreign suppliers in core technologies, as well as achieving global leadership in specific strategic sectors (Zhou & Fang, 2021). It also aims to elaborate on China's complex governance system disposed on multiple levels, which frequently acts on the basis of policy experimentation and pilot-projecting. The chapter will set the necessary background for the following analysis of China's funding for innovation.

Initially, China's innovation policy relied on a centralised approach, strong government intervention in markets, large subsidies and uncompetitive protectionist measures. However, as this approach produced mixed results and sometimes significant downsides, the Chinese government has moved towards more pragmatic, market-orientated policies. Currently, the Chinese government is not anymore the main actor of the NIS or of the domestic economy at large, but it rather increasingly acts as an optimiser, facilitator and strategy-setter. It sets guidelines and policy targets but leaves the room for adaption to subnational authorities. While as regards major reforms, the preferred path is that of policy pilot-projects in limited areas. Therefore, policymaking in China should be seen through the lens of structured uncertainty, rather than a coherent top-down approach. This type of decentralisation and experimentalism, despite shortcomings such as declining central authority and incoherent, sometimes contradicting and even wasteful regional competition, proved to be overall successful in achieving significant results.

However, the central government still intervenes strongly in those sectors considered of maximum priority, which cannot emerge naturally due to the constraints of the market's limited capacities. In such industries, China's government remains ready to provide substantial financial resources, but also to intervene through protectionist policies and picking-winner policies. State support remains crucial also to balance regional development gaps, as there is a high level of discrepancy between regions in terms of innovation capacity and economic development, with the Yangtze River provinces being much better positioned than the Central and Western ones.

Furthermore, Chapter 4 is dedicated to funding as a fundamental input factor for technological innovation. Historically, the USA has long been the world leader in R&D expenditure, from both public and private sources. However, beginning with 2008, China's R&D investment has grown remarkably, at an average annual growth rate that greatly exceeds those of other countries. Overall, China's R&D expenditure has already exceeded that of the EU and is currently the second-largest R&D performing nation in the world, accounting for 20% of the world's total R&D expenditure. China's R&D intensity, measured in R&D expenditure as a percentage of GDP, has also grown rapidly and has long exceeded that of the EU, but compared to the USA, it still has a consistent gap. Moreover, the amount and share of Chinese investment allocated to basic research as part of the total R&D expenditure are still much lower than that of the USA.

Overall, keeping the current tendencies, the country might soon exceed the USA to become the world's largest spender on R&D, while its allocation for basic research is also constantly increasing. Therefore, China's funding for innovation has recently drawn significant attention from international policymakers and researchers. However, to date, systematic research reported in English regarding funding mechanisms, their volumes, shortcomings and historical performances is rather limited (Luong et al., 2021). Moreover, as the landscape is fast evolving, research on the topic needs to be constantly updated. This study attempts to contribute to the field using data from publicly available Chinese-language policy documents and official statements, mass-media, as well as interviews collected personally by the author.

It draws attention to the structure of funding by source and industrial sectors, and finds that R&D funding in China is primarily market-driven, whereas the state has a surprising little contribution. In addition, it describes the burgeoning start-up ecosystem and new emerging methods of funding in public–private partnership. Lastly, it is important to note that the cumulated share of public funding for innovation in China coming from subnational authorities has overtaken that of the central government (the China Statistical Yearbook reveals that, for example, China's local fiscal S&T expenditure increased by an average annual rate of 25.15% between 2011 and 2018). However, given the significant differences in development and available budget between different regions, such a decentralised approach inevitably leads to significant development gaps between regions that are not alleviated by the central government. Based on the above considerations regarding the relationship between public funding and innovation capacity, the *Funding for*

*Innovation* chapter will also examine the scale and effects of government funding on innovation in China and, therefore, make several contributions to the ongoing debate about China's industrial policies and subsidies.

Based on the above considerations regarding the relationship between public funding and innovation capacity, the *Funding for Innovation* chapter will also examine the scale and effects of government funding on innovation in China and, therefore, make several contributions to the ongoing debate about China's industrial policies and subsidies.

Ever since the beginning of the reforms and opening-up, inbound and outbound FDI, alongside international trade activities, have also brought a crucial contribution to China's economic and technological development, especially by the means of technology spillovers (Sapkota & Bastola, 2017). Following Chapter 5 will discuss in detail the effects of FDI and direct foreign technology transfer on China's economic growth and technological innovation capacities, as well as the complex interactions between investing companies and the state.

Multinational companies (MNCs) are the ones that first established the country's modern industrial system, supply chains and management structures, including through direct technology transfers and knowledge spillovers (Bazavan, 2019). However, foreign companies had to comply with restrictive policies imposed by the Chinese government, which require technology transfers, joint ventures (JVs) or other kind of limitations. Such conditions for investment are usually not formally and explicitly required, as this would countervail the World Trade Organisation (WTO) rules (Sykes, 2021). However, China requires foreign investing companies to enter JVs with Chinese partners and imposes equity caps on foreign ownership, thus guaranteeing substantial participation of local enterprises. The chapter highlights the processes through which local firms made use of this context to absorb advanced foreign technologies and skills, beginning from imitation and process innovation, continuing by incremental and radical innovation and finally, achieving to become competitive themselves (Feng & Li, 2021).

While benefiting from the presence of foreign-invested companies in some sectors, China has also deployed a mix of limiting policies, closing and gradually opening up sectors considered strategic. Consequently, after decades of "standing on the predecessor's shoulders" and benefiting from an asymmetrical type of integration within global markets, by having foreign markets open and domestic markets restrictive against foreign companies in discretionary ways, Chinese enterprises started to have the capacity and interest to invest abroad, as a modality to secure brand names, market access, global talentstalent and novel technologies (Joia & Huidumac, 2011). China's outbound FDI (OFDI) has grown rapidly since 2005 and at an even faster pace than inbound FDI (IFDI), which led OFDI to exceed IFDI in 2015 for the first time (Feng & Li, 2021). Therefore, outbound investment became a new core contributor to China's development and technology catching-up (Zhang & Daly, 2011).

In recent years, trade frictions, capital controls in China and increased scrutiny in destination countries against Chinese investment, adding to various 'black swan' events such as the COVID-19 pandemic and a general slowdown in global trade and investment, slowed the growth momentum of both China's IFDI and OFDI (Bazavan, 2019). However, 2021 saw a strong rebound, with China's inbound FDI growing by 20.2% y-o-y and reaching USD 173.5 billion, thus exceeding the USA for the first time as the world's first destination of FDI,after China also became the world's largest source of OFDI in 2020 (UNCTAD, 2021). Therefore, this study will focus on the impact of inbound FDI on China's NIS, as well as the reversed technology spillover effect of OFDI, with the aim of exploring the ways in which attracting IFDI and engaging in OFDI activities improve Chinese firms' innovation abilities.

In order to be comprehensive, Chapter 6 describes five other major systemic factors of China's NIS, mapping them across the industry supply chains and evaluating their strategic implications from different perspectives. The five systemic factors are: talent, intellectual property, patents, public perception towards technology and chosen priority industries that receive all-round support from the Chinese government, including semi-conductors and ICT.

Artificial intelligence, as one of the technologies situated at the top of the agenda and, at the same time, the one where China has the most potential to achieve breakthrough innovation with significant impact across the economy, society and the national security sphere, will be treated separately as a study case in Chapter 7.

Finally, as understanding and navigating China's technological rise has become a critical issue for all policymakers, the final chapter aims to make several policy recommendations to the European Union in a new international relations environment, among which are to increase significantly innovation spending and better coordinate resource allocation, prioritise core technologies such as artificial intelligence, consolidate EU domestic tech giants that can compete on the global market, strengthen talent retention and attraction programmes and make the regulatory environment more innovation-friendly.

Against this background, within the analytical framework of the national innovation system and economic catch-up theories, the conclusions chapter will draw final remarks on China's innovation system, highlighting significant trends that have the potential to reshape the international system and redefine power dynamics. The conclusion section also discusses the limitations of the current research and proposes further prospects.

## References


Alisson, G., & Schmidt, E. (2021, December 7). China will soon lead the U.S. in tech. *Wall Street Journal*. https://www.wsj.com/articles/china-will-soon-lead-the-us-in-tech-global-leader-semiconductors-5g-wireless-green-energy-11638915759. Accessed 2 July 2022.

Bazavan, A. (2019). How does China innovate? A deconstruction of China's national innovation system. *Hyperion International Journal of Econophysics & New Economy*, *12*(1).

Carraro, C., & Galeotti, M. (1997). Economic growth, international competitiveness and environmental protection: R&D and innovation strategies with the WARM model. *Energy Economics*, *19*(1). https://doi.org/10.1016/s0140-9883(96)01005-5

Chu, C. C., Li, Y. L., Li, S. J., & Ji, Y. (2021, September). Uncertainty, venture capital and entrepreneurial enterprise innovation—Evidence from companies listed on China's GEM. *Pacific Basin Finance Journal*, *68*(2020), 101576. Available at: https://doi.org/10.1016/j.pacfin.2021.101576.

Development Solutions Europe Ltd. (2018a). *China's '1+N' funding strategy for artificial intelligence*. http://chinainnovationfunding.eu/china-funding-artificial-intelligence/

Ding, J. (2018, March). *Deciphering China's AI Dream: The context, components, capabilities, and consequences of China's strategy to lead the world in AI* (pp. 1–44). Future of Humanity Institute, University of Oxford.

Feng, W., & Li, J. (2021). International technology spillovers and innovation quality: Evidence from China. *Economic Analysis and Policy*, *72*, 289–308. https://doi.org/10.1016/j.eap.2021.09.003

Gârleanu, N., Panageas, S., & Yu, J. (2012). Technological growth and asset pricing. *Journal of Finance*, *67*(4). https://doi.org/10.1111/j.1540-6261.2012.01747.x

Gong, C. (2021). Government R&D investment, knowledge accumulation, and regional innovation capability: Evidence of a threshold effect model from China. *Complexity*. https://doi.org/10.1155/2021/8963237.

Joia, R. M., & Huidumac, E. (2011). China's geostrategic position—FDI flows and stock analysis. *Hyperion International Journal of Econophysics & New Economy*, 129–140.

Li, Y. (2017) *Innovation pathways in the Chinese economy* (Doctoral Dissertation). Georgia Institute of Technology. http://hdl.handle.net/1853/59127

Lin, F. (2017). Industrial policy and China's economic development: A perspective of new structural economics. *Journal of Fudan University, 59*(2).

Lundvall, B. Å., & Rikap, C. (2022). China's catching-up in artificial intelligence seen as a co-evolution of corporate and national innovation systems. *Research Policy, 51*(1), 104395. https://doi.org/10.1016/J.RESPOL.2021.104395

Luong, N., Arnold, Z., & Murphy, B. (2021, March). Understanding Chinese government guidance funds. *Center for Security and* ... [Preprint]. https://cset.georgetown.edu/wp-content/uploads/CSET-Understanding-Chinese-Government-Guidance-Funds.pdf

National Science Board (2018). 'Science & Engineering Indicators 2018'. Available at: https://www.nsf.gov/statistics/2018/nsb20181/assets/nsb20181.pdf.

Sapkota, P., & Bastola, U. (2017). Foreign direct investment, income, and environmental pollution in developing countries: Panel data analysis of Latin America. *Energy Economics, 64*. https://doi.org/10.1016/j.eneco.2017.04.001

Schmidt, E. (2020) *I Used to Run Google. Silicon Valley Could Lose to China. We can't win the technology wars without the federal government's help*. https://www.nytimes.com/2020/02/27/opinion/eric-schmidt-ai-china.html. Accessed 1 July 2022.

State Council of the People's Republic of China and The Central Committee of Communist Party of China (CPC). (2016). *国家创新驱动发展战略纲要 (National Strategy of Innovation-Driven Development)*.

Sun, Y., & Cao, C. (2020). *The dynamics of the studies of China's science, technology and innovation (STI): A bibliometric analysis of an emerging field, Scientometrics*. Springer International Publishing. https://doi.org/10.1007/s11192-020-03500-x

Sykes, A. O. (2021) The law and economics of 'forced' technology transfer and its implications for trade and investment policy (and the U.S.-China Trade War). *Journal of Legal Analysis*. https://doi.org/10.1093/jla/laaa007

Tambosi, S. S. V., Gomes, G., & Amal, M. (2019). Organisational learning capability and innovation: Study on companies located in regional cluster. *International Journal of Innovation Management, 24*(6). https://doi.org/10.1142/S1363919620500577.

UNCTAD. (2021). World investment report 2021| UNCTAD. *United Nations Conference on Trade and Development*. [Preprint].

Wang, F., & Zhu, D. (2021). The influence of industrial policy on innovation in startup enterprises: An empirical study based on China's GEM listed companies. *Complexity*. https://doi.org/10.1155/2021/9650741

WIPO. (2021). *Global Innovation Index 2021: Tracking innovation through the COVID-19 crisis*. Geneva. https://www.wipo.int/edocs/pubdocs/en/wipo_pub_gii_2021.pdf

World Bank. (2022). *Eurostat-OECD PPP Programme, World Development Indicators database*. https://data.worldbank.org/indicator/NY.GDP.MKTP.PP.CD?locations=CN. Accessed 1 July 2022.

Zenglein, M.J., & Holzmann, A. (2019). *Evolving Made in China 2025: China's industrial policy in the quest for global tech leadership, Merics*.

Zhang, X., & Daly, K. (2011). The determinants of China's outward foreign direct investment. *Emerging Markets Review, 12*(4). https://doi.org/10.1016/j.ememar.2011.06.001

Zhang, Y. (2021). The regional disparity of influencing factors of technological innovation in china: Evidence from high-tech industry. *Technological and Economic Development of Economy, 27*(4), 811–832. https://doi.org/10.3846/tede.2021.14828

Zhang, Y., & Zhou, Y. (2015). *The source of innovation in China: Highly innovative systems*. Palgrave Macmillan.

Zhou, W., & Fang, M. M. (2021) *Subsidizing Technology Competition: China's Evolving Practices and International Trade Regulation Technological competition is one of the most defining elements in United States-China trade tensions. China is unwaveringly committed to a new growth mod*.

Zou, L., Cao, X. Z., & Zhu, Y. W. (2021). Research on regional high-tech innovation efficiency and influence factors: Evidence from Yangtze River economic belt in China. *Complexity*. https://doi.org/10.1155/2021/9946098

CHAPTER 2

# Literature Review

Innovation is a necessary condition for the sustainable development of companies and economies. Understanding its nature and influencing variables allows decision-makers and private actors to design and implement efficient innovation policies. This chapter will review the most influential perspectives about the nature of innovation, its relation to economic development and the mechanisms that enable innovation to spread and spill between companies and among industries. Furthermore, it will prepare theoretical grounds to analyse the relationship between different fundamental factors of the Chinese national innovation system, such as public policies, funding and investment.

## 1 The Nature of Innovation

Joseph Schumpeter is the pioneer in the study of innovation, a concept that he first proposed in his *Theory of Economic Development* (1934). He defined innovation as "new combinations" of new or existing knowledge, resources and other factors, that are situated in the economic sphere and have commercialisation purpose, as opposed to mere invention. Schumpeter also described innovation as a breakthrough exploratory process that can create and exploit market disequilibrium in order to earn abnormal returns. With his book *Capitalism, Socialism and Democracy*


A. Băzăvan, *China's National Innovation System*,
https://doi.org/10.1007/978-981-97-3266-1_2

(1942), Schumpeter further refined the definition of innovation as "creative destruction", or the "process of industrial mutation that incessantly revolutionises the economic structure from within, incessantly destroying the old one, incessantly creating a new one". To summarise, in Schumpeter's view, innovation is the process through which new methods, products and ideas are transformed into economic outcomes, leading to the creation of new industries and markets and the destruction of old ones.

Freeman and Soete (2012) further built upon the works of Joseph Schumpeter, defining innovation as a complex process involving various actors, such as firms, universities, government organisations and others, split into 3 elements: knowledge creation, knowledge diffusion and knowledge application. Knowledge creation refers to the development of new scientific and technological knowledge through R&D activities. Knowledge diffusion refers to the spread of new knowledge across individuals, organisations and geography. Finally, knowledge application involves the transformation of new knowledge into novel products, processes or services that create economic value. As regards the innovation actors, Freeman and Soete strongly emphasised the role of institutions. They highlight the fact that innovation is not only the result of individual creativity or entrepreneurship but also depends significantly on the institutional framework in which innovation takes place. Institutions such as universities, research institutes and government agencies play a critical role in creating and diffusing knowledge, while firms and other organisations are responsible for using the knowledge to develop new products and services. Finally, Freeman and Soete consider that innovation is influenced by a range of factors, including market structure, competition and government policies. Consequently, innovation is not a linear process, but is shaped by complex interactions among these factors.

Chesbrough and Crowther (2006) emphasise the necessity to integrate enterprises' internal and external resources, as well as the importance of open innovation and collaboration between different organisations, in order to disseminate the benefits of innovation to a wider range of stakeholders. On the other hand, this implicitly draws on the role of power and politics in shaping the innovation process. Building upon Chesbrough's earlier work (Chesbrough, 2003), Laursen and Salter's theory of open innovation (2006) provides a framework for understanding the different forms and drivers of open innovation. The authors define open innovation as the process of innovation that involves the exchange of ideas and knowledge between organisations, which can be either inbound or outbound. Inbound open innovation refers to the process of sourcing external knowledge and ideas to complement the knowledge found within the firm. Outbound open innovation refers to the process of leveraging the firm's internal knowledge and ideas to create value for external partners and stakeholders.

Finally, Keith Rothwell (1992) proposed the technological innovation chain, a framework describing the different stages of the innovation process, from initial research to commercialisation. The framework is based on the idea that innovation is a sequential process that involves a series of interconnected stages. The main stages include basic research, applied research, development, demonstration and commercialisation, all of which require different sets of resources, skills and expertise.

After reviewing different ways of defining innovation, it is important to categorise it. An important distinction is between incremental and radical innovation. Incremental innovation refers to the process of generating gradual improvements on the basis of previous methods and products. In turn, radical innovation is the process of creating new concepts and technologies that are highly different from the existing ones, having the capacity to revolutionise industries or even create new ones (Wilhelm & Dolfsma, 2018). Performing different types of innovation involves different levels of difficulty and of course, achieving incremental innovation is easier and can bring quick wins (Bessant et al., 2014). At the same time, radical innovation is strategically more important as it can bring the breakthrough competitive edges, but faces considerable challenges such as prohibitive costs, long gestation period and higher risks.

The Organisation for Economic Cooperation and Development—OECD (OECD/Eurostat, 2005) further categorises innovation into product, process, marketing and organisational innovation, while Geldes et al. (2017) make a further distinction between innovation that is technological and innovation that is non-technological (organisational or structural). From a different angle, Hage and Hollingsworth's (2000) framework for understanding the different types of research, consists of three main categories: basic research, applied research and development research.

## 1.1 *Innovation as a Driver of Economic Growth and "Catching-Up"*

Technological improvement and innovation have long been identified as important driving forces for increasing productivity and building a modern and reliable model of economic growth, especially in emerging economies (Amankwah-Amoah etal., 2018; Choi & Yi, 2017; Schniederjans, 2017). It can be argued that there is consensus in the regard that domestic innovation, in the sense of technological development, is one among the primary sources of sustainable growth, gains in productivity and competitiveness, irrespective of the particular context (Eichengreen et al., 2011).

However, economists have different views regarding the exact nature of the relationship between innovation and economic growth, as was reflected by Arrow (1962), Grossman and Helpman (1994) and Romer (1994). Theorists are currently making efforts to keep pace with the fast-evolving empirical reality, as after the digital revolution, technology evolution has become increasingly complex and wide-encompassing, including in the social sphere (for example, how people interact), which opens new fronts and brings new challenges to existing theories (Lacasa et al., 2019; Sheng et al., 2019).

Schumpeter (1934) argued that "economic growth is a process of creative destruction, whereby new products and processes replace outdated ones". Other endogenous growth theorists also highlight the strong causality between technological development and economic growth (Grossman & Helpman, 1994; Romer, 1994). In turn, according to Solow's theory of exogenous technological progress (1957), economic growth is the result of changes in production inputs, technological progress and productivity levels, the latter two being strongly related.

In their effort to reduce income and technological gaps, developing countries make efforts to 'catch-up' with advanced economies (Lee, 2014). Amankwah-Amoah and Hinson (2019) show that innovation has the great capacity of alleviating economic disparities, as it allows developing countries and regions to catch up faster. In the process of industrialisation, important factors that contribute to catching-up are technology introduction and FDI, which can improve the technological innovation ability, raise productivity and accelerate economic growth. In the early stages of catching-up, factor accumulation is crucial, in the sense of acquisition of machinery, raising human capital and building infrastructure (Bazavan, 2020). In this period, domestic innovation is not feasible in terms of costs and time. Therefore, the only way to narrow the technological gap is to import mature technology.

As the economy grows and reaches the middle-income stage, the marginal effect of factor accumulation investment decreases (Liu et al., 2017). Therefore, maintaining growth becomes a challenge, as countries face the risk of falling into the middle-income trap, as happened to many countries in Central and Latin America (Gill & Kharas, 2007). Therefore, a new strategy is needed, focusing on domestic innovation and the increase in the value supply chains of local companies. Moreover, Lee and Kim (2009) argue that innovation is especially important for economic growth in countries beyond the middle-income stage, as for the lower middle- or low-income countries it is more important to establish strong, functional political institutions, improving governance performance and the quality of education, while also lowering corruption for instance (Liu et al., 2017).

From a different perspective, the diffusion of innovation leads to structural shifts in the industrial system. Technological innovation that is isolated in one organisational unit cannot produce productivity growth and therefore Andergassen et al. (2018) highlights the necessity of insuring seamless technological flows between organisational units. In general, technological flows are directed towards the most efficient departments, which ultimately leads to the rationalisation and optimisation of the industrial structure. On the other hand, technological flows and progress cause productivity imbalances between departments and between industries. These imbalances grow faster than the speed of structural change, leading to unforeseen costs and actually damaging innovation efficiency (Zhou et al., 2021). The acceleration of structural changes and therefore the reduction of societal and economic costs can be addressed by governments through dedicated policies. However, Gong (2021) warns that industrial policies are subject to government failures which can be more harmful than market failures.

### *1.2 Theoretical Framework for Studying Innovation*

The National Innovation System (NIS), one of the key concepts in Schumpeterian economics, is a central approach within innovation studies (Fagerberg & Sapprasert, 2011). The framework was first proposed by Freeman (1987), whose research aimed to achieve two goals: to create an alternative to the neoclassical economic growth theory and to provide a better understanding of the evolution of the world order. According to Freeman, technological revolutions are linked to changes in global leadership. For example, he studies the specific characteristics and coherence of the NIS of the United Kingdom in the eighteenth century that made possible the emergence of steam power and textiles. Following, with the rise of new technological systems powered by electricity and chemistry, Germany and the United States surged ahead and surpassed Britain. Following, in the era of information technology, Japan took precedence.

The concept was further expanded by Lundvall (1992), who argued that "the NIS is a set of institutions and organisations that generate, diffuse, and utilise new knowledge and technologies". Lundvall also emphasised the role of education and training in the innovation process. Teixeira (2014) conducted a bibliometric analysis to examine the origins, development and impact of the National Innovation System (NIS) literature. Grimes and Sun (2016) extended this line of research to the field of national innovation, using bibliometrics to identify the most influential countries, institutions, journals, seminal works and authors, as well as clusters within national innovation studies.

NIS can be best defined as 'the network of institutions in the public and private sectors whose activities and interactions initiate, import, modify, and diffuse new technologies' (Freeman, 1987). To simplify, NIS frames innovation in a national institutional environment, where actors at different levels are engaged in a constant interaction for the production, diffusion and use of new, and economically useful knowledge (Lee & Lee, 2021). These interactions constitute the fabric of the system and are shaped in turn by factors such as culture, norms, institutional arrangements, policies, etc. (Richard R. Nelson, 1993).

The main actors of NIS are companies, as they have the motivation to accumulate innovation capabilities. However, firms do not innovate alone (Lundvall & Rikap, 2022). Their ability to innovate is affected by the quality of their relationships with other organisations, state and private actors, suppliers, customers and markets (Li, 2017). The government also contributes significantly by stimulating the ability of companies to absorb new technologies, by providing the needed infrastructure and by ensuring an enabling environment for knowledge diffusion (Filippetti & Archibugi, 2011). Moreover, the Government also has the responsibility to provide and improve education and training, as well as to carry and finance its own-led research, particularly in fundamental sectors (Fagerberg & Srholec, 2008). Freeman, in his study over Japan's industrial modernisation during the ICT revolution, has emphasised the role of the government within the labour market, the education system and the unique industrial organisation (the Keiretsu).

Complementarily, Freeman and Louçã (2003) introduce the framework of Corporate innovation system (CIS), which highlights the formation of networks among various industry and innovation stakeholders, studying the dynamics of power relations among them. While networks are pervasive and constantly evolving, it is rare for a network to consist of partners that are balanced. Therefore, the question of power dynamics becomes relevant, as networks may serve as a way for a dominant firm to exert control over its suppliers, such as those providing materials, components or technology. Implicitly, the success of a CIS depends on the one hand on the lead firm's internal efforts, while on the other hand on its ability to gain access to external knowledge. Freeman has actually foreseen that the growing importance of transnational corporate innovation networks may come to challenge the relevance of NIS, which is rather focused on developments within the national level.

Evolutionary economists such as Dosi (1997) and Metcalfe (1998), have proposed the Learning Model as another valuable theoretical approach. According to this model, firms acquire innovation gradually by developing and accumulating their existing capabilities, utilising their available resources and opportunities. The learning process typically begins with low-end manufacturing, and through a series of incremental steps, firms acquire new designs and skills that enable them to improve their processes, products and marketing. Eventually, they ascend to the top of the production chain. Evolution includes "variety creation [..], replication including imitation[..] and selection (that reduce variety in the economic system and discourages the inefficient or ineffective utilization of resources)".

Finally, the concept of 'leapfrogging', introduced by Prahalad and Mashelkar (2010) in the context of emerging economies, will also prove useful for understanding the evolution of the Chinese innovation system, especially in areas such as fintech and e-commerce, where all-encompassing platforms with innovative business models are emerging. The view emphasises the advantage of the latecomer, who can benefit from using the already achieved innovation without having to undertake the costly stages of research (Lu, 2000). In the final stage of catching-up, the latecomer may actually be better positioned to make small adaptations or use other advantages which enable it to pass ahead of the incumbents

(Lee, 2019). The approach is particularly significant when explaining China's leadership in areas such as fintech and e-commerce, where all-encompassing platforms with innovative business models are emerging. In the case of electronic payment systems, they emerged in the context of an underdeveloped financial market, as well as low financial education. China skipped over the stage of checks and credit/debit cards directly to Alipay and WeChat Wallet, while the former became world's largest mobile payment platform. On the contrary, financial markets in US and Europe are well established and thus, resilient to change and innovation.

As a summary regarding the frameworks for studying innovation, the NIS emphasises the importance of collaboration and education in fostering innovation, the evolutionary Learning Models highlights the importance of networks in the innovation process, whereas "leapfrogging" introduces a new perspective on innovation in emerging economies, where the adoption of new technologies can burn development stages. For the scope of this paper, the NIS allows us to tackle the complexity of emerging innovation environments and draw significant insights that may not be easily accessible through other methods.

## 2 Foreign Direct Investment and Internationalisation

The following section will explore how FDI and international technology spillovers impact economic growth and innovation. Scholars have studied the effects and influence of IFDI and internationalisation on domestic innovation in developing countries from many perspectives. The evidence is mixed across contexts, but can be largely summarised into two opposite views.

On the one hand, some scholars believe that IFDI has a positive 'agglomeration effect' brought about by knowledge spillovers, the introduction and absorption of foreign technology, input sharing, increased capital and labour pooling (Lin et al., 2021; Smith & Thomas, 2017; Wang et al., 2014). This stimulates economic growth and assists local enterprises' technological development capacity in promoting from imitation to independent innovation (Dazheng, 2009).

On the other hand, the results of other studies are not as optimistic towards IFDI, highlighting the negative effects of technology spillovers (Feng & Li, 2021; Zeng & Zhou, 2021) and the crowding-out effect on technological innovation of local enterprise (Alfaro, 2017; Wu et al.,

2017). The most commonly mentioned negative effect is the pressure of increased market competition over domestic companies brought about by more advanced foreign peers (Zhang, 2021). This pressure, rather than improving the performance of domestic companies, can actually drive them out of the market (Wang et al., 2014).

From a different point of view, Degbey and Pelto (2013) and Bertrand and Capron (2015) look at the reverse knowledge transfer towards the source countries of investment. In recent decades, OFDI performed by latecomers from developing countries, including China, has grown rapidly, serving also as a means of seeking technology (Ai & Tan, 2020). While outbound investments have the potential to reconfigure the global networks of mother companies, optimise resource allocations, obtain new technologies and tap into new markets, talents and ideas, the success of doing so depends considerably on the capacity of the institution of the home country to integrate the new acquisitions (Zhu et al., 2019). As opposed to MNCs with long tradition, latecomers who start investing abroad might lack the competence to transfer acquired technology and combine it effectively with their current capacities (Luo & Tung, 2018; Yakob et al., 2018).

## 3 Investment in Research & Development (R&D)

Innovation-driven enterprises are seeking to develop new products that keep up with the changing needs of their customers, which leads them to improve market shares and productivity (Berman & Hagan, 2006). In order to do so, a firm needs to acquire technological advantages and perform R&D investment (Kim et al., 2021).

R&D investment, composed of R&D expenditure and R&D personnel (Zhang, 2021), has received significant attention from researchers as the main driving force of technological innovation within companies (Alarcón & Sánchez, 2013; Koc & Ceylan, 2007; Xin et al., 2019). R&D investment is usually measured by R&D intensity (Kim et al., 2021). The higher the R&D intensity of an enterprise is, the more likely it is to obtain better innovation outputs (Anzola-Román et al., 2018).

At the same time, given the fact that long-term and risky projects, with large capital requirements, are the ones leading to radical innovation, Szopik-Depczynska et al. (2020), as well as Pereira Cabral et al. (2020) argue that financial challenges are some of the most common barriers faced by companies in undertaking innovation activities. It is only a small number of large companies financially strong enough to carry breakthrough innovation, while medium-sized companies limit themselves to lower impact innovation. As regards SOEs, some scholars such as Pfeffer and Salancik (2003) and Hu (2001) believe that SOEs have higher likelihood of conducting breakthrough innovation, while others like Li et al. (2010) and (Zhang & Shi, 2011) argue that SOEs have a principal-agency problem and are therefore less likely to innovate.

The fact that breakthrough innovation is a public good with society-wide externalities makes the case of government direct investment in innovation, or support for companies that carry innovation activities. Moreover, fundamental research activities that can determine breakthrough achievements require large-scale funding, which frequently exceed the capacity of the private sector. Therefore, public-led investments have a significant impact on the capacity of the NIS to deliver and have received extensive attention from international scholars. On the one hand, public funding for innovation has the potential to stimulate R&D investment by compensating for the 'innovation inertia' of firms, reducing financing constraints, decreasing uncertainty, and alleviating innovation risks (Hall & Bagchi-Sen, 2002).

However, some scholars are sceptical towards public funding for innovation, arguing that it may be problematic in at least four ways: Firstly, Li et al. (2016) believe that the serious information asymmetry between the state and private actors, adding to the rent-seeking behaviour of companies with the deepest political connections, inevitably poses the challenges of resources mismatch, frauds and wasteful investments. Secondly, public funding also raises concerns regarding the potential to create an illusion of innovation and a "patent bubble", as companies could tend to devote their efforts to achieving quantity and neglect innovation quality, in the pursuit of meeting government's targets for the scale and speed of innovation (Li & Zheng, 2016). Thirdly, it might be the case that public funding acts as a form of subsidising corporate profits, improving their balance and survival prospects even if they make low R&D efforts, and thus creating over-capacity and reducing the motivation for performing genuine R&D. In other words, government funding could bring a crowding-out effect (Hall, 2002).

### *3.1 Government Financial Incentives for Innovation Activities Performed by Private Companies*

In addition to directly investing in innovation through its own SOEs and institutions, the government can also have a significant positive or negative impact on the innovation capability of enterprises through tax incentives, financial loans and government subsidies. There are two opposing views on the impact of government funding on the quantity and quality of private-led innovation.

On the one hand, some scholars believe that, at least in the short term, government financial support can promote firm innovation activities (Yu, 2013). Accordingly, government financial incentive can correct the 'innovation inertia' of companies caused by positive externalities, ease the constraint of innovation resources, reduce uncertainty, share the burden of innovation risks and, overall, stimulate the innovation power of firms (Bai et al., 2019; Dai & Liu, 2008). Especially as regards high-quality innovation activities, while being a public good, its pronounced characteristics of risk, long cycles, and great capital demand make it vulnerable to market failures. Government preferential policies and financial subsidies can help alleviate the problems of insufficient capital resources, while also exerting a leverage effect throughout the market (Szczygielski et al., 2017).

On the contrary, other scholars reach opposite conclusions, arguing that the positive impact of public funds is overestimated, if not negative. One reason is the fact that government investment can lead to a squeezing-out effect of enterprises' own R&D funds, which will further inhibit innovation capability and reduce the efficiency of firms' technological innovation (Hong et al., 2016; Huang et al., 2016). According to this view, subsidies are distorting, directly increasing corporate profits, which reduces the motivation of companies to strive for innovation (Wang & Zhu, 2021). As innovation is not carried out based on real market demand, short-term achievements would not be sustainable and would translate into commercially useful products in the long term (Zeng, 2021).

Finally, Hitt et al. (2019) try to reach a compromise, arguing that a mix of diversified resources reduces the risk of R&D investments and creates the potential for higher achievements.

## 4 Summary

This chapter examined the predominant viewpoints on the character of innovation, its connection to economic growth and the means by which it disseminates and spreads across industries and companies, thus laying the groundwork for examining the interplay between critical components of the Chinese national innovation system, such as public policies, funding and investment, through a theoretical lens. Together, these diverse points of view will support the analysis on China's funding of innovation activities, backed by data and insights obtained from private stakeholders, government sources, fund managers, and external researchers.

For the purpose of this paper, NIS is the most suitable framework for exploring the intricacies of emerging innovation environments and extracting valuable insights that may not be easily attainable through other approaches. The Learning Models and "leapfrogging" will also be deployed to underscore the role of networks in the innovation process and to approach innovation in China's emerging economy, where the adoption of new technologies accelerated developmental stages.

## References

Ai, Q., & Tan, H. (2020). Uncovering neglected success factors in post-acquisition reverse capability transfer: Evidence from Chinese multinational corporations in Europe. *Journal of World Business, 55*(3). https://doi.org/10.1016/j.jwb.2019.101053

Alarcón, S., & Sánchez, M. (2013). External and internal R&D, capital investment and business performance in the Spanish agri-food industry. *Journal of Agricultural Economics, 64*(3), 654–675. https://doi.org/10.1111/1477-9552.12015

Alfaro, L. (2017). Gains from foreign direct investment: Macro and micro approaches. *World Bank Economic Review, 30*. https://doi.org/10.1093/wber/lhw007

Amankwah-Amoah, J., & Hinson, R. E. (2019). Contextual influences on new technology ventures: A study of domestic firms in Ghana. *Technological Forecasting and Social Change, 143*, 289–296. https://doi.org/10.1016/j.techfore.2019.01.019

Amankwah-Amoah, J., Osabutey, E. L. C., & Egbetokun, A. (2018). Contemporary challenges and opportunities of doing business in Africa: The emerging roles and effects of technologies. *Technological Forecasting and Social Change, 131*, 171–174. https://doi.org/10.1016/j.techfore.2018.01.003

Andergassen, R., Nardini, F., & Ricottilli, M. (2018). Innovation, specialization and growth in a model of structural change. *B.E. Journal of Macroeconomics, 18*(2). https://doi.org/10.1515/bejm-2017-0095

Anzola-Román, P., Bayona-Sáez, C., & García-Marco, T. (2018). Organizational innovation, internal R&D and externally sourced innovation practices: Effects on technological innovation outcomes. *Journal of Business Research, 91*, 233–247. https://doi.org/10.1016/J.JBUSRES.2018.06.014

Arrow, K. J. (1962). *Economic welfare and the allocation of resources for invention. The rate and direction of inventive activity: Economic and social factors*. Princeton University Press [Preprint]. https://www.nber.org/chapters/c2144.pdf

Bai, X., Wang, Y., & Su, X. (2019). R&D subsidies or tax incentives: An empirical analysis of government intervention on enterprise innovation performance and innovation quality. *Science Research Management, 40*(6), 9–18.

Bazavan, A. (2020). China's transition to a knowledge economy—Institutional mechanisms, public policies and private investment. In C. R. Pamfilie, V. Dinu, L. Tăchiciu, D. Pleșea, & C. Vasiliu (Eds.), *5th BASIQ international conference on new trends in sustainable business and consumption*. ASE Bucharest.

Berman, S. J., & Hagan, J. (2006). How technology-driven business strategy can spur innovation and growth. *Strategy and Leadership, 34*(2). https://doi.org/10.1108/10878570610700848

Bertrand, O., & Capron, L. (2015). Productivity enhancement at home via cross-border acquisitions: The roles of learning and contemporaneous domestic investments. *Strategic Management Journal, 36*(5). https://doi.org/10.1002/smj.2256

Bessant, J., Öberg, C., & Trifilova, A. (2014). Framing problems in radical innovation. *Industrial Marketing Management, 43*(8), 1284–1292. https://doi.org/10.1016/J.INDMARMAN.2014.09.003

Chesbrough, H., & Crowther, A. K. (2006). Beyond high tech: Early adopters of open innovation in other industries. *R and D Management, 36*(3). https://doi.org/10.1111/j.1467-9310.2006.00428.x

Chesbrough, H. W. (2003). The era of open innovation. *MIT Sloan Management Review, 44*(3), 35–41.

Choi, C., & Yi, M. H. (2017). The Internet, R&D expenditure and economic growth. *Applied Economics Letters, 25*(4), 264–267. https://doi.org/10.1080/13504851.2017.1316819

Dai, C., & Liu, Y. (2008). Comparative analysis of the impact of tax incentives and financial subsidies on corporate R&D. *Economic Science, 3*, 58–71.

Dazheng, W. (2009). Encourage the introduction of technology or encourage self-innovation. *Science & Technology Progress and Policy* [Preprint].

Degbey, W., & Pelto, E. (2013). Cross-border M&A as a trigger for network change in the Russian bakery industry. *Journal of Business and Industrial Marketing, 28*(3). https://doi.org/10.1108/08858621311302831

Dominguez Lacasa, I., et al. (2019). Paths of technology upgrading in the BRICS economies. *Research Policy, 48*(1). https://doi.org/10.1016/j.respol.2018.08.016

Dosi, G. (1997). Opportunities, incentives and collective patterns of technological change. *Economic Journal* [Preprint]. https://doi.org/10.1111/1468-0297.00239

Eichengreen, B., Park, D., & Shin, K. (2011). When fast growing economies slow down. *NBER Working Paper Series* [Preprint].

Fagerberg, J., & Sapprasert, K. (2011). National innovation systems: the emergence of a new approach. *Science and Public Policy, 38*(9), 669–679. https://doi.org/10.3152/030234211X13070021633369

Fagerberg, J., & Srholec, M. (2008). National innovation systems, capabilities and economic development. *Research Policy* [Preprint]. https://doi.org/10.1016/j.respol.2008.06.003

Feng, W., & Li, J. (2021). International technology spillovers and innovation quality: Evidence from China. *Economic Analysis and Policy, 72*, 289–308. https://doi.org/10.1016/j.eap.2021.09.003

Filippetti, A., & Archibugi, D. (2011). Innovation in times of crisis: National systems of innovation, structure, and demand. *Research Policy, 40*(2), 179–192. https://doi.org/10.1016/J.RESPOL.2010.09.001

Freeman, C. (1987). *Technology and economic performance: Lessons from Japan*. Pinter Publishers.

Freeman, C., & Louçã, F. (2003). The emergence of a new techno-economic paradigm: The age of Information and Communication Technology (ICT). In *As time goes by: From the industrial revolutions to the information revolution* (pp. 301–335). Oxford University Press. https://doi.org/10.1093/0199251053.003.0009

Freeman, C., & Soete, L. (2012). *The economics of industrial innovation* (pp. 1–470). Routledge. https://doi.org/10.4324/9780203357637

Geldes, C., et al. (2017). Proximity as determinant of business cooperation for technological and non-technological innovations: A study of an agribusiness cluster. *Journal of Business and Industrial Marketing, 32*(1), 167–178. https://doi.org/10.1108/JBIM-01-2016-0003

Gill, I., & Kharas, H. (2007). *An East Asian renaissance ideas for economic growth*. World Bank.

Gong, C. (2021). Government R&D investment, knowledge accumulation, and regional innovation capability: Evidence of a threshold effect model from China. *Complexity*. https://doi.org/10.1155/2021/8963237

Grimes, S., & Sun, Y. (2016). China's evolving role in Apple's global value chain. *Area Development and Policy, 1*(1). https://doi.org/10.1080/23792949.2016.1149434

Grossman, G. M., & Helpman, E. (1994). Endogenous innovation in the theory of growth. *Journal of Economic Perspectives, 8*, 23–44.

Hage, J., & Rogers Hollingsworth, J. (2000). A strategy for the analysis of idea innovation networks and institutions. *Organization Studies* [Preprint]. https://doi.org/10.1177/0170840600215006

Hall, B. H. (2002). The financing of research and development. *Oxford Review of Economic Policy, 18*(1). https://doi.org/10.1093/oxrep/18.1.35

Hall, L. A., & Bagchi-Sen, S. (2002). A study of R&D, innovation, and business performance in the Canadian biotechnology industry. *Technovation, 22*(4). https://doi.org/10.1016/S0166-4972(01)00016-5

Hitt, M. A., Hoskisson, R. E., & Ireland, R. D. (2019). *Strategic management: Competitiveness & globalization: Concepts and cases 12e*. Cengage Learning Asia.

Hong, J., et al. (2016). Do government grants promote innovation efficiency in China's high-tech industries? *Technovation, 57–58*(4), 4–13. https://doi.org/10.1016/J.TECHNOVATION.2016.06.001

Hu, A. G. (2001). Ownership, government R&D, private R&D, and productivity in Chinese industry. *Journal of Comparative Economics, 29*(1). https://doi.org/10.1006/jcec.2000.1704

Huang, Q., Jiang, M. S., & Miao, J. (2016). Effect of government subsidization on Chinese industrial firms' technological innovation efficiency: A stochastic frontier analysis. *Journal of Business Economics and Management, 17*(2), 187–200. https://doi.org/10.3846/16111699.2015.1061590

Kim, W.-H., Chen, B., & Hwang, J.-S. (2021). Imitation, technology, and firm performance: The Korean firms case in China. *Journal of Korea Trade, 25*(4), 128–145. https://doi.org/10.35611/jkt.2021.25.4.128

Koc, T., & Ceylan, C. (2007). Factors impacting the innovative capacity in large-scale companies. *Technovation, 27*(3), 105–114. https://doi.org/10.1016/J.TECHNOVATION.2005.10.002

Laursen, K., & Salter, A. (2006). Open for innovation: The role of openness in explaining innovation performance among U.K. manufacturing firms. *Strategic Management Journal, 27*(2). https://doi.org/10.1002/smj.507

Lee, J., & Lee, K. (2021). Catching-up national innovations systems (NIS) in China and post-catching-up NIS in Korea and Taiwan: Verifying the detour hypothesis and policy implications. *Innovation and Development, 11*(2–3), 387–411. https://doi.org/10.1080/2157930X.2021.1932062

Lee, K. (2014). *Schumpeterian analysis of economic catch-up*. Cambridge University Press. https://doi.org/10.1017/cbo9781107337244

Lee, K., & Kim, B. Y. (2009). Both institutions and policies matter but differently for different income groups of countries: Determinants of long-run economic growth revisited. *World Development, 37*(3). https://doi.org/10.1016/j.worlddev.2008.07.004

Lee, L. (2019). *The art of economic catch-up: Barriers, detours and leapfrogging in innovation systems*. https://doi.org/10.1017/9781108588232

Li, D., Chau, P. Y. K., & Lai, F. (2010). Market orientation, ownership type, and E-business assimilation: Evidence from Chinese firms. *Decision Sciences, 41*(1). https://doi.org/10.1111/j.1540-5915.2009.00261.x

Li, W., Li, H., & Li, H. (2016). Innovation incentives or tax shield? A study of the tax preferences of high tech enterprises. *Science Research Management, 37*(11). http://journal26.magtechjournal.com/Jwk3_kygl/EN/abstract/abstract11193.shtml. Accessed 1 July 2022.

Li, W., & Zheng, M. (2016). Is it substantive innovation or strategic innovation?—Impact of macroeconomic policies on micro-enterprises' innovation. *Economic Research Journal, 51*(4), 60–73.

Li, Y. (2017). *Innovation pathways in the Chinese economy* (Doctoral dissertation, Georgia Institute of Technology). http://hdl.handle.net/1853/59127

Lin, Y., Qin, Y., & Xie, Z. (2021). Does foreign technology transfer spur domestic innovation? Evidence from the high-speed rail sector in China. *Journal of Comparative Economics, 49*(1), 212–229. https://doi.org/10.1016/j.jce.2020.08.004

Liu, X., et al. (2017). Beyond catch-up—Can a new innovation policy help China overcome the middle income trap? *Science and Public Policy, 44*(5), 656–669. https://doi.org/10.1093/scipol/scw092

Lu, Q. (2000). *China's leap into the information age: Innovation and organization in the computer industry*. Oxford University Press.

Lundvall, B. (1992). *National innovation system, toward theory of innovation and interactive learning*. Pinter Publisher.

Lundvall, B. Å., & Rikap, C. (2022). China's catching-up in artificial intelligence seen as a co-evolution of corporate and national innovation systems. *Research Policy, 51*(1), 104395. https://doi.org/10.1016/J.RESPOL.2021.104395

Luo, Y., & Tung, R. L. (2018). A general theory of springboard MNEs. *Journal of International Business Studies*. https://doi.org/10.1057/s41267-017-0114-8

Metcalfe, J. S. (1998). *Evolutionary economics and creative destruction* (1st ed.). Routledge. https://doi.org/10.4324/9780203275146

Nelson, R. R. (Ed.). (1993). *National innovation systems: A comparative analysis*. Oxford University Press.

OECD/Eurostat. (2005). *Oslo Manual: Guidelines for collecting and interpreting innovation data. The measurement of scientific and technological activities, Oslo Manual*.

Pereira Cabral, B., Lage de Sousa, F., & Canêdo-Pinheiro, M. (2020). Assessing the impacts of innovation barriers: A qualitative analysis of Brazil's natural resources industry. *Resources Policy, 68*. https://doi.org/10.1016/j.resourpol.2020.101736

Pfeffer, J., & Salancik, G. R. (2003). *The external control of organizations: A resource dependence perspective*. Stanford University Press.

Prahalad, C. K., & Mashelkar, R. A. (2010). Innovation's holy grail. *Harvard Business Review, 88*(7–8), 134–141.

Romer, P. M. (1994). The origins of endogenous growth. *Journal of Economic Perspectives, 8*(1), 3–22. https://doi.org/10.1257/JEP.8.1.3

Rothwell, R. (1992). Successful industrial innovation: Critical factors for the 1990s. *R&D Management, 22*(3). https://doi.org/10.1111/j.1467-9310.1992.tb00812.x

Schniederjans, D. G. (2017). Adoption of 3D-printing technologies in manufacturing: A survey analysis. *International Journal of Production Economics, 183*, 287–298. https://doi.org/10.1016/j.ijpe.2016.11.008

Schumpeter, J. (1934). The theory of economic development—An inquiry into profits, capital, credit, interest, and the business cycle. *Regional Studies*.

Schumpeter, J. A. (1942). Creative destruction from capitalism, socialism and democracy (1942). *Democracy* [Preprint].

Sheng, J., Amankwah-Amoah, J., & Wang, X. (2019). Technology in the 21st century: New challenges and opportunities. *Technological Forecasting and Social Change, 143*, 321–335. https://doi.org/10.1016/j.techfore.2018.06.009

Smith, N., & Thomas, E. (2017). Regional conditions and innovation in Russia: The impact of foreign direct investment and absorptive capacity. *Regional Studies, 51*(9), 1412–1428. https://doi.org/10.1080/00343404.2016.1164307

Solow, R. M. (1957). Technical change and the aggregate production function. *The Review of Economics and Statistics, 39*(3), 312. https://doi.org/10.2307/1926047

Szczygielski, K., et al. (2017). Does government support for private innovation matter? Firm-level evidence from two catching-up countries. *Research Policy, 46*(1), 219–237. https://doi.org/10.1016/j.respol.2016.10.009

Szopik-Depczynska, K., Cheba, K., & Wiśniewska, J. (2020). Innovation, R&D and user-driven innovation activity in R&D Departments in Poland. The multi-criteria analysis. *Procedia Computer Science, 176*, 2705–2713. https://doi.org/10.1016/j.procs.2020.09.290

Teixeira, A. A. C. (2014). Evolution, roots and influence of the literature on national systems of innovation: A bibliometric account. *Cambridge Journal of Economics, 38*(1), 181–214. https://doi.org/10.1093/cje/bet022

Wang, F., & Zhu, D. (2021). The influence of industrial policy on innovation in startup enterprises: An empirical study based on China's GEM listed companies. *Complexity*. https://doi.org/10.1155/2021/9650741

Wang, Y., et al. (2014). Foreign direct investment spillovers and the geography of innovation in Chinese regions: The role of regional industrial specialization and diversity. *Regional Studies, 50*(5), 805–822. https://doi.org/10.1080/00343404.2014.933800

Wilhelm, M., & Dolfsma, W. (2018). Managing knowledge boundaries for open innovation—Lessons from the automotive industry. *International Journal of Operations and Production Management, 38*(1), 230–248. https://doi.org/10.1108/IJOPM-06-2015-0337

Wu, J., Ma, Z., & Zhuo, S. (2017). Enhancing national innovative capacity: The impact of high-tech international trade and inward foreign direct investment. *International Business Review, 26*(3), 502–514. https://doi.org/10.1016/j.ibusrev.2016.11.001

Xin, K., et al. (2019). R&D intensity, free cash flow, and technological innovation: evidence from high-tech manufacturing firms in China. *Asian Journal of Technology Innovation, 27*(2), 214–238. https://doi.org/10.1080/19761597.2019.1635894

Yakob, R., Nakamura, H. R., & Ström, P. (2018). Chinese foreign acquisitions aimed for strategic asset-creation and innovation upgrading: The case of Geely and Volvo Cars. *Technovation*, 70–71. https://doi.org/10.1016/j.technovation.2018.02.011

Yu, F. (2013). Government R&D subsidies, political relations and technological SMEs innovation transformation. *iBusiness, 05*(03). https://doi.org/10.4236/ib.2013.53b022

Zeng, J. (2021). China's artificial intelligence innovation: A top-down national command approach? *Global Policy, 12*(3), 399–409. https://doi.org/10.1111/1758-5899.12914

Zeng, S., & Zhou, Y. (2021). Foreign direct investment's impact on china's economic growth, technological innovation and pollution. *International Journal of Environmental Research and Public Health, 18*(6), 1–25. https://doi.org/10.3390/ijerph18062839

Zhang, Y. (2021). The regional disparity of influencing factors of technological innovation in china: Evidence from high-tech industry. *Technological and Economic Development of Economy, 27*(4), 811–832. https://doi.org/10.3846/tede.2021.14828

Zhang, H., & Shi, J. (2011). On the technical efficiency of new product in Chinese provincial industry. *Economic Research Journal, 1.*

Zhou, X., et al. (2021, February). Technological innovation and structural change for economic development in China as an emerging market. *Technological Forecasting and Social Change, 167*, 120671. https://doi.org/10.1016/j.techfore.2021.120671

Zhu, H. (Susan), et al. (2019). Home country institutions behind cross-border acquisition performance. *Journal of Management, 45*(4). https://doi.org/10.1177/0149206317699520

CHAPTER 3

# Methodology

Using the NIS framework, this exploratory research aims to provide a macro understanding of the mechanisms and processes that drive innovation in China, across industries, by examining the following principal elements: the role of the government and the structure of public policies; innovation funding priorities and main funding channels; inward and the role of foreign companies invested in the national innovation system; innovation of Chinese outward FDI; and other systemic factors. Although in several instances comparative innovation indexes are mentioned, such as the WIPO Global Innovation Index, the current study does not aim to measure and compare China's innovation capacity, which would require a different set of quantitative indicators and analysis methods. It limits its scope to China on the whole, but draws attention to the significant differences among regions in terms of economic development and capacity to deploy innovation capacities. The study is a result of document analysis and research on the ground, conducted during the period 2017–2021.

The research commenced with an extensive review of relevant academic publications covering innovation in general and innovation in China in particular, from both international and Chinese sources. The review identified and collected relevant academic works within a wide range of high-quality publications in the field of technology and innovation management, indexed by the Science Citation Index Expanded (SCI-E), Social Science Citation Index (SSCI), Conference Proceedings Citation



A. Băzăvan, *China's National Innovation System*,
https://doi.org/10.1007/978-981-97-3266-1_3

Index—Science (CPCI-S) and Conference Proceedings Citation Index—Social Science and Humanities (CPCI-SSH), included in the Web of Science. The review included all articles in which the title mentioned the words: ("China" OR "Chinese") AND ("innovation" OR "technology"). While it attempted to include as many resources as possible in order to ensure a significant coverage, the scope is limited by the fact that the database favours English-language journals and does not contain books. Although incomprehensive, the literature review might not have missed a significant amount of relevant documents given the fact that many scholars publish journal articles before book-length analysis. In terms of time scope, given the highly dynamic nature of the topic under investigation, the search covered all academic works more recent than 2017, up to 2021. The initial search yielded a total of 631 articles. Furthermore, of course, the theoretical framework and fundamental concepts are based on earlier literature, beginning with Schumpeter's theory *of economic development* (1934).

After reviewing the literature on the approach to the national innovation system and its suitability for the particular case of China, the next step was to systematically review the China innovation policy formation process. Therefore, a comprehensive quantitative and qualitative analysis of state and party policy documents was carried out, at national, provincial and local levels. Although the review of national policies included all relevant innovation initiatives published between 2012 and 2021, for subnational policies, the study selected major initiatives from tier 1 cities (Beijing, Shanghai, Shenzhen and Guangzhou) and several selected tier 2 (Tianjin, Wuhan, Hangzhou and Chengdu). Policy documents were collected in Chinese, from the official websites of the central and local government agencies, as well as of the central party, local branches and party-related organisations.

Third, explicit or implicit political statements were obtained from more than two hundreds of open-source Chinese and English-language documents, such as press releases, interviews, news articles, blogs and think-tank reports. The collected data were published between December 2017 and December 2021. The research used keyword screening methods in a professional Chinese media content database that provides access even to items that have been currently removed from the internet.

In addition, financial firm-level data, macro information on foreign investment, as well as basic calculation data of government R&D expenditure are drawn from and verified between national and international databases such as the Statistics Yearbook on Science and Technology Activities of Industrial Enterprises, China Statistical Yearbook on High Technology Industry, the China Stock Market and Accounting Research (CSMAR) database for publicly listed firms, the List of China's Outward Foreign Direct Investment Projects, which contains detailed information on OFDI activities of companies, the World Economic Outlook Database (IMF), The Main Science and Technology Indicators (OECD), the UIS online database (UNESCO Institute for Statistics) and The Science and Engineering Indicators in the US National Science Foundation (NSF). In addition, industry financial indicators, including venture capital investments, have been drawn from specialised commercial databases. In addition, other quantitative data are obtained from composite measurements such as The Global Innovation Index 2021 (WIPO, 2021) and the 2021 EU Industrial R&D Investment Scoreboard (Grassano et al., 2021). R&D expenditures are denominated in US dollars at constant prices and purchasing power parities (PPPs).

Finally, qualitative data were collected through 31 informal interviews with leading industry players, investors, policymakers and researchers, conducted between March 2018 and April 2020 in China's major innovation clusters: Beijing, Guangzhou, Hong Kong, Shanghai and Shenzhen. These allowed both open-ended and Likert-scale answers. To obtain valid and reliable data, the interviews were primarily conducted face-to-face, as well as by telephone and video calls. To maximise results, anonymity was ensured and interviews were conducted mainly in Chinese. Interviews have been informal and unstructured, the personal factor contributing to the trustfulness and in-depth of the data provided. The interviewees were distributed among government, industry and academia as follows: 8 directors or deputy directors working in governmental institutions among which 1 head and 1 deputy head of the department in central administration, 2 directors and 1 deputy director of decentralised authorities, 2 secretary-generals of province-level Communist Party organisations and 1 mayor of a major municipality; 15 general managers or equivalents in technology-intensive industries out of which 4 at national-level large companies, 5 at small or medium companies, 3 founders at start-ups and 3 directors of venture capital funds; and ultimately, 8 high-level researcher managers in 4 top-tier universities from Beijing and Shanghai. The questions were qualitative in nature, asking for opinions, plans and personal evaluations on China's innovation policies and programmes. The fact that the interview answers are inherently distorted by subjective biases and self-censorship has been taken into account in the final results.

To the furthest extent possible, input data, regardless of its source, has been verified through data-triangulation. It has also been winsorized to eliminate the influence of extreme values and opinions. However, due to the fast-changing innovation landscape, the search for timely data is challenging, while its sensitive nature limits the broadness and accuracy of data possible to be obtained.

The research is exploratory, contributing by updating and broadening the scope of previous research on the NIS of China. However, it does not attempt to be comprehensive. Given the complexity of the matter, many other aspects remain due to the following contributions including.

## References

Grassano, N., Hernandez Guevara, H., Fako, P., Tübke, A., Amoroso, S., Georgakaki, A., Napolitano, L., Pasimeni, F., Rentocchini, F., Compaño, R., Fatica, S., & Panzica, R. (2021). *The 2021 EU industrial R&D investment scoreboard*. Publications Office of the EU. Luxembourg. https://doi.org/10.2760/559391

WIPO. (2021). *Global innovation index 2021: Tracking innovation through the COVID-19 crisis*. Geneva. https://www.wipo.int/edocs/pubdocs/en/wipo_pub_gii_2021.pdf

CHAPTER 4

# Government and Public Policies

China engages openly in industrial policy as it seeks to become a self-sufficient power in a variety of industries. Scientific and technological development has long been considered by intellectual elites as critical for China's nation-building and rejuvenation, economic development and modernisation (Elman, 2006). As China has missed the industrial revolution and suffered heavy losses in the consecutive wars of the second half of the nineteenth century, in the beginning of the twentieth century nation-building movements considered the adoption of foreign technology to be "the primary task" for "self-strengthening (自强)" (Kuo & Liu, 1978). During the May Fourth Movement in 1919, the newly introduced ideas of 'Mr. De'—standing for democracy—and 'Mr. Sai'—standing for science—became the only way forward for China (Poo, 2019).

Later, after the founding of the People's Republic of China, during Chairman Mao Zedong's era, China has started to pursue science and technology (S&T) innovation by the means of centrally coordinated policies and allocated resources. In 1978, with the beginning of the opening-up, Chairman Deng Xiaoping designated S&T as "the first productive force",[1] and in the 1980s, the Chinese state launched a mass propaganda campaign to promote his idea. Since 1995, the concept of

[1] Third Plenary Session of the 11th CPC Central Committee of the Communist Party of China, 18 December 1978.



A. Băzăvan, *China's National Innovation System*,
https://doi.org/10.1007/978-981-97-3266-1_4

'revitalizing the nation through S&T' has become widely used in policy documents and official statements. In 2003, President Hu Jintao introduced the Innovation-Driven Development Strategy, which became a top priority and was further strengthened during President Xi Jinping's tenure (Zhang, 2021).

As the latter declared in a 2018 speech, 'science and technology have never before so profoundly influenced the future and fate of nations and have never before so profoundly influenced the lives and welfare of people, as they do today'. In the same speech, President Xi has also mentioned that China "must strive to become the world's main centre of science and the high ground of innovation".[2] In 2016, innovation became the first among 5 big principles for development which should lead China to build a moderately prosperous society in all aspects, alongside coordination, green, open and shared development (Ministry of Foreign Affairs of PRC, 2016). As Liu (2008) argues, the narrative "excludes any other alternative version of science and technology and exempts any challenge of the 'power' of science and technology". Therefore, in addition to its pragmatic economic and national security value, innovation also has a strong ideological substance, as technological achievements and catching up contribute to the strengthening of the legitimacy of the Party.

Since establishing its NIS, China tested and developed a variety of plans and programmes that differ significantly between regions and historical times. Sometimes, the central government's targets and policy instruments have been rather vague, granting room for policy experimentation at the subnational level. Moreover, not rarely has the multitude of central initiatives been inconsistent in their outcomes, sometimes succeeding to achieve rapid progress, yet sometimes falling short of meeting their targets.

Following the economic opening-up launched in 1978, the transformation of China's S&T sector truly started picking up steam in 1985 (Sun & Cao, 2020). Initially, central policy planning has attempted to consolidate dissipated initiatives into a more coordinated, whole-of-resources approach (Liu et al., 2011). Over time, policymaking has

[2] "Become the World's Primary Center for Science and High Ground for Innovation" ("努力成为世界主要科学中心和创新高"). trans. by Ben Murphy et al., DigiChina. March 18, 2021. https://digichina.stanford.edu/news/xi-jinping-strive-become-worlds-primary-center-science-and-high-ground-innovation.

gradually recognised the key role of market mechanisms in resource allocation and has begun to design a more market-friendly and business-led "functional industrial policy" (Wang & Zhu, 2021). Therefore, it gradually shifted its interventions to an increasingly sophisticated portfolio of soft supporting policies, including the creation of investment funds, tax incentives and fiscal measures, supportive and discriminative public procurement, export promotion programmes, loans and credit guarantees, among others (Sun & Cao, 2020).

This evolved into a top-down type of experimentalist governance, where the central government sets targets and subnational administrations choose their ways to achieve them (Zhang et al., 2022). However, such a shift is not absolute and many elements of China's planned economy still remain with strong and sometimes arbitrary government intervention in industrial policy (Wang & Zhu, 2021). During this transition from a rather planned innovation governance system to an increasingly business-led one, China's NIS remains dominated by a 'selective industrial policy'. Therefore, in those areas of prime interest, the central government maintains the capacity to deploy large coordinated efforts, integrating and optimising resource distribution, thus overcoming the risks of fragmentation and duplication.

As it hopes to be at the forefront of the Fourth Industrial Revolution, China is striving to reduce its dependence on foreign suppliers and promote independent innovation capacities, especially in high-tech industries, as emphasised in the strategic plan 'Made in China 2025' (Kang & Im, 2021; Liu & Zhao, 2021; Sykes, 2021). This motivation led to the launch of a USD 1.4 trillion programme for "new-type infrastructure", aimed at creating domestic capacities in core technologies such as AI, 5G, big data and the Internet of Things (IoT), among others.

This section reviews the evolution of the Chinese government's role in the national innovation system, in terms of policy priorities, objectives and implementation instruments, at different governance levels. It will also examine the relationship of governments with private and nongovernmental stakeholders, the distribution of authority, as well as the complex dynamics of authority between the central government and subnational authorities. The chapter highlights the fact that China's innovation policy is not monolithic, but consists of a complex network of central and subnational policies and polities, with different capacities and at different levels of development and support, connected or dissipated. The summary will therefore assess the measure to which the government is actually influencing the overall innovation process.

## 1 Decentralisation

Within the available literature, a common assumption about the Chinese state is that it is a 'highly centralised' decision-making system, while its economy has a command-and-control nature (Zeng, 2021). This simplified understanding neglects the nuances of China's multi-layered governance, with regional governments enjoying great degrees of autonomy in certain aspects and especially in economic policy (Bazavan, 2019a).

The administrative system is divided into provinces, autonomous provinces, municipalities and special administrative regions (SARs). The country remains indeed centralised in nature, as the national government intervenes and supervises closely local policy practices, while a single-party governance system seeks to impose political legitimacy through a top-down approach.

However, in order to deliver results and legitimacy, the central government also benefits from and requests subnational governments' input of 'creativity' for innovation in policymaking. Therefore, the central government establishes the global policy goals and their specific targets, thus steering bureaucrats and industry partners at all levels. In turn, local stakeholders must respond with implementation plans and experimentation, which is actually encouraged. This kind of dynamic between national and subnational authorities is an important underlying feature of China's NIS. Most of the time, whether policies are actually implemented and bear the expected results at the local level is related to the local governments' ability and awareness (Zeng, 2021). This mechanism also functions as a public opinion pressure-release for the central government, as when a public policy is not delivering, the public opinion tends to criticise the local authorities for improper implementation, rather than the policy decision makers themselves.

Actually, a persistent feature of China's innovation governance is its high level of regional competition that drives experimentation with different policy approaches. In an effort to align with the objectives of the central government in the shortest possible time, provincial governments are fiercely competing for star projects and building new companies. Moreover, local officials must make sure that their efforts are seen and recognised by their higher authorities in order to aspire for hierarchical promotion (Zhang et al., 2022). This competition can sometimes become highly disordered, bringing about overlaps and mismanagement. Nevertheless, some of the most innovative regions of China are also the ones that enjoy the largest autonomies (SARs, SEZs and municipalities), which makes an argument for the idea that positive effects of decentralisation outmatch the downsides.

In order to better coordinate this mechanism and avoid its shortcomings, *The 13th Five-Year Plan for Science, Technology, and Innovation* called for optimising the working mechanisms and redesigning the division of tasks among national and subnational authorities. However, in the current state, observers should continue to view China's innovation policies through the lens of structured uncertainty.

## 2 Policy Pilot Projecting and Experimentation

While targets are usually set by the central government, many national policies actually start from local initiatives through a bottom-up approach (Heilmann, 2018). In a model of experimentalist governance, in almost every case, when the Chinese government plans to undertake reforms, it launches a pilot project in a limited area that gives local administrations the authority, alongside the responsibility, for policy experimentation (Bazavan, 2019a). Top-down signalling or indirect control of the central government allows local administrations to test new ideas and thus promote institutional innovation (Zhang et al., 2022). The successful ideas are then adapted by the national authorities and scaled across the nation (Zeng, 2021). Thus, policy experimentation is a process of pilot projecting, selection and diffusion, with the overarching aim to create an effective system of innovation governance fit for the country's particularities. Based on a trial-and-error approach, the most successful experiments have gained fame and become book models of governance, while many others have long been rolled back and forgotten (MERICS, 2018). As Heilmann (2008) argues, this model of pilot projecting and policy experimentation at the local level 'minimized the risks and the cost to central policymakers by placing the burden on local governments and providing welcome scapegoats in cases of failure'.

The first Special Economic Zones (SEZs) established in Guangdong and Fujian in 1979 became landmark achievements of experimentalist policymaking, achieving the first outstanding economic and innovation success (Bazavan, 2019a). SEZs have been China's first regions to benefit from liberalised markets and foreign investments. Especially Shenzhen succeeded in turning it first into a manufacturing powerhouse and eventually becoming a world-class innovation and financial hub. In 1980, Shenzhen was just a small fishing village. It has been left free to experiment with policy, independent of central government (although initially surrounded by barbed-wire fences). The city came with many incentives for business people and entrepreneurs, such as tax-exemptions and free land leases to build their premises. The city also offered payments to highly skilled young people to move in, in addition to the salaries they received from companies, which supported 500.000 incoming graduates every year. The Phoenix Talent Program has further incentivised talents in specific interest areas to move to Shenzhen. On its side, the administration proved to be highly efficient, releasing the needed documents for opening businesses in a matter of days at a one-stop shop. Such factors led Shenzhen to grow in less than four decades into one of the most attractive cities for foreign investment and research on the mainland, with an individual GDP exceeding those of Hong Kong, Singapore or Israel (Bazavan, 2019b). Major MNCs emerged from Shenzhen or moved in their headquarters and research centres at a later stage, including Huawei and ZTE, the two top companies in the world by the number of patent applications filled under the Patent Cooperation Treaty (PCT). Shenzhen not only succeeded in attracting foreign investment like Shanghai, but actually grew its own local companies.

Currently, as the city became itself very attractive, the scope of government incentives has been limited to specific sectors of interest, such as high-tech industries. The central government does not support Shenzhen anymore, which is considered to have become mature enough to continue developing independently. The city administration is also not aiming anymore to attract new incoming investment but rather makes efforts to retain companies, despite surging costs. As the city became more expensive, many companies keep their R&D centres in Shenzhen but are moving manufacturing to other cities that became attractive, partly following the Shenzhen earlier model.

Although several lessons can be drawn from the story of Shenzhen, its model cannot be replicated in a different context. Shenzhen benefited from a unique context, especially due to its proximity to Hong Kong, which enabled the latter's manufacturing capacities to move just across the border into Shenzhen. Shenzhen had also benefited from the fact that it was a fully new establishment, without a previous population, such as Zhuhai. This made the social fabric more dynamic, while in an urban environment with a previous population, it would have been harder for newcomers to strive.

Starting from Shenzhen, opening-up reforms have been gradually but carefully expanded across the country, to an ever-increasing number of industries. The SEZ model is now exported to Africa and other areas of Asia, using Chinese expertise, sometimes with the assistance of international financial institutions such as the Asian Infrastructure Investment Bank, the Asian Development Bank, the African Development Bank and the World Bank.

The Torch Programme, launched in 1988, offers another example of early pilot projecting and policy experimentation. The programme launched the first high-tech industrial development zones and science parks, attempting to build Silicon Valley-type hubs for innovation (Liu et al., 2017). As a follow-up, in 2009, the first National Innovation Demonstration Zones (NIDZs) were further established in several cities, with the same aim of serving as experimentation platforms for policymaking (Development Solutions Europe Ltd., 2017).

Conversely, in cases where innovation emerges naturally from the commercial sector, the government may initially provide new technologies with the benefit of the doubt and encourage their free growth (Bazavan, 2019a). Regulatory discussions and safety issues are only addressed later, if at all. This approach, while potentially stimulating experimentation and entrepreneurship, can also have drawbacks. For example, in the case of online money transfers, the government only introduced cap limits on transfers 11 years after Alipay first introduced the service, resulting in a regulatory vacuum that fostered a rapidly growing digital ecosystem with significant productivity gains in the real economy. However, this same lack of regulation also led to devastating losses for many consumers when peer-to-peer lending platforms turned out to be fraudulent.

The government's open attitude towards technologies, which is doubled by positive public perception, is only allowed until technologies reach maturity. Although late, the government might later intervene stronger than foreseen, such as is the case of the recent "crackdown" on tech companies begun in 2021, which will be later discussed in the *Priority Industries* sub-chapter of the *Other Systemic Factors* chapter.

## 3 Priority Technology Areas

Although the Chinese government's share of the overall industrial output of the economy and, particularly, the nation's gross R&D expenditure for R&D (GERD) is steadily decreasing, it continues to lead the investments in strategic technologies that are too risky, expensive and long for the private sector to undertake.

Technological priority areas have been established by the State Council's National Medium and Long-Term Programme for Science and Technology Development (MLP). It was China's most ambitious plan to date in terms of S&T and R&D funding, allocating approximately CNY 500 billion (USD 75 billion) for sixteen national megaprojects. According to the programme, the 16 major special projects covered a range of strategic sectors including: 'core electronic devices, high-end generic chips and basic software, super large-scale integrated circuit manufacturing technology and associated techniques, next-generation broadband mobile telecommunication, high-end numerically controlled machine tools and basic manufacturing technology, the development of large oil-gas fields and coal-bed methane, large advanced pressurised water reactors and nuclear power stations of high temperature gas coolant reactors, control and treatment of water body contamination, new genetically modified varieties, major new drugs, prevention and treatment of major infectious diseases such as HIV/ADIS and viral hepatitis, large passenger aircrafts, high-resolution earth observation systems, manned space flights, and the moon probe' (State Council of the People's Republic of China, 2006).

2015 marked the launch of the ongoing *Made in China 2025* strategy that aims to upgrade China's industry in all sectors, with an emphasis on intelligent manufacturing. Aligned with MLP and the Thirteen Five-Year Plan, it updated the list of sectors that are prioritised for investment and regulatory work:

- next-generation, information technology, high-end numerical control machinery and automation;
- aerospace and aeronautical equipment;
- maritime equipment and high-tech vessel manufacturing;
- rail transport equipment;
- new energy vehicles;
- electrical power equipment;
- new materials;

- biomedicine and advanced medical equipment;
- agricultural equipment.

2015 also marked the launch of a new focal point in policy planning, artificial intelligence (AI), emphasised in the *Internet Plus* strategy. On 20 July 2017, the Chinese government further released the *Next Generation Artificial Intelligence Development Plan*, a road map targeting a related market worth of USD 150 billion by 2030 (see Webster et al., 2017 for an English translation of the Plan). At a similar time, the Ministry of Science and Technology (MOST) has appointed four domestic companies, Baidu, Alibaba Group, Tencent and iFlyTek to each lead one AI-related industry: self-driving cars, smart cities, computer optics for medical diagnosis and voice intelligence, respectively, awarding them privileged access to critical infrastructures and data, regulatory exceptions and funding.

Therefore, for strategic areas, government support extends beyond mere funding, to regulation (or non-regulation) and all-round support through formal or ad hoc means (Development Solutions Europe Ltd., 2016). Responsibility is shared between central and subnational authorities for both successes and failures. Successful examples include high-speed trains, ICT and green technologies. A notable failure to date is represented by semiconductors, which will be further discussed in the *Other Systemic Factors Chapter, Priority Industries Subchapter.*

## 4 Technology Independency and Self-Sufficiency

Since the beginning of his tenure, President Xi Jinping identified his nation's greatest hidden danger to be its dependencies in core technologies on foreign suppliers. Technological self-sufficiency became a key policy goal, as the fundamental guard against economic and trade disruptions. This view has gained even more traction during the last five years, as the debate around industrial policy in the USA, Japan and the EU took scale and invited trade policy actions against China (Schneider, 2021). Furthermore, the post-COVID-19's focus on supply chain resilience and the global chip shortage has led to even more events beyond China's control.

Trade tensions regarding China have first started after its entry into the WTO, determined by the perception that growing import competition from China and offshoring of production facilities are hurting the jobs market in the USA and elsewhere (Autor et al., 2013). Tensions rose steadily during President Obama's tenure and transformed into a "trade war" during the Trump administration. Since the beginning of President Joe Biden's tenure, despite the expectations of some experts of a policy change, the approach towards China has continued unaffected.

Over the years, the USA imposed Section 301 tariffs on imported goods from China, banned the sale of specific hardware and software to Chinese companies, enacted the 'China Initiative' comprising laws preventing technology theft and restricted joint R&D activities with Chinese partners. Restrictions affected even individual students from China who are now finding it increasingly difficult to study in the USA.

For example, in one of the latest rounds of bans adopted in June 2021, 59 Chinese suspected of links to the military and surveillance apparatus were prohibited from investing in the USA. In July 2021, an additional 14 Chinese entities were sanctioned on the basis of alleged human rights abuses in Xinjiang. In November 2021, 10 new Chinese companies were added to the Entity List because they allegedly carried activities that are contrary to national security or foreign policy interest (Rühlig, 2021).

The concerns of the USA regarding China span a wide range of issues, but some of the most salient are infringements of intellectual property rights (IPR) and of forced technology transfers (Mulloy, 2019). These two aspects are perceived by the USA as serious threats to its own economy and security. The USA also criticises China's centralised economic model, with a strong government push that would provide unfair subsidies along with other types of support to establish national high-tech champions (Office of the U.S. Trade Representative, 2019). This perspective led the USA to pursue sanctioning China through all instruments at its disposal, in an attempt to prevent further technology diversion, especially in those sectors that have the potential to promote China's military advancement (Rühlig, 2021). Over time, export bans became increasingly targeted and "specialised". Their scope is narrowing towards specific hi-tech and defence-related sectors, while steadily advancing technology decoupling. For example, against the global expansion of Huawei, ZTE and other ICT companies, bans on trading with semiconductors have proved to be an effective retaliatory tool from the USA perspective.

There appear to be no signs of a change of policy in the near future in Washington D.C. As increasingly more Chinese companies are sanctioned by the USA, global technological development might indeed become divided on a dual track global market, centred around the USA or centred around China. Decoupling has a significant impact, especially on China's high-tech industries. Therefore, for Beijing, the stakes are high, perceiving US policies as a direct threat to China's capacity to import critical inputs for its economy (Wyne, 2020). At the National Cybersecurity and Informatisation Work Conference in April 2018, President Xi Jinping declared that the reliance on foreign technology is China's 'Achilles' heel' (China Policy, 2018). In April 2020, during his remarks to the CPC Politburo, Xi Jinping urged for "independent, controllable, safe, and reliable" value chains in fields related to national security.[3] *Made in China 2025* and the latest two five-year plans also emphasise the need for technological autonomy, independent manufacturing capacities and indigenous cutting-edge technologies that can support the entire production cycle. At the same time, the government has been advancing the "dual circulation" strategy, intended to prioritise domestic consumption as a primary source of economic development, working as a hedge against external shocks and promoting supply chain indigenisation.

Therefore, current trade tensions constitute a renewed stimulus for China to move towards self-reliance, and in recent years, policy documents and official statements display an evolving confidence in the country's own capabilities. While concerned about pertaining vulnerabilities, at the same time, China sees itself closer than ever to achieving technological parity with other countries and even a soon-to-become leader.

In empirical reality, the country has indeed already made significant progress across industries. There are sectors, such as artificial intelligence, information and communication technologies, high-speed rail and NEVs, where China has already become one of the creators. However, for many other industries, China is still in a position to seek independence. In areas such as semiconductors and microprocessors, which China perceives as one of its most vulnerable points, despite positive signs, success is beyond palpable boundaries (Bazavan, 2019a).

Finally, the dream of technological independence and self-reliance, shared to a certain extent by both China and the USA, might be impossible to attain by anyone in a (still) deeply connected global economy, that is moving faster than ever.

[3] Several Major Issues in the National Medium and Long-Term Economic and Social Development Strategy, Seeking Truth, October 31, 2020. http://www.ccdi.gov.cn/ldhd/gcsy/202011/t20201103_229231.html.

## 5 The Scale of Government Intervention

In markets where domestic firms face challenges in competing with foreign companies, the state often intervenes strongly through protective measures. However, this approach raises concerns among foreign companies about fairness in competition and equal opportunities. For instance, China restricts the services of American companies, including Facebook, Alphabet and Twitter, in order to protect its domestic firms. While this policy may benefit the established companies, it could also harm the emergence of new companies and innovation in the Chinese market.

On the other hand, as will be discussed more broadly in the following chapter **Funding for Innovation**, government direct funding accounts for less than 22% of total R&D (GERD) spending in China, while the large majority of funds are provided by the business sector (Bazavan, 2020). Moreover, business-led R&D is rather negligibly supported formally, in terms of subsidies and favourable tax policies.

The low share of publicly funded R&D is consistent with the unexpected low contribution of state-owned enterprises (SOEs) in the total industrial output, as seen in the graphic below. Following the economic reforms of the late 1990s, the number and capacity of private companies have exploded, leading the share of SOEs in the total number of firms operating in China to drop significantly, from 24% in 1995 to 3% in 2014. However, most of the surviving SOEs are relatively large and are located in upstream or strategically important industries (Bazavan, 2019b) (Fig. 1).

Indeed, the Chinese government acknowledges and welcomes the fact that resource allocation is primarily determined by the market and sees its role rather as a platform enabler and close partner for innovation (Bazavan, 2019a). State influence remains concentrated, as it only invests in selected sectors that exceed the capabilities of businesses (Zhou & Fang, 2021). At the same time, it is important to note that the distinction between private and state-owned companies is not clear-cut in China (Ding, 2018). In many industries of interest, the state could assert control over and influence companies by owning 'special management shares', establishing party committees and possessing other types of dependency relations (Li, 2017).

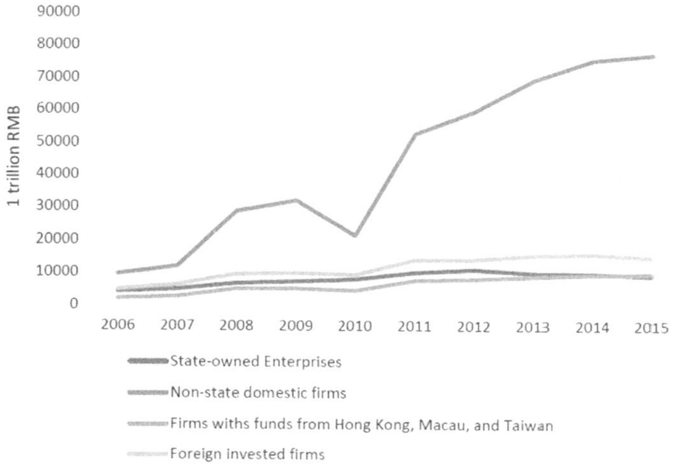


**Fig. 1** Total value of industrial output by ownership types of firms (*Source* China S&T Statistical Yearbook 2007–2016, compiled by Li [2017])

## 6 Standardisation

International technical standards, acting as frameworks for regularising technologies in order to ensure interconnectivity and compatibility across products and regions, have long been considered a niche expert topic. However, given the emerging geopolitical competition with consequences in the technology sector, standards have also made their way to the central stage of political attention. The capacity of a state to participate in, influence and lead the formulation of international standards became a reflexion of national technological prowess and key to gaining the upper hand.

The process of negotiating and deciding on international technical standards has traditionally been a stronghold of American and European industry actors (Berger & Russel, 2021). Led by the principle that standard setting should be an open, bottom-up process led by industry players, the US and EU companies created a systematic, cumulative advantage and have a greater say. However, more recently, given its domestic technological progress and industrial development, China's influence on the formulation of international standards has gradually advanced. The USA-China Economic and Security Review Commission

(USCC) considers that the "dominance of technical standards underpinning ICT and other emerging fields is integral to Beijing's ambitions" and deliberate push to obtain influence in the standards developing organisations (SDOs) (U.S.-China Economic & Security Review Commission, 2020). Evidence of China's growing role in standard setting includes more numerous submissions to key SDOs as well as the strengthened representation of Chinese nationals in leadership positions. Significant breakthroughs and contributions achieved are evident in certain fields of standardisation where China has emerged as a new leader, such as in AI, 5G and the broader telecom industry.

China is currently undertaking a reform of the standardisation system (Rühlig, 2021). In 2021, the Central Committee of the Chinese Communist Party and the State Council released the *National Standardisation Development Outline*, as part of the broader *China Standards 2035* initiative. With a name that sounds similar to 'Made in China 2025', the strategy calls for increasing the participation of China in global standards setting and the shift away from a state-controlled standard setting model towards one that is on the one hand state-centric, while on the other hand more closely aligned with market forces. Despite the fact that the strategy contains several positive regarding the minimisation of state intervention in standards development, that add to repetead official calls, our interview results showed that standardisation remains and actually increasingly becomes to be considered a key element to promote national aims (Berger and Russel, 2021). These goals go beyond gaining a commercial advantage, but spread into the strategic and security realm, for example, using Beijing's concept of 'cyber sovereignty' to impede the free flow of information. It appears that China's standardisation system remains subordinated to China's industrial policy agenda, dominated by SOEs and state-affiliated research institutions.

Therefore, there is no doubt that in recent years China has made concentrated efforts and achieved significant breakthroughs to increase its standard setting influence in an increasing number of fields, especially in emerging digital technologies such as 5G, AI and ICT. At the same time, it should be avoided to unrealistically overstate China's already attained influence on standards governance, while also noting that China's participation can equally bring benefits, not only risks. Although this percentage is growing rapidly, China is currently responsible for only 1.8% of international technical standards, according to the European Chamber of Commerce in China (Rühlig, 2021).

However, it is a fact that as China expands its influence within SDOs and through bilateral trade and investment relations, its ability to influence technical standardisation is likely to increase. At the same time, there is a growing frustration among international partners with the perceived Chinese state-centric approach to standardisation that serves the country's industrial agenda, which grows the risk of fragmentation or even decoupling of international technical standards into two or more spheres riddled with incompatibilities.

In this competitive environment, the EU should engage with China in a manner that makes clear the need for international rules and reciprocity. At the same time, the EU must ensure that it continues to be a global standard setter, and that SDO evolutions are not infringing upon its strategic autonomy, technological sovereignty and fundamental values. Among several ways of doing so, the EU should increase its own engagement with SDOs, including by providing more resources, hosting meetings and encouraging its experts to participate. While acting in a more EU-wide coordinated approach, the EU should also keep away from further politicising a process that is technical in nature. In their turn, SDOs should also take measures to check undue government influence of China or of any other party, by means such as strengthening anonymous voting procedures.

## 7 Summary

In summary, the Chinese government identifies innovation as a top priority for national development. The mechanisms to design and implement innovation policy are complex. On the one hand, targets are established with a top-down approach, while on the other hand, China deploys a variety of policy experiments, strategies and measures—sometimes hardly compatible with each other—at multiple levels of government, in an effort to put into practice relevant initiatives. This reflects a unique model of experimental policymaking at subnational levels, with the goal of rolling successful initiatives across the country (Arenal et al., 2020).

Overall, China's policies include but are not limited to awarding priority industries generous funding and a favourable regulatory environment, attracting international talents, promoting technological national independency, incentivising or pressuring the transfer of foreign technology, designing innovation-friendly policies and improving institutional efficiency, encouraging technology-seeking investments abroad and intervening in the market to protect domestic companies from foreign competitors.

In sectors considered to be strategic, the state owns itself participations in enterprises or possesses other types of dependency relations (Li, 2017). It does not refrain from strongly intervening with protectionist measures in industries where Chinese companies are less competitive than their foreign peers. More recently, there has been a growing tendency to assert control over big technology companies and a request from authorities that the latter should contribute to national policy goals, even at the expense of undercutting their credibility and capacity to be trusted in global markets. Such returns of the state in economy, opposed to the general trend of disengagement, are criticised as "国进民退" (the state advances, the private sector retreats) (Breslin, 2011). Furthermore, China's stronger push for technology independence and autonomy, mirroring that of other players, may also disrupt connectivity critical to global growth and progress.

However, the role of government is limited in its capacity and willingness to intervene. Both economic data and policy sources show that the government is, in the majority of cases, a facilitator, an end customer and a provider of an enabling environment, rather than a primary actor itself on the innovation scene. Policymaking in China requires the coordination of governments at different levels with companies and the alignment of public and private interests. Moreover, unlike previously, the most recent S&T strategies strongly emphasise the central role of industry-led innovation policy and the primary goal of commercialising technology.

Therefore, on the one hand, the Chinese government considers that its ability to play a leading role is critical to achieving the goal of "national rejuvenation", especially by retaining control and autonomy. But this comes into tension with the aim of unleashing private creativity and market efficiency, which would also allow domestic companies to become global trusted sources of technological products. This overlapping complexity leads the government to act in a multitude of ways and methods, which differ greatly between regions and political contexts.

## References

Arenal, A., et al. (2020). Innovation ecosystems theory revisited: The case of artificial intelligence in China. *Telecommunications Policy, 44*(6). https://doi.org/10.1016/j.telpol.2020.101960

Autor, D. H., Dorn, D., & Hanson, G. H. (2013). The China syndrome: Local labor market effects of import competition in the United States. *American Economic Review, 103*(6). https://doi.org/10.1257/aer.103.6.2121

Bazavan, A. (2019a, September). Chinese government's shifting role in the national innovation system. *Technological Forecasting and Social Change, 148*. https://doi.org/10.1016/j.techfore.2019.119738

Bazavan, A. (2019b). How does China innovate? A deconstruction of China's national innovation system. *Hyperion International Journal of Econophysics & New Economy, 12*(1), 99–107.

Bazavan, A. (2020). China's transition to a knowledge economy—Institutional mechanisms, public policies and private investment. In C. R. Pamfilie, V. Dinu, L. Tăchiciu, D. Pleşea, & C. Vasiliu (Eds.), *6th BASIQ international conference on new trends in sustainable business and consumption*. ASE Bucharest.

Berger, B., & Russel, D. (2021, December 2). *Is China stacking the technology deck by setting international standards?* https://thediplomat.com/2021/12/is-china-stacking-the-technology-deck-by-setting-international-standards/. Accessed 2 July 2022.

Breslin, S. (2011). China and the crisis: Global power, domestic caution and local initiative. *Contemporary Politics* [Preprint]. https://doi.org/10.1080/13569775.2011.565987

China Policy. (2018). *April: Circuit breaker. Roundup from our portfolios*. https://mailchi.mp/policycn/observer-2746697?e=95d012ca4e

Development Solutions Europe Ltd. (2016). *Comparison of the 12th five-year plan for S&T development, and the 13th five-year plan for S&T innovation.*

Development Solutions Europe Ltd. (2017). *Fifth ad hoc study—Analysis of national high- and new-technology zones.*

Ding, J. (2018, March). *Deciphering China's AI dream: The context, components, capabilities, and consequences of China's strategy to lead the world in AI* (pp. 1–44). Future of Humanity Institute, University of Oxford.

Elman, B. A. (2006). *A cultural history of modern science in China*. Harvard University Press. https://doi.org/10.4159/9780674036482

Heilmann, S. (2008). Policy experimentation in China's economic rise. *Studies in Comparative International Development, 43*(1), 1–26. https://doi.org/10.1007/S12116-007-9014-4/FIGURES/2

Heilmann, S. (2018). *Red Swan: How unorthodox policy making facilitated China's rise*. The Chinese University of Hong Kong Press.

Kang, J., & Im, Y. (2021). Competition for TECHNOLOGY HEGEMONY between the U.S., & China from a Geopolitical Point of View. *J-Institute, 6*(1), 20–26. https://doi.org/10.22471/military.2021.6.1.20

Kuo, T., & Liu, K.-C. (1978). Self-strengthening: The pursuit of Western technology. *The Cambridge History of China*, 491–542. https://doi.org/10.1017/CHOL9780521214476.011

Li, Y. (2017). *Innovation pathways in the Chinese economy* (Doctoral dissertation, Georgia Institute of Technology). http://hdl.handle.net/1853/59127

Liu, F. C., et al. (2011). China's innovation policies: Evolution, institutional structure, and trajectory. *Research Policy, 40*(7). https://doi.org/10.1016/j.respol.2011.05.005

Liu, J., & Zhao, H. (2021). Privacy lost: Appropriating surveillance technology in China's fight against COVID-19. *Business Horizons, 64*(6), 743–756. https://doi.org/10.1016/j.bushor.2021.07.004

Liu, X., et al. (2017). Beyond catch-up—Can a new innovation policy help China overcome the middle income trap? *Science and Public Policy, 44*(5), 656–669. https://doi.org/10.1093/scipol/scw092

Liu, Y. (2008). The construction of pro-science and technology discourse in chinese language textbooks. *Language and Education, 19*(4), 304–321. https://doi.org/10.1080/09500780508668683

MERICS. (2018). *Serve the people: Innovation and IT in China's social development agenda*. MERICS Papers on China [Preprint], (6).

Ministry of Foreign Affairs of PRC. (2016). *No Title*, *China's Position Paper on the Implementation of the 2030 Agenda for Sustainable Development*. https://www.fmprc.gov.cn/mfa_eng/topics_665678/xjpdmgjxgsfwbcxlhgcl70znxlfh/t1357701.shtml

Mulloy, P. (2019). Coerced tech transfer: The heart of the China problem. *The American Prospect*. https://prospect.org/world/coerced-tech-transfer-heart-china-problem/. Accessed 1 July 2022.

Office of the U.S. Trade Representative. (2019). *2019 Report to the congress on China's WTO compliance*.

Poo, M. M. (2019). Culture and history of Chinese science. *National Science Review, 6*(4), 607. https://doi.org/10.1093/NSR/NWZ074

Rühlig, T. (2021). *The shape of things to come: The race to control technical standardisation*. Beijing.

Schneider, J. (2021). *China's chip industry: Running faster but still falling behind*. https://rhg.com/research/china-chips/. Accessed 1 July 2022.

State Council of the People's Republic of China. (2006). *The national medium- and long-term program for science and technology development (2006–2020)—An Outline*.

Sun, Y., & Cao, C. (2020). The dynamics of the studies of China's science, technology and innovation (STI): A bibliometric analysis of an emerging field.

*Scientometrics, 124*, 1335–1365. https://doi.org/10.1007/s11192-020-03500-x

Sykes, A. O. (2021). The law and economics of 'forced' technology transfer and its implications for trade and investment policy (and the U.S.-China Trade War). *Journal of Legal Analysis*. https://doi.org/10.1093/jla/laaa007

U.S.-China Economic and Security Review Commission. (2020). *2020 Report to Congress of the US-China Economic and Security Review Commission*. https://www.uscc.gov/sites/default/files/2020-12/2020_Annual_Report_to_Congress.pdf. Accessed 1 July 2022.

Wang, F., & Zhu, D. (2021). The influence of industrial policy on innovation in startup enterprises: An empirical study based on China's GEM listed companies. *Complexity*. https://doi.org/10.1155/2021/9650741

Webster, G., Creemers, R., Triolo, P., & Kania, E. (2017). *Full translation: China's "New Generation Artificial Intelligence Development Plan"*. https://www.newamerica.org/cybersecurity-initiative/digichina/blog/full-translation-chinas-new-generation-artificial-intelligence-development-plan-2017/

Wyne, A. (2020). How to think about potentially decoupling from China. *Washington Quarterly, 43*(1). https://doi.org/10.1080/0163660X.2020.1735854

Zeng, J. (2021). China's artificial intelligence innovation: A top-down national command approach? *Global Policy, 12*(3), 399–409. https://doi.org/10.1111/1758-5899.12914

Zhang, W., et al. (2022). Experimentalist governance in China: The National Innovation System, 2003–2018. *Journal of Chinese Governance, 7*(1), 1–26. https://doi.org/10.1080/23812346.2021.1934328

Zhang, Y. (2021). The regional disparity of influencing factors of technological innovation in China: Evidence from high-tech industry. *Technological and Economic Development of Economy, 27*(4), 811–832. https://doi.org/10.3846/tede.2021.14828

Zhou, W., & Fang, M. M. (2021). Subsidizing technology competition: China's evolving practices and international trade regulation. *Washington International Law Journal, 30*(3), 470–544.

CHAPTER 5

# Funding for Innovation

Aiming to enhance technological capabilities from domestic sources, the Chinese government and companies are determined to increase funding for research and innovation (Wei et al., 2016). Beyond funding, China is also in the middle of reforms aimed at optimising resource allocation and addressing pertaining issues, especially by shifting to more competitive mechanisms of funding disbursement (Lundvall & Rikap, 2022). Such mechanisms include the creation of investment funds that allocate resources according to market principles, alongside various tax incentives and subsidies. This chapter analyses China's funding for innovation in terms of volume, distribution of sources and destination by sector.

## 1 Funding for R&D

### *1.1 Gross Expenditure for R&D (GERD)*

In 2000, the USA was leading global R&D expenditures, with an annual spending of USD 270 billion at current PPP. It was followed by the EU with USD 180 billion. China's expenditure was a distant USD 33 billion current PPP. Between 2000 and 2015, China's GERD has increased on average by approximately 18% annually (Ministry of Science and Technology, various years). The growth rate has decreased over the last years in relative terms but still remains high. This fast growth led China to become the second-biggest spending country in the world in 2008 and surpassed



A. Băzăvan, *China's National Innovation System*,
https://doi.org/10.1007/978-981-97-3266-1_5

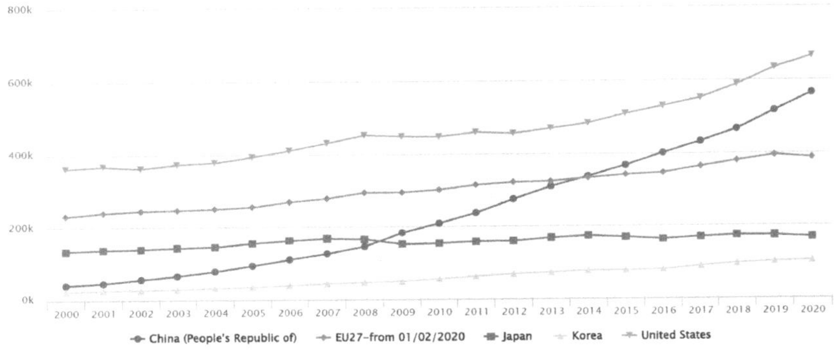


**Fig. 1** GERD in constant USD PPP, million (*Source* OECD Main Science and Technology Indicators 2022)

the EU as a whole in 2014. By 2020, China's expenditure accounted for 90% of the USA's. Following the current trajectory, China could overtake the USA and become the world's largest nation by GERD before 2030. In his 2021 work report, Premier Li Keqiang called for continuing with over 7% annual growth between 2021 and 2025, exceeding the GDP growth target of 6% (Fig. 1).[1]

Therefore, the increase in GERD was a consequence not only of economic growth but also of prioritisation of R&D spending. R&D intensity, measured in GERD as a percentage of GDP, has increased from 0.83% in 2000 to 2.4% in 2020 (slightly below the 13th 5-Year Plan target set at 2.5%). Although still behind the USA, Japan and the OECD average, China is progressing quickly and has exceeded the EU since 2019 (Fig. 2).

### *1.2 Basic vs. Applied Research*

If we refer only to fundamental research, which involves the greatest costs but can also achieve the greatest breakthroughs, the USA holds a dominant position, accounting for 60% of global spending on basic research (OECD, 2021). In turn, funding for basic research in China accounts

[1] "China's Beefed Up R&D Spending to Narrow Tech Gap with U.S., Ease 'Stranglehold Problems'" Global Times, March 5, 2021, https://www.globaltimes.cn/page/202103/1217469.shtm.

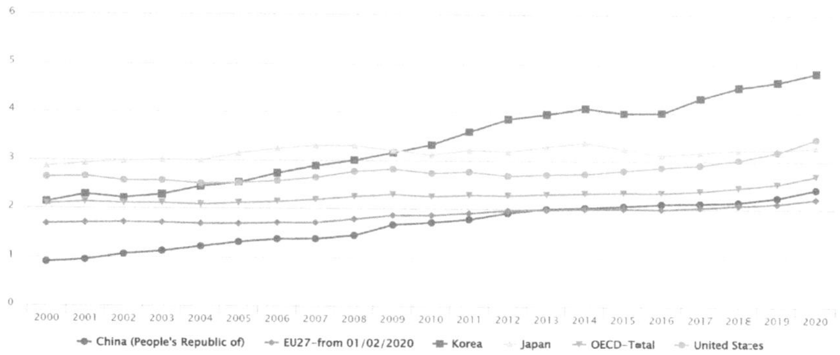


**Fig. 2** R&D Intensity in several countries, GERD as % of GDP (*Source* OECD estimates based on the OECD Main Science and Technology Indicators Database, March 2022)

for only 20% of the global total, as the country has rather focused on the short term, practical side of R&D, that translates innovation into commercial products and applications (Allison et al., 2021). According to the latest data from the National Bureau of Statistics of China, in 2020, the 82.7% lion share of GERD belonged to experimental development, 11.3% to applied research and only 6% to basic research.

But China aims to change that. Over recent years, the share of R&D expenditure with basic research has steadily increased (National Bureau of Statistics of China, 2021). In his 2021 work report, Premier Li Keqiang has also called for raising basic research spending by 10.6%, therefore at a higher rate than the GERD target.[2] As such, by 2025, basic research spending is expected to reach 8% of the overall government R&D expenditure.[3]

[2] "China's Beefed Up R&D Spending to Narrow Tech Gap with U.S., Ease 'Stranglehold Problems" *Global Times*, March 5, 2021, available at https://www.globaltimes.cn/page/202103/1217469.shtml.

[3] "China's R&D Expenditure Expected to Reach 3.758 Trillion Yuan in 2025," CGTN, March 8, 2021 https://www.ecns.cn/news/sci-tech/2021-03-08/detail-ihaihrwe3352341.shtml.

### 1.3 *R&D Funding by Source (Public and Private)*

As opposed to the general perception, Chinese R&D expenditure is led by the business sector, to an even greater extent than in the USA, the EU and Korea, being exceeded only by Japan. According to OECD data for 2018 or the latest available year, business expenditures on R&D (BERD) in China accounted for 76.6% of total R&D spending, second only to Japan (79.1%) among the world's largest R&D spenders, but ahead of Korea (76.6%), USA (62.4%) and the EU 28 (54.7%).

Consequently, Chinese government funding as a share of GERD has decreased steadily in previous years and reached 20.2% in 2018. This figure is lower than those of the EU (31.7%),[4] the USA (23%), South Korea (20.5%) and Russia (a massive 67%). Therefore, among the top research and development (R&D) performing nations, it is only the Japan government with an even lower share of government spending in national GERD (14.6%) than the Chinese.

These numbers are, of course, consistent with the fact that China allocates a relatively large proportion of expenditure to experimental development and applied research, which companies need to produce profits. However, basic research usually exceeds the capacity or interest of private companies and is usually carried out by the public sector.

It is worth noting that foreign-funded research also has a contribution to China's NIS (Bazavan, 2019). The number of research centres established in China by MNCs has exceeded 1.500 in 2014 (Yip & McKern, 2016). However, according to OECD data for 2018, only 0.4% of GERD was financed from overseas sources, lower than all other reviewed countries (Fig. 3).

In addition to spending comparatively little on R&D, the government also awards limited fiscal benefits to stimulate firms that carry R&D, with the exception of several limited initiatives such as the High- and New-Technology Enterprise (HNTE) (Development Solutions Europe Ltd., 2017a). Therefore, despite limited growth in recent years, the direct funding and tax incentives of the Chinese government for BERD as a percentage of GDP are lower than those of most other countries (Bazavan, 2019a). Situated at 0.13% in 2017 (latest available), government direct funding for BERD accounts for 0.06% and tax incentives for 0.07% (OECD, 2021). As mentioned in the introduction, this low level

[4] OECD estimate for 2015.

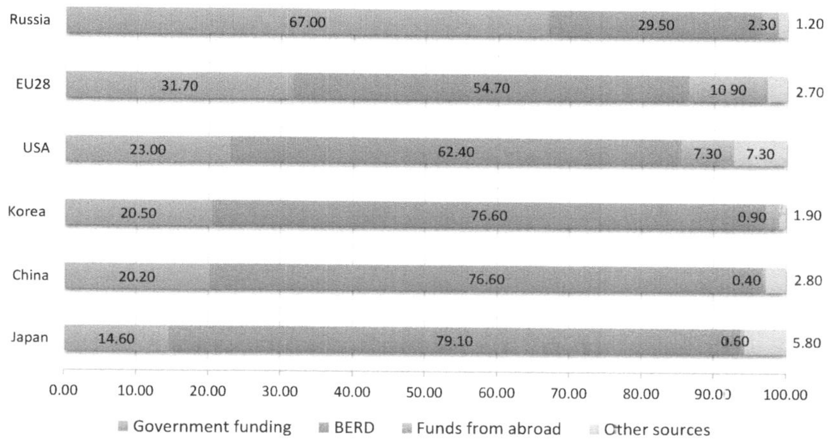


**Fig. 3** R&D by Funding Source as a % of GERD, 2018 or latest available year (*Source* Author's compilation, based on data from OECD [2019])

of government support for BERD is little known to those studying the effects of subsidies on business-led R&D in China (Boeing, 2016; Chen et al., 2018; Guan & Yam, 2015; Guo et al., 2016; Howell, 2017; Liu et al., 2016; Wei et al., 2016) (Figs. 4 and 5).

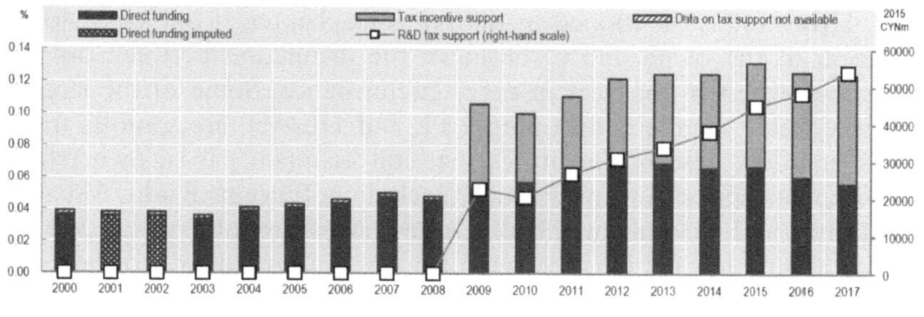


**Fig. 4** Government direct funding and tax incentives for BERD, China, 2000–17 as a percentage of GDP, 2015 prices (right-hand scale) (*Source* OECD, R&D Tax Incentives Database, http://oe.cd/rdtax, December 2021)

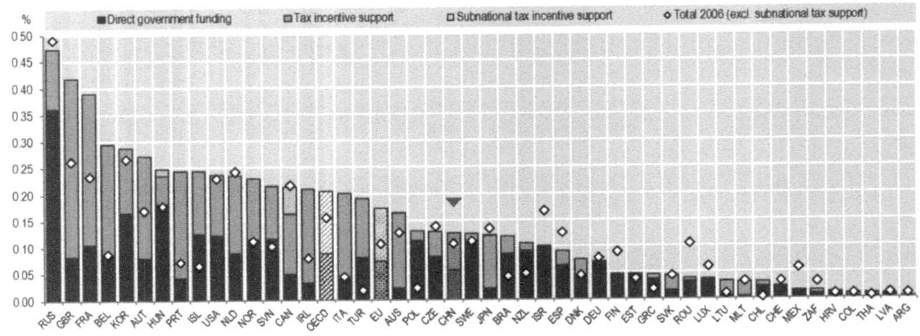


**Fig. 5** Direct government funding of business R&D and tax incentives for R&D, 2019 (latest available) as a percentage of GDP (*Source* OECD, R&D Tax Incentives Database, http://oe.cd/rdtax, December 2021)

The above data do not imply that the Chinese government is not investing in R&D. As mentioned previously, public spending has actually increased fast and constantly over the last decades and is expected to reach USD 580 billion by 2025. However, this growth is outpaced by an even faster growth of BERD. On the other hand, as it was discussed in the *Government and Public Policies* chapter, the government prefers to concentrate extensive resources towards a limited number of priority sectors.

Therefore, R&D expenditure is, to a significant extent, market-driven, while the state contributes with little, if any, financial and fiscal incentives. However, as mentioned in the previous chapter, if one pays closer attention to the ownership of business, the distinction between private and state-owned is not clear in every circumstance. Some of the largest industry R&D spenders, including ZTE and Huawei, are spinoffs from SOEs or public research institutes that still maintain partial ownership. Newer giants emerged from start-ups, including Tencent, Baidu, Alibaba, ByteDance and Xiaomi, might also have state shareholders (Li, 2017). But we should not fall into the trap of overstating the degree of government ownership. Baidu, Tencent, Alibaba and Xiaomi, as well as most of China's tech giants, are (still) publicly traded companies traded on foreign exchanges. In fact, according to all data, research funding is overwhelmingly led by private funds, including foreign ones. Government-financed research and state ownership across industries are further discussed in the *Government and Public Policies* chapter.

### 1.4 Business Expenditure for R&D (BERD)

As shown in the previous sections, BERD is the core support for R&D expenditure of most countries, including China. If we compare R&D spending of Chinese companies to the rest of the world (ROW), the *2021 EU Industrial R&D Investment Scoreboard*, which lists the firms that spend the most on R&D worldwide, reveals that out of 2500 top world spenders with over EUR 36.5 million each and a combined amount of EUR 908.9 billion, 597 companies are from China (combined amount of EUR 140.95 billion, 15.6% of total expenditure), while 799 companies are from the USA (EUR 343.56 billion, 37.8% total expenditure), 401 from the EU (EUR 184.1 billion). 20.2%), 293 from Japan (EUR 111.06 bn., 12.2%) and 410 from the ROW (EUR 129,23 bn., 14.2% total expenditure). Given its economic size, the number of Chinese companies and the overall value of R&D are still relatively limited compared to those of the USA and the EU. However, the gaps are rapidly reducing. The study records a fast growth in cumulated expenditure by Chinese firms included in the ranking, with 18.1% y–o-y in 2020 alone. China exceeded the EU in 2018 and the gap has been widening ever since.

The growth is the fastest among all countries and is distributed across almost all sectors considered, as well as in the large overall number of Chinese companies. Chinese companies are particularly increasing their investments in the ICT industry. One example is Huawei, which over a short period of time became the second largest R&D spender worldwide all sectors considered and the first in the ICT industry. Huawei has also become in recent years the largest source of patent applications with the World Intellectual Property Organisation (WIPO) (Fig. 6).

If we narrow the ranking to top 1000 R&D business spenders in the world, 194 firms are from China, whereas 321 companies are from the USA, 199 from the EU and 135 from Japan. If we narrow the ranking even further to the 158 companies that invest in R&D more than €1 billion, 24 firms are from China, whereas 54 from the USA, 37 from the EU (out of which at least one is a subsidiary of a Chinese company, Geely Holdings) and 26 from Japan. Ultimately, in the top 50 R&D spenders, there are only 4 Chinese companies.

It can be noticed that Chinese BERD accounts for an important share of top global R&D spending and is growing rapidly. However, China is still largely under-represented compared to its economic size, potential and global share of GERD. If we further analyse the distribution of firms,

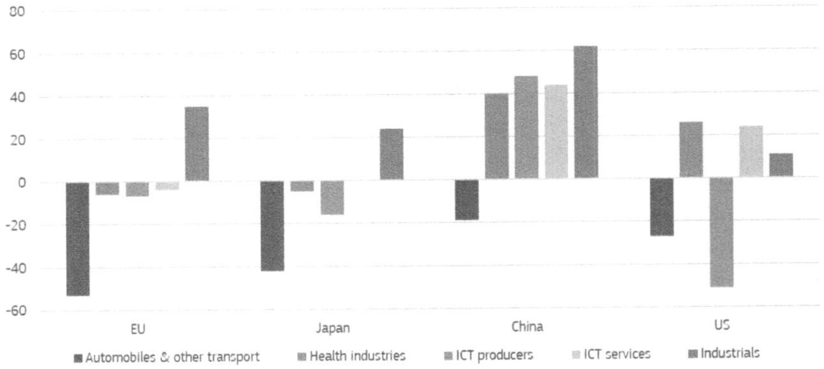


**Fig. 6** Main changes of presence (number of companies) of the main geographic regions between 2016 and 2021 (*Source* The 2021 EU Industrial R&D Investment Scoreboard, European Commission, JRC/DG RTD)

we find that the more we narrow the rankings towards top spenders, the more the ratio of Chinese companies decreases. In the top 2500 largest R&D spenders, 23.9% are Chinese companies. In top 1000, the ratio decreases to 19.4%, in top 158 to 15.2% and in top 50 to 8%. The opposite is valid for United States, which hosts approximately 32% of top 2500 companies, 32.1% of top 1000, 34.7% of top 158, 38% of top 50 R&D and 5 out of 10 first spenders. At the same time, the global BERD of USA and China is comparable, and experts even expect China to exceed the USA in the next few years.

The above data reflect the fact that BERD in China is atomised and well distributed among a large population of companies, especially outside top 2500. Therefore, the number of firms involved in R&D activities is relatively large, with most of them investing relatively little (Bazavan, 2020). On the contrary, in the USA, BERD is more concentrated, weighting on the big tech giants.

Moreover, research efforts of Chinese companies in the top 2500 are largely distributed across sectors. ICT production is the only dominant, accounting for 27.1% of all research spending. If we exclude Huawei, which accounts alone for 12.3% of all input, then R&D expenditure in the ICT sector decreases to 14.9% of all research spending, followed by ICT services with 18.4%, construction with 13.3%, industrials with 9.5% automobiles and other transport with 9.3% and health industries with 6%. All other industries individually account for less than 5% of research spending.

The fragmented distribution of R&D expenditure among companies and sectors fosters competition and dynamism across low-tech sectors, leading to incremental innovation by enhancing production processes, supply chains, business models and marketing strategies. Nevertheless, Chinese firms encounter limitations in their ability to pursue costly basic research that involves high risks and long-term benefits, which is precisely the type of research that may eventually lead to radical breakthroughs (Bazavan, 2020). However, as a tendency, Chinese businesses are redirecting increasingly more funding towards basic and applied research.

## 2 The Venture Capital and Start-Up Scene

Significant research supports the idea that disruptive innovation frequently arises in start-ups (for example Chandy & Tellis, 2000; Christensen, 2011). China is one of the main actors on the global venture capital (VC) scene. Its flourishing ecosystem is comprised of crowdfunding investment platforms, angel investors, start-up incubators and accelerators, foreign investors, large VC funds sometimes belonging to tech giants Baidu, Alibaba and Tencent (the BAT), as well as "government guidance funds" (GGFs) (Bazavan, 2019b).

Chinese policymakers began to recognise the flaws of subsidy schemes and other traditional funding mechanisms for innovation, including inefficiency, poor allocation or even outright corruption.[5] For example, in the case of special funds for the AI industry, according to Deloitte (2018), "90% or even 99%" of companies asserting to be in the business of AI are not actually doing so, using the word AI to deceive the government and obtain state subsidies—a problem that is likely to persist in other industries as well. Therefore, alongside direct funding for R&D and innovation

[5] "'The Interim Measures of the Administration of Government Investment Funds was Promulgated" [《政府投资基金暂行管理办法》发布], People's Daily[人民日报], December 16, 2015, available at http://www.cssn.cn/fx/fx_fxxf/201512/t20151216_2783644.shtml?COLLCC=1949694195&COLLCC=3905747674 & archived at https://perma.cc/QH7G-K5FH.

projects, the government has started to experiment with a new "hands-off" approach that is currently gaining traction (Bazavan, 2019a). This approach uses capital markets to drive innovation in priority sectors (Chu et al., 2021). In order to bring the profit motive into industrial policy, the government is co-investing with profit-driven investors in start-ups and SMEs, by the means of equity, VC and risk compensations (Development Solutions Europe Ltd., 2018a). In other words, rather than picking winners itself, the government partners with experienced private funds to leverage market discipline and pool resources (Luong et al., 2021).

Therefore, the government expects that its profit-orientated partners can provide additional complementary capital as well as inside information, contacts and expertise. In turn, as a coinvestor, the government provides capital contributions (usually approximately 1/3), reduces investors' exposure, provides policy support, signals policy commitment to priority industries and, in some cases, guarantees minimum returns (Ding, 2018). While the state entity holds equity or creditor rights, the private partner takes the lead on investment decisions and day-to-day management (Development Solutions Europe Ltd., 2017b). The state would eventually recover the initial investment, but leaves the profits to the private investor.

This is how public funds are deployed to build an extensive support mechanism for the start-up ecosystem (Allison et al., 2021). The funds come primarily from the Technology Innovation Guiding Fund, a system of funds-of-funds (FOF), which invests in other 'sub-funds', which are further disbursed to actual projects and businesses (Zero2IPO, 2019). The central government usually provides approximately 30% of the FOF's volume, while the remaining might be covered by local governments, banks, companies, private funds, venture angels, etc.

Most of the downstream sub-funds are constituted as 'Government Guidance Funds' (GGFs). These are public-private instruments with a dual purpose: to generate profit and to stimulate the transfer, capitalisation and commercialisation of technology results. Funds are raised from both public and private sources and further invested in start-ups and SMEs in priority industries and at different stages. GGFs are usually specialised on specific industries or particular types of business activities that are prioritised. As of the first quarter of 2020, 1,741 GGFs were functioning in China, raising more than CNY 4.76 trillion (USD 672 billion) (Zero2IPO, 2020). The ultimate goal is to multiply and mobilise investments from the market in the sectors viewed as a policy priority (Development Solutions Europe Ltd., 2018b).

## 3 Summary

One of the highlights of this chapter is the fact that R&D expenditure in China is primarily carried out by the private sector, while government direct funding accounts for only 20.2% of GERD, which stands lower than in the EU, the USA or Korea. Besides direct R&D expenditure, public support for BERD in the form of direct funding and tax incentives is also unexpectedly limited, accounting for only 0.13% of GDP.

Research spending is highly distributed across sectors and the number of firms. Relatively many companies are engaged in experimental development and applied research that produces incremental innovation across all sectors of economy, but very few have sufficient resources to engage in fundamental research, the one leading to breakthrough innovations. With a few exceptions concentrated in the ICT sector such as Huawei and Alibaba, China has few champions in other industries to compete with American high-tech giants.

Overall, research and innovation expenditure in China is massive and rapidly increasing (Bazavan, 2019a). On the one hand, China is already the world's second-highest R&D spender and the gap with the USA is bound to narrow, as the current trends point towards China becoming the world's biggest R&D spender within two years.[6] On the other hand, the venture capital scene and the start-up ecosystem, both essential for transforming innovation into commercial-useful ideas, have taken proportions in recent years and are able to genuinely compete with those of the USA (Normile, 2018).

It is self-explanatory that funding inputs are closely correlated with innovation outputs (Shelton, 2008). For R&D funding to effectively contribute to improving China's innovation results, certain shortcomings must be addressed (Bazavan, 2019b). Given the fact that achieving breakthrough innovation requires long gestation times and intensive funding, by far the most persistent challenge of China's innovation funding system is the low allocation of resources to basic R&D. Therefore, China should

[6] Measured in USD PPP.

continue to shift its balance of expenditure towards basic innovation, among other priorities.

## References


Allison, G., et al. (2021). *The Great Tech Rivalry: China vs the U.S.* https://www.belfercenter.org/publication/great-tech-rivalry-china-vs-us. Accessed 2 July 2022.

Bazavan, A. (2019a, September). Chinese government's shifting role in the national innovation system. *Technological Forecasting and Social Change, 148*. https://doi.org/10.1016/j.techfore.2019.119738

Bazavan, A. (2019b). How does China innovate? A deconstruction of China's national innovation system. *Hyperion International Journal of Econophysics & New Economy, 12*(1), 99–107.

Bazavan, A. (2020). China's transition to a knowledge economy—Institutional mechanisms, public policies and private investment. In C. R. Pamfilie, V. Dinu, L. Tăchiciu, D. Pleșea, & C. Vasiliu (Eds.), *6th BASIQ international conference on new trends in sustainable business and consumption*. ASE Bucharest.

Boeing, P. (2016). The allocation and effectiveness of China's R&D subsidies—Evidence from listed firms. *Research Policy* [Preprint]. https://doi.org/10.1016/j.respol.2016.05.007

Chandy, R. K., & Tellis, G. J. (2000). The incumbent's curse? Incumbency, size, and radical product innovation. *Journal of Marketing, 64*(3). https://doi.org/10.1509/jmkg.64.3.1.18033

Chen, J., et al. (2018). The distinct signaling effects of R&D subsidy and non-R&D subsidy on IPO performance of IT entrepreneurial firms in China. *Research Policy, 47*(1), 108–120. https://doi.org/10.1016/j.respol.2017.10.004

Christensen, C. M. (2011). *The Innovator's Dilemma*. Vahlen. https://doi.org/10.15358/9783800642816

Chu, C. C., et al. (2021). Uncertainty, venture capital and entrepreneurial enterprise innovation—Evidence from companies listed on China's GEM. *Pacific Basin Finance Journal, 68*(September 2020), 101576. https://doi.org/10.1016/j.pacfin.2021.101576

Deloitte. (2018). *中国人工智能产业白皮书* [White Paper on China's AI Industry].

Development Solutions Europe Ltd. (2017a). *Fifth ad hoc study—Analysis of national high- and new-technology zones*.

Development Solutions Europe Ltd. (2017b). *Technology innovation guiding fund in China*. http://chinainnovationfunding.eu/technology-innovation-guiding-fund/. Accessed 4 December 2018.

Development Solutions Europe Ltd. (2018a). *China's '1+N' funding strategy for Artificial Intelligence*. http://chinainnovationfunding.eu/china-funding-artificial-intelligence/

Development Solutions Europe Ltd. (2018b). *China's funding for innovative start-ups: Three key systemic approaches* (pp. 1–12).

Ding, J. (2018, March). *Deciphering China's AI dream: The context, components, capabilities, and consequences of China's strategy to lead the world in AI* (pp. 1–44). Future of Humanity Institute, University of Oxford.

Guan, J. C., & Yam, R. C. M. (2015). Effects of government financial incentives on firms' innovation performance in China: Evidences from Beijing in the 1990s. *Research Policy* [Preprint]. https://doi.org/10.1016/j.respol.2014.09.001

Guo, D., Guo, Y., & Jiang, K. (2016). Government-subsidized R&D and firm innovation: Evidence from China. *Research Policy, 45*(6), 1129–1144. https://doi.org/10.1016/j.respol.2016.03.002

Howell, A. (2017). Picking "winners" in China: Do subsidies matter for indigenous innovation and firm productivity? *China Economic Review, 44*, 154–165. https://doi.org/10.1016/j.chieco.2017.04.005

Li, Y. (2017). *Innovation pathways in the Chinese economy* (Doctoral dissertation, Georgia Institute of Technology). http://hdl.handle.net/1853/59127

Liu, X., Li, X., & Li, H. (2016). R&D subsidies and business R&D: Evidence from high-tech manufacturing firms in Jiangsu. *China Economic Review* [Preprint]. https://doi.org/10.1016/j.chieco.2016.08.003

Lundvall, B. Å., & Rikap, C. (2022). China's catching-up in artificial intelligence seen as a co-evolution of corporate and national innovation systems. *Research Policy, 51*(1), 104395. https://doi.org/10.1016/J.RESPOL.2021.104395

Luong, N., Arnold, Z., & Murphy, B. (2021, March). Understanding Chinese government guidance funds. *Center for Security and …* [Preprint]. https://cset.georgetown.edu/wp-content/uploads/CSET-Understanding-Chinese-Government-Guidance-Funds.pdf

National Bureau of Statistics of China. (2021). *Communiqué on National Expenditures on Science and Technology in 2020*.

Normile, D. (2018). China narrows U.S. lead in R&D spending. *Science, 362*(6412), 276–276. https://doi.org/10.1126/science.362.6412.276

OECD. (2019). *Gross domestic spending on R&D (indicator)*. https://doi.org/10.1787/d8b068b4-en

OECD. (2021). *Main science and technology indicators, Volume 2021 Issue 1*. https://doi.org/10.1787/eea67efc-en. Accessed 1 July 2022.

Shelton, R. D. (2008). Relations between national research investment and publication output: Application to an American Paradox. *Scientometrics* [Preprint]. https://doi.org/10.1007/s11192-008-0212-2

Wei, S.-J., Xie, Z., & Zhang, X. (2016). From “Made in China” to “Innovated in China”: Necessity, prospect, and challenges. *Journal of Economic Perspectives*. https://doi.org/10.3386/w22854

Yip, G. S., & McKern, B. (2016). China’s next strategic advantage: From imitation to innovation. *Asian Pacific Economic Literature*. https://doi.org/10.1142/S1363919616800025

Zero2IPO. (2019). *Report China’s Government Guidance Funds in 2019, From ‘Large Scale Blossom’ to ‘Intensive Cultivation’* [2019年我国政府引导基金由“遍地开花”到“精耕细作”].

Zero2IPO. (2020). *Report on performance evaluation of Chinese government guidance funds 2020* [2020年中国政府引导基金绩效评价研究报告].

CHAPTER 6

# Foreign Direct Investment and Internationalisation

After the opening-up, China became a large receiver of FDI and technological input. This drastically transformed China's NIS, as foreign companies brought the needed capital, technology and know-how, creating a modern industrial system from scratch. Chinese domestic companies initially emerged as providing support and low value-added inputs to the manufacturing needs of foreign companies. The former gradually climbed up the value chains and became increasingly competitive in higher value-added sectors. As they accumulated technological and financial capacities, at a later stage, Chinese companies started to invest abroad themselves in order to gain access to international markets, key technologies, world-leading talent and even data (Lundvall & Rikaph, 2022). Currently, China became a source to a larger extent than a destination for FDI, but Chinese tech giants still have a gap to fill regarding their degree of openness and internationalisation. This chapter will analyse the effects of IFDI and OFDI on the transformation of China's NIS.

## 1 Inbound FDI

China holds the largest consumer market in the world in terms of PPP. Such a scale brings unique opportunities to both domestic and foreign companies, allowing them to constantly identify new niches and test new



A. Băzăvan, *China's National Innovation System*,
https://doi.org/10.1007/978-981-97-3266-1_6

products. Therefore, the market acts as a multi-layered arena of interaction between Chinese companies, MNCs and governments (Li, 2017). This section is dedicated to these interactions and their role in the Chinese innovation system.

### *1.1 From Process Innovation to Radical Innovation*

The learning curve of Chinese companies started when markets were suddenly opened in the 1980s and later scaled up beginning with 1990s. Before the *Open-Door Policy*, China had limited access to foreign currency and a small export capacity, which could not provide sufficient financial resource for direct technology imports. Following Deng Xiaoping's liberalisation of trade and capital, China benefited from both increased technology imports and capital inflows (Feng & Li, 2021). The new favourable policies attracted MNCs to move production to China, open branches and subcontract local companies (Bazavan, 2020). But there were still strict regulatory requirements in place, as markets and access to resources were still managed by SOEs. Therefore, a significant proportion of IFDI took the form of JVs between MNCs, that brought the know-how and capital, and SOEs that leveraged another important asset—huge human resources.

Domestic innovation is closely related to domestic market capacity and demand. At the beginning of economic development, there was very little consuming power inside China, and therefore manufacturing started by exporting on foreign markets. Chinese companies had to first produce inputs for MNCs exporting to the ROW, before producing final products for China's market. At this stage, innovation relied primarily on imitation and direct import of technology. The speed was fast, given the necessity to adapt to MNCs' requirements for costs, performance and quality (Steiber, 2018).

At a second stage, as the domestic market started to matter, Chinese companies began to adjust some of their products and services in order to sell also on the national market (Yip & McKern, 2016). This type of process can be called "frugal innovation", which is to downgrade premium features designed for external markets, reduce costs and also make adaptations that meet the needs of local demand (Li, 2017). During a trial-and-error learning process, Chinese companies gradually developed best or near best-practice technologies and enhanced their know-how (Yu et al., 2017).

Gradually, a new stage emerged when the Chinese domestic market became so large and attractive that MNCs have shifted from producing in China in order to sell abroad, to producing in China in order to sell in China, or even to producing outside China in order to sell inside. The uptake of the domestic market by MNCs brought significant new competitive pressures to local enterprises. In order to compete with foreign products on their home-turf and avoid being driven out, domestic enterprises had not only to learn from MNCs, but also to start driving technological innovation themselves and to improve production efficiency (Feng & Li, 2021).

This brought several challenges. Firstly, MNCs benefited from better technology, managing skills and a global network of resources. Secondly, Chinese customers did not trust local brands and therefore Chinese companies had to make significant additional efforts to gain market. The solution was to adapt products to such an extent that they are clearly more focused on Chinese consumers and better fitted to their needs, as well as to the cultural and economic context. On the other hand, Chinese companies had the natural advantage of a better understanding of local markets. As for Chinese consumers, price was a more important criterion than quality at the time, local firms responded by adjusting products to the configuration that provides the best quality possible for a significantly lower price than equivalent foreign products. In this process, domestic companies used the value chains built already by MNCs, including component suppliers, subcontracted manufacturers and even their skilled workers and talents.

Therefore, MNCs created both the fundamental industrial system and the competition incentive needed to stimulate the emergence of successful domestic firms. At the same time, Chinese firms also learnt to collaborate and associate, building networks that reduce costs and enable them to better serve the market. In the process, technology spillovers started to flow not only from MNCs to local companies, but also between the local companies themselves (Yano & Shiraishi, 2022).

### *1.2 Market Restrictions*

Today, Chinese firms like Huawei, ZTE and Hikvision denounce recently introduced trade and procurement restrictions in the USA and the EU as arbitrary, uncompetitive, politically motivated and outright anti-Chinese.

However, China has also systematically maintained or created obstacles and restrictions for MNCs in several fields, including by motivating national security concerns. Such market restrictions have played an important role in strengthening the ability of Chinese companies to resist competitive pressures in sectors where they could not reach maturity otherwise (Bazavan, 2019).

An important restricting policy implemented by the Chinese government to leverage the advantage of its huge internal market was the 'technology trading market' (TMFT) (e.g. Xia, 2012). TMFT specifies technology transfer as a precondition for the entry into Chinese markets of MNCs (Lin et al., 2021). The expectation is, of course, to help domestic firms acquire advanced technology from foreign multinationals and therefore upgrade their capabilities and competitiveness (Holmes et al., 2013). As the Chinese domestic market gradually became one of the most important markets in the world to many European, American or Japanese companies (for example for most automobile manufacturers China is the first global market, including for Volkswagen, BMW and Daimler), many technology-intensive companies accepted the compromise. In exchange, MNCs could secure very profitable market shares or even state-granted monopolies, at least temporarily.

Beyond the different stances pro or against the TMFT, its practical efficiency has to be assessed on a case-by-case basis, as it has not always been the case that local partners succeeded to absorb the technology and operational knowledge (Li, 2017). The successful example of high-speed rail (HSR) technology transfer best reflects the capacity of Chinese JV partners to internalise acquired technologies and scale up operations fast (Homme & Von Zedtwitz, 2018). On the other hand, in the case of combustion engine automobiles, Chinese producers have never succeeded to become competitors to their global peers (Feng, 2016), and MNCs like Volkswagen have continued to benefit from large market shares in China that can only be challenged by the new NEVs revolution. Currently, the government is easing restrictions, as in the case of FDI in NEVs production facilities, JVs are no longer needed. A similar steady opening-up of the combustion engine automobiles sector is in progress as well and European producers of trucks and buses have already announced opening fully-owned production facilities.

On the other hand, there are also strategic sectors where Chinese companies failed to become competitive with MNCs and where the state decided to intervene with market restrictions going as far as completely excluding foreign companies from the domestic market. Such an evolution is maybe most visible in the ICT industry where companies like Baidu, Alibaba and Tencent have emerged as national champions (Steiber, 2018). On a market that completely excluded foreign competitors, they started by imitating business models from outside China, benefited from strong state support, conquered initially their huge home market void of competition and went forward to adapt their products to global markets, enabled by large accumulated resources.

Nonetheless, there are increasingly less restrictions, as Chinese companies become sufficiently competitive by themselves and do not need state intervention anymore. As mentioned, some of the best well-known recent openings include the sectors of automobiles, banking and financial services. Before 2018, the sectors where OFDI was allowed were mentioned in the *Foreign Investment Catalogue*, acting as a positive list. In 2018, market restrictions were shifted to the *Foreign Investment Negative List*, which defines only those sectors that are restricted in some way. In 2020, the number of restricted sectors decreased from 40 to 33, and in 2021 it further decreased to 31. Free trade zones (FTZs) benefit from a more limited negative list that comprises only 27 sectors, virtually eliminating all restrictions on manufacturing and providing more access in for services. At the same time, sectors related to national security will continue to remain closed across the spectrum and a new restriction on investments in the media industry will enter into force in 2022.

### *1.3 International Concerns*

China's practices and policies regarding foreign investment have stirred numerous controversies and concerns, especially in the USA. China is perceived to be unfairly subsiding domestic companies to enter foreign markets and discriminating against foreign companies on its internal market, which the USA Information Technology and Innovation Foundation describes as 'state mercantilism' (Atkinson, 2017). Other international allegations against the Chinese government include the practice of forced technology transfers which, according to the Trump administration, cause billions of dollars of losses annually to US companies; unequal enforcement of IPR legislation; arbitrary market restrictions on grounds of national security; the adoption of national standards divergent from international ones; unjustified export controls, etc. (Atkinson, 2017; Hout & Ghemawat, 2010).

As a result, according to OECD's *FDI Regulatory Restrictiveness Index* (OECD, 2021), China ranks as the 11th most restrictive country in the world towards inbound FDI. The indicator accounts for foreign equity limitations, approval mechanisms, rules on the employment of foreigners and other operational restrictions. Data following the 2020–2022 pandemic will likely significantly increase China's position at the top of the index, despite the fact that the volume of IFDI has reached record levels.

From China's point of view, there is no forced technology transfer, as foreign companies enter agreements voluntarily, explicitly agreeing to provisions of JV and the transfer of know-how.[1] China also considers that it has made fast progress in terms of improving legislation and ensuring a level playing field on a number of issues, including IPR. Moreover, there are some who argue that such market restrictions are not specific to China, as they have been widely used by other economies as well, including Korea and Japan (Zhou & Fang, 2021). Finally, as previously mentioned, in exchange of accepting several "compromises" to enter the Chinese market, some MNCs have been conferred by the Chinese government substantial privileges, subsidies and even unfair advantages in some cases, in the detriment of domestic firms.

## 2 Outbound FDI

Over the last two decades, China has steadily become an important source of FDI, as a growing number of Chinese companies that have achieved success in domestic markets are looking to expand abroad. Accumulated financial resources enable them to invest in developed countries, securing brand names, accessing global talent and new technologies, and improving their prospects for growth and financial performance (Steiber, 2018).

[1] Cai, J., & Elmer, K. (2019, January 14). Is the US right to cry foul about forced technology transfer to business in China—And what is Beijing's position? *South China Morning Post*. https://www.scmp.com/news/china/diplomacy/article/2181528/us-right-cry-foul-about-forced-technology-transfer-do-business.

In 1986, China[2] accounted for 0.1% of global OFDI stock. This share steadily rose to 0.48% by 2001, when China joined the WTO (Lundvall & Rikap, 2022). However, OFDI only has taken a form since 2005, after the release of the 'Go Global' policy. The policy, which encouraged Chinese companies to invest abroad, constituted a fundamental paradigm change, as before it, China was only seen as a destination and not a source of FDI. As Chinese firms responded rapidly, outbound investments have experienced explosive growth rates, especially towards developed markets, and reached 4.9% of global outward FDI stock in 2016 (Buckley et al., 2018). By 2018, more than 27,000 companies had established 43,000 subsidiaries and JVs in 188 countries across the globe (Dong et al., 2021). In 2020, after a 86.3 times growth from 2001 levels, China became the second largest holder of FDI assets globally, after the USA (UNCTAD, 2021).

In terms of investment flows, Chinese OFDI peaked in 2016, when in just one year, FDI doubled towards Europe and tripled towards North America. However, according to the public figures released by China's Ministry of Commerce, investment flows decreased for three consecutive years in 2017, 2018 and 2019, before picking up again in 2020, despite the global pandemic, which made China, in 2020, for the first time, the world's largest source of foreign investment outflows. The 2017–2019 decrease was caused by several internal and external factors. On the one hand, China's government became worried about a decreasing level of currency reserves, as well as by the perception that Chinese companies are using OFDI as a means to conduct money-laundering. These concerns determined the government to introduce capital controls and limits on the scope of investments, designating policies that aimed to drive OFDI towards chosen priority sectors, including those that have the potential to produce reverse technology effects. At the same time, as it will be mentioned later, Chinese OFDI has started to confront increased regulatory obstacles and public opinion concerns in destination countries, which led to the cancellation of several investment deals (Fig. 1).

Therefore, despite recent setbacks 2020 and 2021 showed the capacity of Chinese OFDI to rebound and maintain, and a tempered growth is expected in the following period. Direct exposure to and involvement in overseas markets allows Chinese companies to enhance their innovation

[2] All data in this chapter refers to Mainland China, excluding Hong Kong, Macao and Taiwan.

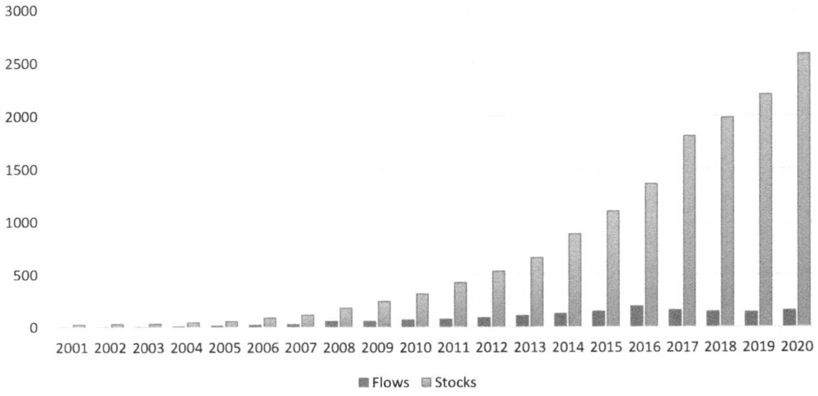


**Fig. 1** China's flows and stocks of OFDI (billions USD) (*Source* China 2020 Statistical Bulletin of Outbound Direct Investment)

capacity as a result of increased competition and the reverse spillover effect from their subsidiaries (Piperopoulos et al., 2018). In fact, as explained in the following section, many investments take the form of direct acquisitions or take-overs, with one of the primary goals being to acquire technology that is absorbed in the mother company in China.

### *2.1 Investment Outflows by Type and Destination*

Originally, Chinese OFDI was focused on energy, commodities and resources. Between 2010 and 2016, the focus switched towards high-tech industries in developed economies, which could be partly explained by a governmental push (Wang & Miao, 2016). The Chinese regulatory framework was adapted since 2017 to hinder outward investments in fields such as real estate, hospitality and entertainment, while openly encouraging sectors that have the potential of acquiring new technologies. Revealing examples include investments in the USA made by the BAT and several large VC funds (Sykes, 2021). These include both acquisitions and green field investments in Silicon Valley, some of which have obtained USA government procurement contracts.

Following, after suffering several setbacks and raising regulatory concerns in host countries regarding investments in rather technology-intensive sectors, more recently, Chinese OFDI was reoriented towards consumer products and entertainment industries, which together make up almost half of the total, followed by transport and infrastructure, financial and business services, basic materials and health (Baker McKenzie & Rhodium Group, 2022).

A large part of investments abroad falls in the category of M&As. The volume of M&As has grown at an average rate of 33% year-on-year between 2013 and 2017 accounting for 11% of all global deals (Bazavan, 2019). In 2016 alone, Chinese companies spent USD 22.7 billion on the acquisition of foreign firms, six times more than the total value of foreign-invested M&A in China. Recently however, China's outbound M&A decreased, due to the increased scrutiny and sensitivity abroad, in conjuncture with a growing renewed inward focus of Chinese companies that prioritised M&As at home. In 2020, global M&A deals, including China's, have decreased understandably due to the global pandemic. However, in 2021, global deals picked-up, while China's continued to decrease and reached a low USD 23.7 billion in 2021, partly because of China's stricter COVID-19 control rules, but also because of a more fundamental shift.

Some of the most well-known technology-intensive Chinese investments abroad include the acquisition of IBM PC branch by Lenovo, Volvo Cars and 10% of Daimler by Geely, certain product lines of Ericsson by Huawei, German Kuka Robotics by Midea, GE Appliances by Haier, Lexmark by Apex Technology and Swiss Syngenta by Chem China. Even better known is a series of failed acquisition attempts blocked by the governments of host countries: Money Gram by Ant Financial, Lattice Semiconductor by Canyon Bridge Capital Partners, Genworth Financial Incorporated by China Oceanwide Holdings Group, German equipment maker Aixtron by the Fujian Grand Chip Investment Fund and Magnachip by China's Wise Road Capital.

In addition to M&As, Chinese companies are also carrying greenfield investment in self-owned research facilities in clusters such as Silicon Valley. For example, Baidu operates two AI and deep learning research centres in Sunnyvale, Tencent owns a data centre in Silicon Valley and an AI research facility in Seattle, Didi Chuxing owns "Didi Labs" in Silicon Valley and Alibaba develops "Damo Academy" in California, Moscow, Tel Aviv and Singapore.

As China was aggressively pursuing venture capital investments, US-China FDI flows have inversed since 2014, when Chinese investments to USA exceeded USA investments to China (Saiidi, 2019). Therefore, the United States used to be by far the largest destination for Chinese outbound foreign investment, accounting for 17.44% on average between 2005 and 2015 and peaking in 2016 when China's FDI outflows to the USA reached USD 46.5 bn., or 23.7% of all Chinese investment flows abroad. M&As dominated Chinese investments to the USA, especially in the fields of software & IT services, electronic components, communications, industrial machinery, business services and auto components (Select USA, 2017), with the most active Chinese company in USA-tech deals being Tencent.

However, increasing regulatory scrutiny on the mainland, as well as sustained hostility and new restrictions in the USA, has led Chinese FDI to USA to decrease sharply, from a peak value of USD 46.5 bn. in 2016 to only USD 6 billion in 2020 (The Ministry of Commerce, the National Bureau of Statistics and the State Administration of Foreign Exchange, 2021). In the same year, overall investment flows to Asia (excluding Hong Kong) reached USD 23.2 bn., to Latin America USD 16.7 bn., to Europe USD 12.7 bn. and to Africa USD 4.2 bn. As recently Europe has also increased scrutiny on Chinese investments, in recent years a tendency of Chinese OFDI to shift towards Latin America, where regulators and public opinion are still largely favourable, it can be noticed.

The ranking changes when referring to the values to M&A activity only, where Europe remains the first destination, followed by Asia, North America and Latin America. According to Baker McKenzie and Rhodium Group (2022), in 2021, Chinese M&A deals in Europe rose by 5% to USD 8.4 billion, while decreasing at the same time by 37% to USD 4.7 billion in North America. In the same year, M&As in Asia reached $5.4 billion, while deals in Latin America remained constant at approximately USD 3 billion.

Finally, perceptions about Chinese investments highly vary from one country to another. Whereas some countries put high expectations around economic benefits brought by new capital, other countries are rather concerned about potential risks, including to their national security, especially as, in some cases, the ownership structure of Chinese investors is rather opaque. Chinese investments can certainly provide opportunities, but the balance between risks and opportunities should be considered on a case-by-case basis, depending on the sector, the context and the magnitude.

The "Go Global" strategy involves expanding operations abroad and exporting domestically-developed technology. However, in certain industries that are heavily influenced by international politics, the success of Chinese companies' expansion depends on the state's efforts in the international arena, regardless of their technological maturity and cost-effectiveness (Bazavan, 2019). An example is high-speed rail, where China's competitive technology is accompanied by prohibitive infrastructure costs for most nations. The state-owned banks' willingness to offer cheap credits enables partner countries to contract Chinese-built infrastructure, ultimately enhancing China's international prestige and strengthening ties with the partner country. Similarly, in the case of 5G telecommunication network, Huawei's superior technology and cost-effectiveness may not be enough to secure the export of its technology due to international scrutiny and the Chinese government's political ability to defend the company's interests abroad. Additionally, as the competition to set global standards for new technologies becomes increasingly politicised, the Chinese government's capacity to negotiate these standards internationally greatly influences Chinese companies' ability to access foreign markets.

## 3 Summary

This chapter reviewed the impact of investing foreign companies in the Chinese innovation system, as well as the impact of technology-seeking Chinese outbound investments. It all started in the stage of low-end manufacture, when MNCs investing in China brought technology and know-how, re-shaped institutions and created a modern industrial system from scratch. Chinese companies first emerged as providers of intermediate inputs, but gradually absorbed technology, undertook reverse-cycle engineering, performed creative imitation and achieved incremental improvements in their production processes, as well as marketing and distribution techniques. Making use of the resources provided by MNCs, including networks of suppliers but also talents and know-how, adding to the increased competitive pressure stemming also from MNCs, domestic companies gradually became global competitors. This was, of course, strongly supported by the government which, through a variety of policies at different levels, stimulated technology absorption and protected domestic firms from the negative aspects of competition. Some of the measures taken by the government have been highly uncompetitive and protectionist, such as the TMFT policy, leading to considerable international tensions, especially within the USA business and political community, but the appetite of foreign companies to invest in China has always remained strong. Ultimately, the local market acted as a stepping-stone for successful Chinese companies, before venturing into competition at a global scale.

As it accumulated resources, China's NIS started to shift from a net receiver of investment to a net supplier. Encouraged by the state, Chinese firms began since early 2000s to venture into outbound investments with the goal of securing brand names, market access, global talent and fresh technologies. M&As, rather than greenfield investments, proved to be the most common method of doing so. Technology-oriented investments have become predominant in Chinese outbound FDI flows especially since 2017, when the Chinese government imposed restrictions to other categories of ventures. However, new internal regulations had a strong negative effect on all spectrum of Chinese outbound investments, adding to increasing scrutiny in USA and EU directed against Chinese investments, which impeded a series of agreed deals. Therefore, between 2016 and 2020, the volume of Chinese investments abroad has suffered drawbacks, but after positive signs in 2021 when China became the largest investor in the world by outflows, and given the underlying fundamentals, it is expected that volumes will continue to grow on the medium and long term, at a normalised pace.

## References

Atkinson, R. D. (2017). *Testimony of Robert D. Atkinson, President, Information Technology and Innovation Foundation, Before the U.S.-China Economic and Security Review Commission. Hearing on Chinese Investment in the United States: Impacts and issues for policymakers*. Information Technology & Innovation Foundation. https://www.uscc.gov/sites/default/files/Atkinson_USCC%20Hearing%20Testimony012617.pdf

Baker McKenzie and Rhodium Group. (2022). *Trends and spotlights of the Chinese investment landscape*. https://www.bakermckenzie.com/-/media/files/insight/publications/2022/02/fdi-china-report-2022-english.pdf?sc_lang=en&hash=054A2FD520CD9CB19224E661D8A777E8. Accessed 1 July 2022.

Bazavan, A. (2019, September). Chinese government's shifting role in the national innovation system. *Technological Forecasting and Social Change, 148*. https://doi.org/10.1016/j.techfore.2019.119738

Bazavan, A. (2020). China's transition to a knowledge economy—Institutional mechanisms, public policies and private investment. In C. R. Pamfilie, V. Dinu, L. Tăchiciu, D. Pleşea, & C. Vasiliu (Eds.), *6th BASIQ international conference on new trends in sustainable business and consumption*. ASE Bucharest.

Buckley, P. J., et al. (2018). A retrospective and agenda for future research on Chinese outward foreign direct investment. *Journal of International Business Studies, 49*(1). https://doi.org/10.1057/s41267-017-0129-1

Dong, Z., Miao, Z., & Zhang, Y. (2021). The impact of China's outward foreign direct investment on domestic innovation. *Journal of Asian Economics, 75*, 101307. https://doi.org/10.1016/j.asieco.2021.101307

Feng, K. (2016). Chinese indigenous innovation in the car sector. In Y. Zhou et al. (Eds.), *China as an innovation nation* (pp. 133–164). https://doi.org/10.1093/acprof:oso/9780198753568.003.0005

Feng, W., & Li, J. (2021). International technology spillovers and innovation quality: Evidence from China. *Economic Analysis and Policy, 72*, 289–308. https://doi.org/10.1016/j.eap.2021.09.003

Holmes, T. J., McGrattan, E. R., & Prescott, E. C. (2013). Quid pro quo: Technology capital transfers for market access in China. *Review of Economic Studies, 82*(3). https://doi.org/10.1093/restud/rdv008

Homme, D. P., & Von Zedtwitz, M. (2018). The changing face of innovation in China—Foreign companies must Retool their R&D strategies to keep pace with newly innovative Chinese Entreprises. *MIT Sloan Management Review, 59*(4), 24–32.

Hout, T. M., & Ghemawat, P. (2010). China vs the world: Whose technology is it? *Harvard Business Review* [Preprint].

Li, Y. (2017). *Innovation pathways in the Chinese economy* (Doctoral dissertation, Georgia Institute of Technology). http://hdl.handle.net/1853/59127

Lin, Y., Qin, Y., & Xie, Z. (2021). Does foreign technology transfer spur domestic innovation? Evidence from the high-speed rail sector in China. *Journal of Comparative Economics, 49*(1), 212–229. https://doi.org/10.1016/j.jce.2020.08.004

Lundvall, B. Å., & Rikap, C. (2022). China's catching-up in artificial intelligence seen as a co-evolution of corporate and national innovation systems. *Research Policy, 51*(1), 104395. https://doi.org/10.1016/J.RESPOL.2021.104395

OECD. (2021). *FDI regulatory restrictiveness index*. www.oecd.org/investment/fdiindex.htm. Accessed 10 May 2018.

Piperopoulos, P., Wu, J., & Wang, C. (2018). Outward FDI, location choices and innovation performance of emerging market enterprises. *Research Policy, 47*(1). https://doi.org/10.1016/j.respol.2017.11.001

Saiidi, U. (2019). *Chinese foreign direct investment to the US falls in 2018: Data, data show*. CNBC. https://www.cnbc.com/2019/01/15/chinese-foreign-direct-investment-to-the-us-falls-in-2018-data.html. Accessed 1 July 2022.

Select USA. (2017). *Foreign Direct Investment (FDI): China*. International Markets Fact Sheets. https://www.selectusa.gov/servlet/servlet.FileDownload?file=015t0000000LKM1

Steiber, A. (2018). *Management in the digital age: Will China surpass Silicon Valley?* SpringerBriefs in Business Management. https://doi.org/10.1007/978-3-319-67489-6

Sykes, A. O. (2021). The law and economics of 'forced' technology transfer and its implications for trade and investment policy (and the U.S.-China Trade War). *Journal of Legal Analysis*. https://doi.org/10.1093/jla/laaa007

The Ministry of Commerce, the National Bureau of Statistics and the State Administration of Foreign Exchange. (2021). *Statistical Bulletin of China's Outbound Direct Investment in 2020 (2020年度中国对外直接投资统计公报).*

UNCTAD. (2021). World investment report 2021|UNCTAD. *United Nations Conference on Trade and Development* [Preprint].

Wang, H., & Miao, L. (2016). *China goes global: How China's overseas investment is transforming its business enterprises*. Palgrave Macmillan.

Xia, L., and Zhao, L.Y. (2012). '市场换技术"方针的历史演变. (Historical evolution of the "Trade Market for Technology" strategy)',当代中国史研究. *Contemporary China History Studies*, *19*(2), pp. 27–36.

Yano, G., & Shiraishi, M. (2022). Innovation spillovers between domestic firms in China. *Emerging Markets Finance and Trade*, *58*(4), 1042–1060. https://doi.org/10.1080/1540496X.2021.1926978

Yip, G. S., & McKern, B. (2016). China's next strategic advantage: From imitation to innovation. *Asian Pacific Economic Literature*. https://doi.org/10.1142/S1363919616800025

Yu, Y., Yu, J., & Pan, X. (2017). Governance and the China innovation economy. *Asia-Pacific Journal of Regional Science*, *1*(1), 63–84. https://doi.org/10.1007/s41685-017-0013-9

Zhou, W., & Fang, M. M. (2021). Subsidizing technology competition: China's evolving practices and international trade regulation. *Washington International Law Journal*, *30*(3), 470–544.

CHAPTER 7

# Other Systemic Factors

## 1 Introduction

This chapter analyses five additional systemic factors of China's NIS, mapping them across the industry supply chains and evaluating their strategic implications from different perspectives. These are: talent, intellectual property, patents, public perception towards technology and chosen priority industries that receive all-around support.

## 2 Talent

A central component of a country's NIS is its capacity to develop, retain and attract talent. In general, it can be stated that the more numerous a country's S&T specialised population is, the larger is the proportion of people that contribute to research and development and consequently, the more likely it is that new knowledge is produced (Bogers et al., 2018). Of course, higher education capacity and the overall development of the scientific system, alongside the volume of available financial resources, are key components for developing, retaining and attracting talent. Other relevant factors include the level of internationalisation and openness of the system, the country's cultural attractiveness, etc.

Given China's recent rise in S&T capacity and its ambition to climb technology-intensive supply chains, the demand for highly skilled R&D workforce and world-class engineers has continuously increased. In 2020,


A. Băzăvan, *China's National Innovation System*,
https://doi.org/10.1007/978-981-97-3266-1_7

the share of China's research personnel in total labour force was only 0.29%, considerably below the levels of the EU, 0.89%; the USA, 0.9% (data for 2019); Japan, 1%; and Korea, 1.6%. China's score has been rising from 0.11% in 2000, but at a slower rate than of its peers (OECD, 2021). However, in nominal values, given China's much larger population, in 2013 (latest available year), the country had more full-time employed researchers than the USA, more than twice the number of Japan, and about 85% more than the EU (Fig. 1).

Over the last decades, China has invested significantly in its higher education system, in an effort to catch up with leading institutions globally. And it has done so with a certain degree of success, as several of its universities, such as Peking University, Tsinghua University and Fudan University, are scoring high in global rankings. Therefore, the higher education system has expanded fast, in both quantity and quality. Most measures are outstanding so just to give an example, between 2015 and 2022, the number of graduated students applying for masters' degrees has grown almost threefold, from 1.65 million to 4.57 million (China

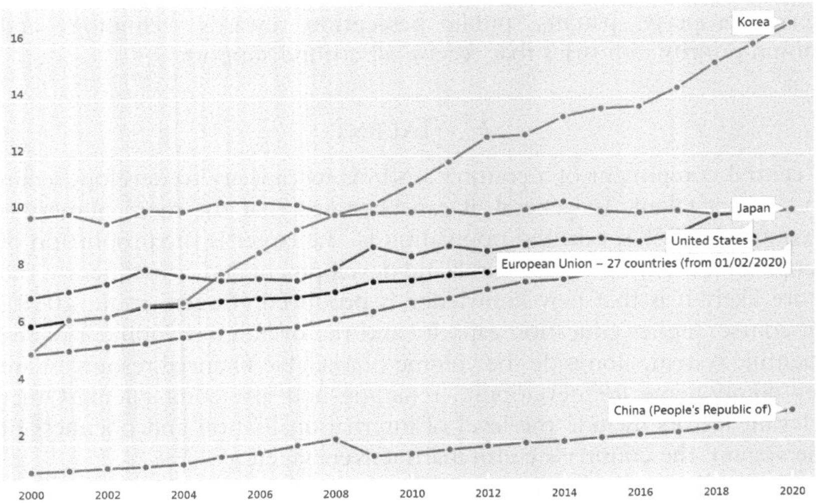


**Fig. 1** Number of researchers per 1 000 employees, 2000–2020 (*Source* OECD [2021], "Researchers" [indicator], https://doi.org/10.1787/20ddfb0f-en, accessed on 29 May 2022)

Daily, 2022). By 2025, according to current tendencies, the number of STEM Ph.D. graduates is expected to be double that of the USA. With regard to Chinese deciding to study abroad, three decades ago, approximately 1/20 of them returned home after graduation, while currently, 4/5 do (Alberts & Narayanamurti, 2019). Historically, the USA has been the favoured destination for Chinese students, but given the increased tensions between the two countries adding to the difficulties caused by the pandemic, the number of Chinese students studying in the USA has generally declined over the past two years.

As the process of globalisation has increasingly impacted the Chinese economy, the government has recognised that in addition to home-grown talent, overseas Chinese as well as foreign non-ethnic Chinese talents are also important resources. In 2016, President Xi Jinping talked about the "global talent competition" and mentioned that "It is necessary to gather talents from all over the world and use them to provide strong talent support for the development of China's industry" (NDRC, 2020).

Employing overseas talent[1] does not only help to bring new ideas and empower domestic innovation, but also creates and strengthens connections with foreign-based leading research institutions and companies (ILO, 2017). Historically, the USA was able to benefit the most from its capacity to recruit talent from the global pool (Allison et al., 2021). However, recently, as the National Security Commission on Artificial Intelligence has recognised, "The competition for international students has accelerated... For the first time in our lifetime, the United States risks losing the competition for talent on scientific frontiers" (NSCAI, 2018).

As such, the attraction of overseas trained talents has become a key component of China's innovation policy. Both the central and subnational governments have created numerous initiatives for attracting overseas talents, whether returning ethnic Chinese or foreigners, particularly those who have studied or worked at the most reputable institutes in the world, after they have fully developed their capabilities and built their network. The programmes offer attractive salaries and research funding that tops the ones received in the country of origin, and come at package with a promotion from the previous position. Such initiatives include centrally-led schemes like the *Thousand Talent Programme* and *The Chinese Academy of Science's Hundred Talents Program*, which are

[1] Foreigners or Chinese that are studying or woring abroad.

further detailed in *ANNEX I National Talent Attraction Programs in China*. Beyond the national government, provincial and city-level authorities are also very active in deploying programmes to attract foreign talent, usually replicating national schemes. Local programmes are complementary to national funding and can usually be earned cumulatively by the same individual/team.

However, the results of these programmes are mixed and China has not yet become a major destination for top talents. Such a transformation will indeed take a significant and concerted effort to achieve, if it is at all realistic. According to the *MORE 3 Global Survey* (European Commission, 2017) which counted a sample of 417 EU researchers currently working abroad, China was just the 16$^{th}$ non-EU country of destination by number of European researchers. In Asia only, China was the third most popular destination, after Japan and Singapore.

Some of the main deficiencies of current talent programmes are: low internationalisation profile of Chinese universities and companies, burdensome immigration procedures, arduous path to permanent residency, academic freedom limitations, inappropriate selection criteria and ongoing evaluation of foreign talents, high costs of sending children to international schools, inflexibility for spouses' work activities, lack of inclusiveness of the academic community and cultural misunderstandings. Other issues include: fragmentation of management and administrative procedures, stiff regulations for spending research funds, difficulties to form research teams and insufficient readiness for the cultural differences to working in China.

Nevertheless, most foreign researchers based in China undertake temporary projects of 1–3 years, and historic data show that it is still very unlikely for them to settle as permanent residents. Moreover, China does not even seem to expect or encourage them in this regard. As such, permanent residences are very difficult to obtain, even if one wishes to. To compare, in 2016 China issued 1.576 permanent residences to all foreigners of all occupations and nationalities, while USA emitted 1 million of them in the same period.[2] Between 2020 and 2022, given the

[2] International Labour Organization and International Organization for Migration & Centre for China and Globalization (CCG). *Attracting skilled international migrants to China. A review and comparison of policies and practices*. 2017. Available at https://www.ilo.org/wcmsp5/groups/public/---asia/---ro-bangkok/---ilo-beijing/documents/publication/wcms_565474.pdf.

strict regulations around the COVID-19 pandemic, this number closed to zero in China. On the other hand, many of Chinese talent programmes propose extended discontinued periods of work in China, such as 4 months every year for a period of several years, which fits a category of foreign researchers that are not willing to renounce their academic positions abroad.

Overall, despite sustained efforts and several achievements, the number of highly qualified foreign talents recruited and the retention rate remain underperforming (ILO, 2017). China still needs to make further improvements to its talent policy and its capacity to integrate foreign researchers. Although China can address some issues through an easy administrative fix, others require more time and are likely to be more difficult to solve. According to interviews results, some of the major issues that impede foreign researchers to work in China include:

- high complexity of immigration procedures and residence requirements;
- ambiguous selection and performance evaluation criteria;
- burdensome paperwork and bureaucratic mechanisms;
- high costs for children's education;
- difficult conditions for spouse employment;
- lack of inclusiveness;
- cultural barriers.

On the other hand, government talent programmes and related policies are just one limited component of a country's competitiveness in attracting skilled foreign personnel. Other important aspects considered by individual talents when deciding whether to relocate to China include cultural inclusion, overall lifestyle, environmental conditions, etc.

## 3 Intellectual Property

Misperceptions about the understanding of China's NIS are frequently caused by analysing limited timeframes and therefore omitting the rate of change, which is higher than most of its global peers. That is particularly evident when discussing IPR legislation. In recent years, there have been numerous examples of IP infringements in China, as weak IPR legislation and enforcement was rather in China's best interest, facilitating fast technology transfers.

However, currently, the trend is very much reversed. Given the increased cumulated native knowledge and the ambition to strengthen the role of innovation as a basis of economic growth, Chinese companies are now patenting increasingly more and became confronted themselves with IP theft internal to China. Therefore, Chinese companies have become very interested in fighting IP infringements and are actively pushing for strengthening legislation and enforcement.

Therefore, as the European Chamber of Commerce in China attests, strong efforts are underway to improve China's IP system (European Union Chamber of Commerce in China, 2021). Unlike merely 10 years ago, today IPR can be meaningfully protected, and many foreign and domestic companies fill and win lawsuits. Compensation for infringement has not yet reached the levels in other advanced economies, as IP legislation is still new and evolving, but the trend is positive. Domestic companies are now using IP to protect themselves, and in certain sectors such as telecommunications and AI, they already produce world-leading IP. Companies such as Huawei are now asking foreign companies to pay for the use of their IP and an increasing number of them are taking foreign competitors to court over infringements.

The IPR legislation in China is likely to continue to see further strengthening, such as by improving compensation for IP infringement. It cannot be excluded that, over time, given the increasing necessity to protect its own innovation, Chinese IP legislation will become even stricter than those of its peers. This said, this transition is lagging behind, especially in lower-value sectors. Furthermore, there are still significant inadequacies in IPR enforcement, as sometimes enforcement mechanisms are governed by political will. Moreover, IP protection is closely related to the overall state of the judicial system, which is particularly lacking in terms of transparency. However, the Chinese IPR legislative system is also reported to be biased towards domestic firms, to the detriment of foreign ones. Therefore, despite recent progress, the current status of IPR legislation and enforcement in China continues, at least for the moment, to act as a hindrance to MNCs in further offshoring high-tech manufacturing and R&D operations to China.

## 4 Patents

The number of international applications and transformations of patents, trademarks and designs filed in each country under the Patent Cooperation Treaty (PCT) of WIPO is widely used as reflexion of a country's technological output scale. According to the annual report of WIPO (2022), despite the pandemic, the organisation received a record number of 277,500 applications, after a 0.9% increase from the previous year. The first 10 countries made up 88.1% of total applications, and as far as regions are concerned, Asia alone accounted for 54.1% of total applications, showing a significant growth up from 38.5% in 2011.

China surpassed the USA as the leading PCT user in 2020 and maintained its position in 2021, when it filed almost 70,000 applications, or 25% of global PCT patent applications. This constitutes outstanding growth, after China accounted for only 0.6% in 2000. Meanwhile, during the same period, the share of the USA fell from 42 to 21%, while the top two EU countries, Germany and France, have seen even sharper decreases (Fig. 2).

According to WIPO data, it is not only the sheer numbers of applications, but China has also achieved the largest share of granted applications among major countries. However, a deeper analysis shows that, despite

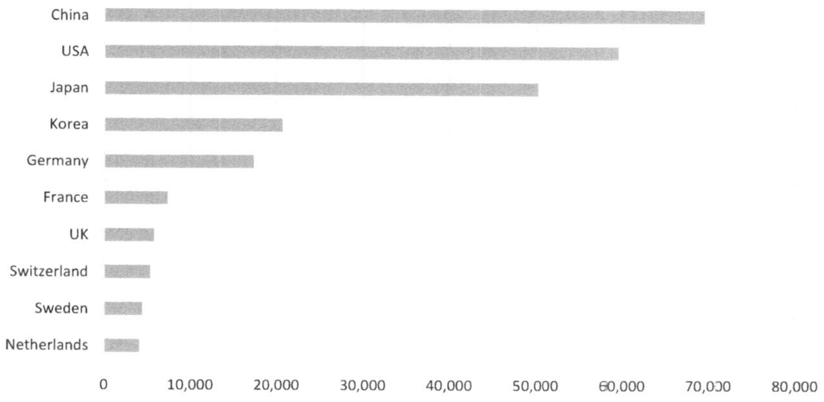


**Fig. 2** Biggest users of the PCT system, by country, 2021 (*Source* WIPO Statistics Database, February 2022, available at https://www.wipo.int/edocs/infogdocs/en/ipfactsandfigures/)

rapid quantitative growth, patent quality has not improved in a similar way. This might be partly explained by a governmental push to meet the numerical targets of patent applications (Hu et al., 2017). In addition, China's patent applications are highly concentrated in several sectors, such as ICT and telecommunications. By comparison, in the USA, patents are better distributed across technology fields and are arguably of a higher quality. A revealing measure is the patent conversion rate and conversion efficiency, by which China, despite a constant positive trend, remains significantly behind the USA. Therefore, despite being a global patent leader by numerous measures, China still needs to prioritise quality over quantity, across a broader category of industrial patents.

## 5 Public Perception Towards Technology Adoption

Another significant factor that provides an enabling environment for the rise of Chinese technologies companies and the adoption of new technologies is positive public perception. China's NIS benefits from a unique resource: a vast population that has experienced economic and social change at unprecedented rates in history, which makes it particularly open to adopting innovation. An important cultural difference between Europe and China is the fact that in the former, people have a general concern about the future and are split whenever a new technology arises, as an important number prefer to be rather cautious. However, in China, the majority of consumers only hope that technology will continue to improve their lives and are less concerned about potential adverse effects. This makes people in China very fast adopters. Given the hugely rapid economic improvements during the last four decades, it became embedded in the culture that the way towards a better life is innovation, technology and industry. As Chinese people are still searching to improve their economic situation, start-ups and new technologies make dreams come true.

Naturally, new technologies also come with embedded flaws. Traditionally, the government in China has rather used a laissez-faire approach, entrusting new technologies with the benefit of doubt and regulating at a later stage. In general, it can be argued that Chinese citizens also expect less privacy of data than people abroad. Finally, Chinese consumers generally trust the government more in taking the necessary measures to protect them.

However, the trend is steadily reversing, as Chinese consumers are also becoming increasingly aware of their rights and pay attention to the means of protecting them. Legislation is following, and in some instances, it can become even stricter than in the other counts. This is the case for certain provisions of the *Data Privacy Regulation*, which are stricter than the GDPR, for example.

## 6 Priority Industries

Before commencing the study case on AI, this section presents two closely related industries that have been a main focus for public policy and funding, as well as for private investments: semiconductors and ICT.

### *6.1 Semiconductors*

Semiconductors are thumbnail-sized devices composed of silicon wafers mounted with billions of transistors that underpin every electronic application around us, from mobile phones to automobiles, and from artificial intelligence to military arsenals. Therefore, semiconductors represent a crucial industry for the world economy and security, with global sales of USD 556 billion in 2021, after a 26.2% increase from 2020. However, despite the expansion of production capacities, in 2020 and 2021, demand has greatly exceeded supply and therefore caused supply chain bottlenecks around the world. This showed again the importance of semiconductors to the economic growth, competitiveness, resilience and national security of every country.

The industry requires highly cumulative knowledge that can be performed by a small number of very few specialised experts. Historically, it has flourished thanks to a large degree of global division of labour that supported enhanced innovation and outputs. At the same time, this division also produced a high degree of transnational interdependencies throughout the supply chains (Lee, 2021). While some countries and corporate actors remain dominant over specific crucial components of the supply chain, such as the US and its giants Intel and Qualcomm that control the software essential for chip design, Taiwan and its Taiwan Semiconductor Manufacturing Company (TSMC) that have a large share of the world's production capacity or the Netherlands and its ASML that leads in essential lithography equipment for production, no region or actor can be autonomous, as it depends on all others at the same time (Crawford, 2020).

The increasing US-China commercial tensions, adding to the COVID-19 pandemic and global shortages in the availability of semiconductors, have recently pushed the industry into the headlines. The ability to develop domestic companies with world-class capabilities is not anymore motivated only by commercial purposes, but became strongly embedded in the national security realm. Therefore, governments around the world, including China, the US, the EU, Japan and Korea, have started to assess their dependencies and vulnerabilities in the semiconductor value chain and decided to intervene strongly in business decisions over production and trade (Schneider, 2021a).

As far as China is concerned, despite benefiting from rapidly expanding production facilities, it remains heavily dependent on imported microchips and semiconductors for most of its goods manufacturing (Normile, 2018). As a result, it developed a number of key policy initiatives and is putting at stake unprecedented public funding to achieve building a leading, independent semiconductor industry by 2030 (Godoi et al., 2015). Although China's chip industry is making fast progress and has reached full coverage of product areas, it is still behind firms headquartered in Taiwan, South Korea and the United States in the higher value-added sectors, while still dependent on many high tech inputs, such as chip design software (EDA) and semiconductor manufacturing equipment (SME).

Therefore, China remains by far the world's largest importer of semiconductors, which is considered an issue that goes beyond the boundaries of economics to the national security realm. In 2015, as part of its *Made in China 2025* plan, China assigned microelectronics as a priority industry for reducing China's reliance of foreign suppliers and set a goal of 70% of internal demand to be supplied by local manufacturers. However, the trade deficit in integrated circuits has continued to grow and by 2020, China was only able to cover 16% of its demand from domestic sources (Bazavan, 2019). As several companies like Huawei began stockpiling supplies due to concerns about renewed US sanctions, Chinese imports of semiconductors surged in 2020 by about 14%, reaching almost USD 380 billion, or 18% of the total goods imported by China (Bloomberg, 2021a). In the same year, China's imports of semiconductor manufacturing equipment also increased by 20% in 2020, topping USD 32 billion, mainly from Japan, South Korea and Taiwan. The scale of these imports underscores both the importance of semiconductors for China and its large degree of dependency on others (Bloomberg, 2021b). Despite policy goals, semiconductor research firm IC Insights predicts that China will only be able to cover 19.4% of its chip demand from domestic sources by 2025 (IC Insights, 2021) (Figs. 3, 4).

While China attempts to build its own production capacities, in recent years, it has found itself blocked by numerous export controls imposed by other countries. Some of these measures target the EDA and SME which provide the most efficient choke points in the supply chain (Lee, 2021). Such restrictions were first considered during the presidency of Obama, but took effect and scale under the Trump administration, which first imposed export controls against Fujian Jinhua Integrated Circuit Co.—one of China's rising semiconductors stars, and against Semiconductor Manufacturing International Corp.—China's largest chipmaker (Crawford, 2020). Further, the USA cut the access of ZTE, Huawei and HiSilicon from the leading-edge technologies of TSMC, making the 3 Chinese companies suffer large losses and submit to undesired compromises (Schneider, 2021d). But for China, more disturbing than

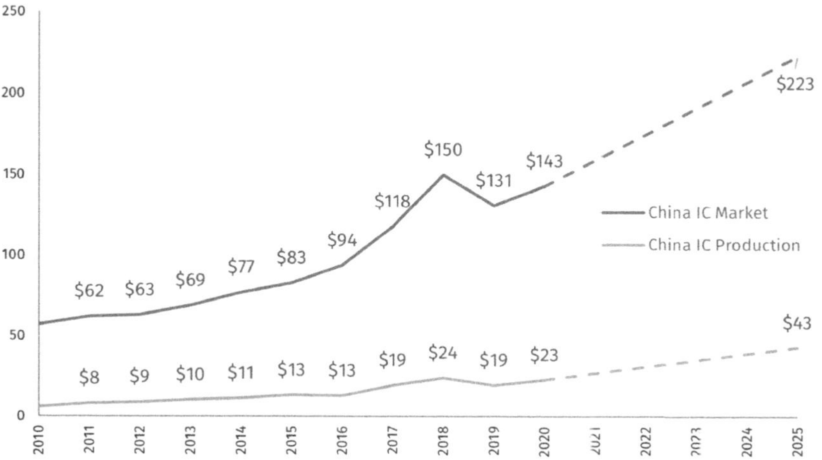


**Fig. 3** China's integrated circuit market and domestic production, USD billion (*Source* IC Insights [2021] in Schneider [2021a])

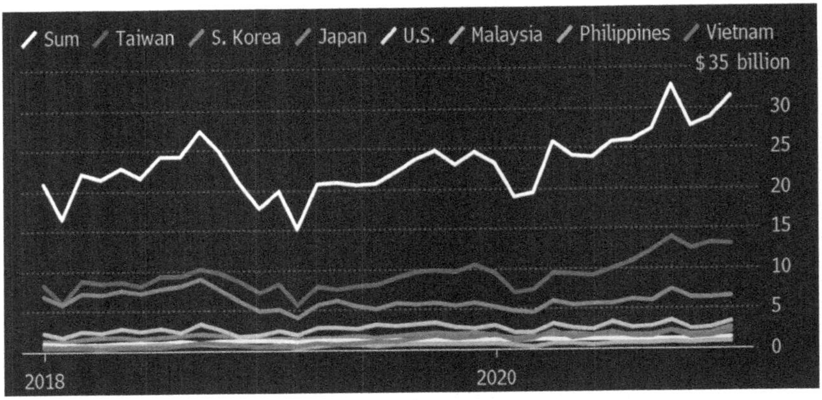


**Fig. 4** China's imports of semiconductors by country of origin, 2018–2020 (*Source* China's general administration of customs in Bloomberg [2021b])

the commercial and technology losses was the idea that the US Department of Commerce has the capacity to basically shut down major Chinese companies in a matter of days.

Preceding to the change of administration in the USA, some analysts expected that the intensity of trade tensions would decrease. However, as far as the semiconductors industry is concerned, the Biden administration has expanded the export backlist on 24 November 2021, when a new series of actors such as New H3C Technologies, Hangzhou Zhongke Microelectronics, Hefei National Laboratory for Physical Sciences at the Microscale and Hunan Goke Microelectronics were added.

Such bans gave the Chinese government a new impetus to develop a leading-edge industry. Anxious grew even more given that, in addition to the USA, China's other main microchip supplier are South Korea and Taiwan, with which relations are also vulnerable as well (Bazavan, 2019). Therefore, the Chinese government has launched multiple initiatives to catch up and create a self-reliant technological ecosystem (Schneider, 2021c).

China is channelling hundreds of billions of dollars into its chip firms through a variety of mechanisms, such as direct funding, government procurement, as well as subsidies. For example, according to OECD data, China provides substantially higher subsidies for semiconductors than any other country in the world. The government also funds and encourages domestic firms to invest overseas in or cooperate with companies that own chip technology and thus obtain access to high-quality chip technology (Ray et al., 2016). It does so especially in those sectors where China is particularly vulnerable and the USA is dominant, such as EDA and SME (O'Keeffe et al., 2021). Another priority is to accelerate research into third generation semiconductors, an emerging sector of semiconductors made of materials such as silicon carbide and gallium nitride, which still no country dominates (Crawford, 2020).

And the results are visible, as China's share of the world's chips production capacity has exceeded that of the USA and reached 15% in 2020, up from less than 1% in 1990. In the same period, the share of the United States has decreased from 37% to 12%. According to the estimates of the Semiconductor Industry Association, by 2030 China will develop 40% of the new global capacity and thus become the world's largest chips producer, with a market share of 24% (in Allison et al., 2021) (Fig. 5).

However, while China's capacity is growing and domestic manufacturing companies are expected to continue progress in certain segments of the industry, due to the particularities of the sector such as the high initial costs, the long creation cycle, the cumulative nature of know-how and the oligopolistic structure of the market that discourages newcomers, heavy capital investments cannot achieve indigenisation on their own (Schneider, 2021a). It takes a very long time for such an industry to grow, not to mention to become profitable, and, at the same time, competitors are advancing increasingly fast (McKinsey & Company, 2017). The

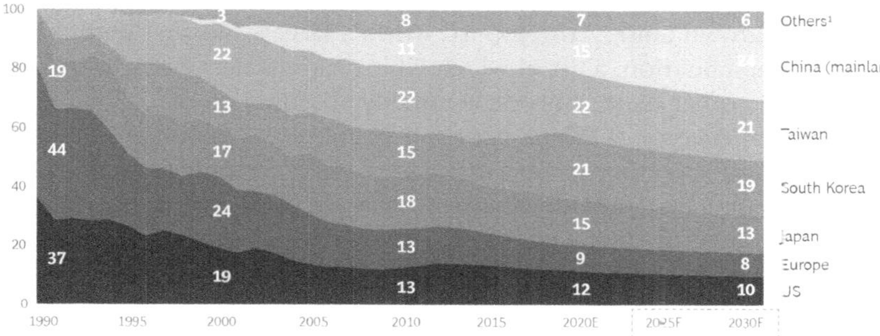


**Fig. 5** Share of global semiconductor manufacturing capacity by location (%) (*Source* Semiconductor industry association in Varas et al. [2020])

country has always remained one or two generations behind and currently is unable to manufacture the most advanced chips with the smallest feature sizes (Lee et al., 2016). Therefore, China's overall semiconductor industry is still lagging behind and it is unlikely to free itself from its sticking bottlenecks anytime soon.

## 6.2 *ICT and the Digital Economy*

As the world has moved to the digital economy, data have become one of the most valuable resources. Digital technologies leverage data to bring efficiency and productivity gains in new and traditional sectors alike (Craglia et al., 2018). China is among the fastest adopters of digital technologies. The scale of its digital economy increased from USD 1.6 trillion in 2012 to more than USD 5 trillion in 2019, accounting for 36.2% of its total GDP.[3] Most likely, these numbers have grown significantly during the COVID-19 pandemic, as they did in other countries as well. MIIT expects that China's big data industry alone will exceed USD 470.79 billion by 2025, up from USD 157 billion today (He & Han, 2021).

A few providers of digital services have ridden the wave of global economic transformation, growing exponentially and succeeding in record time to displace companies from traditional sectors as the world's largest companies. The global competition in the ICT sector is largely taking place between key industrial players from the USA and China, adding to the Korean Samsung. The market was initially dominated by US companies, but Chinese Tencent, Alibaba, Meituan and Jingdong, the leading companies in multiple digital services and platforms, have successfully grown among the top 10 world's largest internet companies by market capitalisation, a list in which China earns a new entry every few years. On the other hand, Europe is notably absent (Fig. 6).

The digital success of China is driven mainly by 3 factors: (1) a vast, young and tech-savvy population that allows rapid commercialisation; (2) a rich ecosystem that provides massive volumes of diverse data; and (3) unparalleled governmental support for companies that gives them sufficient room to experiment, and acts on multiple levels as an enabler, investor, developer and consumer (Breslin, 2011).

[3] Ouyang Shijia, "Digital Economy to Inject Impetus," China Daily, September 7, 2020 https://www.chinadaily.com.cn/a/202009/07/WS5f557848a310675eafc57cf9.html.

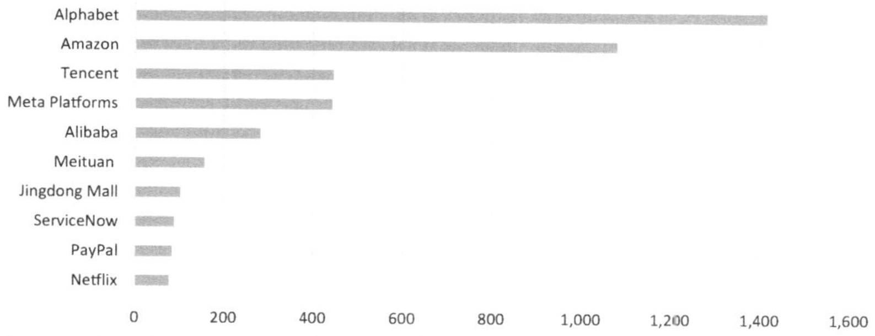


**Fig. 6** Largest internet companies by market capitalisation as of June 2022, US billion (*Source* www.companiesmarketcap.com, accessed on June 18, 2022)

Despite the large number of ICT companies involved in an ever-expanding digital ecosystem, Baidu, Alibaba and Tencent, collectively known as BAT, are the largest platforms, with a highly diversified and wide-reaching business model that touches on every aspect of consumers' lives (McKinsey & Company, 2017). A unique feature that distinguishes them from their USA peers with similar businesses is probably the fact that Alibaba and Tencent fully dominate everyday payments in China, which gives them tremendous economic power and wide-reach across industries (Lundvall & Rikap, 2022).

In the continuing quest to ensure increased economic productivity, Chinese policymakers have sought ways to harness the power of data as an economic resource. In April 2020, the State Council formally designated data as a production factor alongside land, labour, capital and technology. Furthermore, in November 2021, MIIT released the *14th Five-Year Plan for National Informatisation (2021–2025)*, which pushes forward the integration of information technologies with the industrial sector and gives a first priority to the establishment of highly efficient data factor resource systems. This is the second time such a plan has been issued, after the previous 2016–2020. The plan aims to "activate the factor value of data, enhance the role of data as a factor endowment, shape a strong domestic market that is innovation-driven, high-quality, supply-led, and creates new demand". To achieve such aims, one of the provisions affects public data related to demographics, transportation and telecom that should be shared through a unified national open data platform. The plan also foresees new support measures offered to highly specialised manufacturing and IT SMEs, with subnational governments being responsible for offering customised support that ranges from IPO listing to management consulting. With 2020 as the baseline year, the plan targets for 2025 are:

- Investment in ICT infrastructure grows from CNY 2.5 trillion to CNY 3.7 trillion;
- The penetration rate of industrial internet platforms reaches 45%;
- The national integration development index[4] grows by 20%;
- Data centre computing power grows from 90 to 300 ExaFLOPS[5];
- The popularisation rate of digital research, development and design tools grows to 85%;
- The usage rate of digital tools across corporate management and operation reaches 80%;
- 5G user penetration grows from 15 to 56%;
- The number of 5G base towers per 10,000 people grows from 5 to 26;
- The proportion of R&D design tools that are digitalised grows to 85%;
- The proportion of crucial production procedures that are digitally controlled grows to 65%.

In November 2021, MIIT also launched a separate five-year plan to stimulate the nation's big data industry and improve cross-border security management. The strategy reaffirms data as a "factor of production" and a "national strategic resource". Accordingly, by 2025, the data industry would exceed USD 471 billion, with an average compound annual growth rate of approximately 25%. The strategy calls for achieving better "marketisation" of data, strengthening of management of cross-border data flows, providing more support to open-source initiatives, improving computing power and ensuring that China plays a leading role in the global ICT standards setting (Reuters, 2021).

[4] Indicator measuring industrial sector and information technology integration.

[5] Indicator measuring computer performance.

In January 2022, China's State Council has published *The 14th Five-Year Plan on the Digital Economy*. The plan aiming to stimulate industry players to collect and leverage data in order to improve production efficiency sets out tasks and targets covering a large spectrum of sectors, from communications to e-commerce. Data are described as "a key force in the reorganisation of global resources, the reshaping of the global economic structure and the alteration of the global competitive landscape". Among others, the plan envisions that:

- The output of the core industries in the China digital economy will account for 10% of the national GDP by 2025, up from 7.8% in 2020;
- The adoption rate of industrial internet platforms will grow to 45% by 2025, up from 14.7% in 2020;
- The number of residents registered for online government services with their real identity will grow to 800 million, up from 400 million in 2020.

While many of these specific targets have also been included in previous policy documents, the Digital Economy Plan again emphasises the government's approach to data as a key factor of production, critical to generating high value added.

The key actors in China's booming internet economy are the internet tech giants BAT (Zeng, 2021). For many years, these companies have grown virtually unhindered, benefiting from strong government support, including through deregulation. However, the tides changed in 2021, which proved to be a very challenging year for tech companies.

Calls and debates for limiting the growth of internet companies in China have always been present, but the government prioritised economic development and efficiency. However, as China transitioned to prioritise higher-quality growth over fast growth, the government took abrupt measures to "strengthen anti-monopoly and prevent the disorderly expansion of capital",[6] while also securing China's cybersecurity system (Schneider, 2021b). China now aims to place tech companies within the

[6] One of the eight key tasks identified by the Central Economic Work Conference in 2021.

boundaries of compliance with the rule of law (Arenal et al., 2020). Moreover, in addition to complying with regulations, the government also expects companies to provide public goods to society and align with the broader ideological and political agenda.

And that entails addressing the issue of foreign ownership for companies that deal with sensitive data. The backlash focused on Didi Chuxing, which raised USD 4.4 billion by listing on the New York Stock Exchange (NYSE) in early July 2021, in spite of official warnings preventing it from doing so. Shortly after, Didi was reportedly ordered to delist from the US stock exchange due to data security concerns and was announced by the China Cyberspace Administration that it would be investigated for violations of data legislation. As a consequence, Didi had to stop new user registration and was removed from app stores. Further, an anti-monopoly investigation was also launched. At the time of writing this study, Didi is undertaking preparations to delist from NYSE in an attempt to calm the regulatory storm.

In turn, given repeated alleged violations of consumer rights and interests, Tencent was banned from launching new applications or updating existing ones, while the use of its flagship application, WeChat, has been banned among several SOEs due to data security concerns. In addition, Meituan was also fined CNY 3.4 billion by regulators after a six-month investigation on anticompetitive practises.

On another front, new tax schemes proposals indicate that mobile internet platforms are soon to lose state financial aid. For example, Alibaba's last quarterly earnings reports indicate a steady rise in its income tax levels, as subsidiaries are gradually losing tax benefits designed for key software enterprises.

Moreover, the legislation around the collection, use and trade of data has been tightened after the entry into force in 2021 of two key pieces of legislation: *The Data Security Law* and The *Personal Information Protection Law*. Their coverage is broad-reaching across industries and topics, and in certain aspects, it can be argued that they are stricter than the GDPR of the EU.

Overall, China's new approach to limit big tech has been surprisingly wide-reaching. 2021 has changed, at least temporarily, the outlook of the internet platform economy, with major actors in need to comply with a broader set of regulatory, financial and ideological requirements. For the moment, China's internet lost in 2021 and the gap with USA peers has widened. However, it is important to note that China's crackdown did not target hardware companies, which currently remain at the top of the agenda.

## 7 Summary

This chapter examined in detail additional five systemic factors of China's NIS, evaluating their significance from different perspectives, across industry supply chains. These factors include talent policies and talent attraction programmes, the situation of intellectual property rights and the foreseen evolutions, the number and quality of patents across different criteria, the positive public perception towards technology and the prioritisation of strategic industries that receive all-round support.

China has invested heavily in its higher education system, resulting in significant improvements and global recognition for STEM programmes at top universities like Peking, Tsinghua and Fudan. As a result, China is expected to have double the number of STEM Ph.D. graduates compared to the US by 2025. In addition to developing domestic talent, China has implemented various programmes to attract non-ethnic Chinese and overseas Chinese individuals who have acquired valuable skills and established networks at leading global institutions.

Regarding IPR, China is expected to continue strengthening its legislation, but the process is slow. Inadequacies in enforcement mechanisms, sometimes influenced by political factors, are still significant. Furthermore, transparency is lacking in the judicial system, which affects IP protection. The Chinese IPR legislative system is also reportedly biased towards domestic firms, making it difficult for foreign firms to offshore high-tech manufacturing and R&D operations to China. This continues to be a hindrance MNCs, despite recent progress in IPR legislation and enforcement.

The country's share in patent numbers is growing fast and China became a global patent leader by many measures. However, patent quality has not improved proportionally due to a government push for quantity over quality. Furthermore, China's patents are concentrated in a few sectors, unlike in the USA where patents are better distributed across fields and are of higher quality. China needs to further focus on improving the quality of industrial patents across a broader range of fields.

The positive public perception of technology is a key factor enabling the growth of Chinese tech companies and the adoption of new technologies. However, this trend is changing as Chinese consumers become more aware of their rights and seek greater protection. This is leading to the introduction of stricter legislation which has the potential to slow down the pace of innovation.

Finally, the chapter explores two industries that are highly-prioritised by the political establishment: semiconductors and ICT. Both receive all-round support, including through strong financing, favourable tax schemes and political advantages. However, while China is becoming a global leader in ICT technologies, it is still lagging in semiconductors, due to the very cumulative nature of the industry.

## References


Alberts, B., & Narayanamurti, V. (2019). Two threats to U.S. Science. *Science*. https://doi.org/10.1126/science.aax9846

Allison, G., et al. (2021). *The Great Tech Rivalry: China vs the U.S.* https://www.belfercenter.org/publication/great-tech-rivalry-china-vs-us. Accessed 2 July 2022.

Arenal, A., et al. (2020). Innovation ecosystems theory revisited: The case of artificial intelligence in China. *Telecommunications Policy, 44*(6). https://doi.org/10.1016/j.telpol.2020.101960

Bazavan, A. (2019, September). Chinese government's shifting role in the national innovation system. *Technological Forecasting and Social Change, 148*. https://doi.org/10.1016/j.techfore.2019.119738

Bloomberg. (2021a, February 2). *China stockpiles chips, chip-making machines to resist U.S.* https://www.bloomberg.com/news/articles/2021-02-02/china-stockpiles-chips-and-chip-making-machines-to-resist-u-s. Accessed 2 July 2022.

Bloomberg. (2021b, February 5). *One thing China and the U.S. can agree on*. Bloomberg. https://www.bloomberg.com/news/newsletters/2021-02-05/top-china-stories-this-week-ant-overhaul-semiconductor-self-sufficiency. Accessed 2 July 2022.

Bogers, M., Foss, N. J., & Lyngsie, J. (2018). The "human side" of open innovation: The role of employee diversity in firm-level openness. *Research Policy, 47*(1). https://doi.org/10.1016/j.respol.2017.10.012

Breslin, S. (2011). China and the crisis: Global power, domestic caution and local initiative. *Contemporary Politics* [Preprint]. https://doi.org/10.1080/13569775.2011.565987

*China Daily*. (2022). Postgraduate exam more competitive. https://www.chinadaily.com.cn/a/202203/30/WS62439074a310fd2b29e54042.html. Accessed 2 July 2022.

Craglia, M., et al. (2018). *Artificial Intelligence: A European perspective, European Union*. https://doi.org/10.2760/11251

Crawford, A. (2020). *The U.S.-China conflict over chips is about to get uglier*. Bloomberg. https://news.bloomberglaw.com/tech-and-telecom-law/the-u-s-china-conflict-over-chips-is-about-to-get-uglier. Accessed 2 July 2022.

European Commission. (2017). *Survey on researchers outside of Europe—Annex to MORE3 study: Support data collection and analysis concerning mobility patterns and career paths of researchers*. Brussels. https://cdn5.euraxess.org/sites/default/files/policy_library/survey_on_researchers_outside_of_europe_0.pdf. Accessed 1 July 2022.

European Union Chamber of Commerce in China. (2021). *European Business in China Position Paper 2021/2022*. https://europeanchamber.oss-cn-beijing.aliyuncs.com/upload/documents/documents/European_Business_in_China_Position_Paper_2021_2022[964].pdf. Accessed 2 July 2022.

Godoi, F. C., Prakash, S., & Bhandari, B. R. (2015, February). Final report: National Security Commission on Artificial Intelligence. *Public*, 12–15.

He, S., & Han, W. (2021). *China's big data industry to top $470 billion by 2025*. Caixin Global. https://www.caixinglobal.com/2021-12-01/chinas-big-data-industry-to-top-470-billion-by-2025-101812002.html. Accessed 2 July 2022.

Hu, A. G. Z., Zhang, P., & Zhao, L. (2017). China as number one? Evidence from China's most recent patenting surge. *Journal of Development Economics, 124*, 107–119. https://doi.org/10.1016/j.jdeveco.2016.09.004

IC Insights. (2021). *China forecast to fall far short of its "Made in China 2025" goals for ICs*. https://www.icinsights.com/news/bulletins/China-Forecast-To-Fall-Far-Short-Of-Its-Made-In-China-2025-Goals-For-ICs/. Accessed 2 July 2022.

International Labour Organisation (ILO). (2017). *Attracting skilled international migrants to China: A review and comparison of policies and practices*. https://publications.iom.int/system/files/pdf/attracting_skilled_en_0.pdf

Lee, J. (2021). *Mapping China's place in the global semiconductor industry*. https://merics.org/en/short-analysis/mapping-chinas-place-global-semiconductor-industry. Accessed 2 July 2022.

Lee, K., Gao, X., & Li, X. (2016, December). Industrial catch-up in China: A sectoral systems of innovation perspective. *Cambridge Journal of Regions, Economy and Society*, rsw037. https://doi.org/10.1093/cjres/rsw037

Lundvall, B. Å., & Rikap, C. (2022a). China's catching-up in artificial intelligence seen as a co-evolution of corporate and national innovation systems. *Research Policy, 51*(1), 104395. https://doi.org/10.1016/J.RESPOL.2021.104395

McKinsey & Company. (2017, December). *Digital China: Powering the economy to global competitiveness*. https://www.mckinsey.com/%7B~%7D/media/McKinsey/Global

National Development and Reform Commission (NDRC). (2020). *The national development and reform commission answers reporters' questions on the "Guiding Opinions on Expanding Investment in Strategic Emerging Industries and Cultivating Strengthened New Growth Points and Growth Poles"*. http://www.gov.cn/zhengce/2020-09/24/content_5546618.htm. Accessed 2 July 2022.

National Security Commission on Artificial Intelligence (NSCAI). (2018). *Immigrant founders of the fortune 500*. http://startupsusa.org/fortune500/. Accessed 2 July 2022.

Normile, D. (2018). China narrows U.S. lead in R&D spending. *Science, 362*(6412), 276–276. https://doi.org/10.1126/science.362.6412.276

OECD. (2021). *Main science and technology indicators, Volume 2021 Issue 1*. https://doi.org/10.1787/eea67efc-en. Accessed 1 July 2022.

O'Keeffe, K., Somerville, H., & Yang, J. (2021, November 12). *U.S. companies aid China's bid for chip dominance despite security concerns*. https://www.wsj.com/articles/u-s-firms-aid-chinas-bid-for-chip-dominance-despite-security-concerns-11636718400. Accessed 2 July 2022.

Ray, J., et al. (2016, October). China's industrial and military robotics development. *Research Report Prepared on Behalf of the U.S.-China Economic and Security Review Commission* [Preprint].

Reuters. (2021). *China seeks better cross-border control of big data with new plan*. Reuters. https://www.reuters.com/article/china-regulation-data-idCAKBN2IF09S. Accessed 2 July 2022.

Schneider, J. (2021a). *China's chip industry: Running faster but still falling behind*. https://rhg.com/research/china-chips/. Accessed 1 July 2022.

Schneider, J. (2021b). *DiDi's troubles, Tweets of the week (Corruption, Waluigi+Mao, Fish Hugging, Which Ministry Works the Hardest?)*. China Talk. https://chinatalk.substack.com/p/didis-troubles-tweets-of-the-week. Accessed 2 July 2022.

Schneider, J. (2021c). *Labs over fabs: Support the future, not the past*. https://chinatalk.substack.com/p/labs-over-fabs-support-the-future?s=r. Accessed 2 July 2022.

Schneider, J. (2021d). *Will China hit back on chips?* China Talk. https://chinatalk.substack.com/p/will-china-hit-back-on-chips?s=r. Accessed 2 July 2022.

Varas, B. A., et al. (2020, September). *Government incentives and US competitiveness in semiconductor manufacturing* (pp. 1–32). Semiconductor Industry Association.

World Intellectual Property Organisation (WIPO). (2022). *World Intellectual Property Report 2022*. https://www.wipo.int/publications/en/details.jsp?id=4594&plang=EN. Accessed 2 July 2022.

Zeng, J. (2021). China's artificial intelligence innovation: A top-down national command approach? *Global Policy, 12*(3), 399–409. https://doi.org/10.1111/1758-5899.12914

CHAPTER 8

# Case Study on Artificial Intelligence

Artificial intelligence, or the idea that computers can act as general-purpose machines capable of autonomous perception and cognition, taking decisions and learning independently in a way similar to the human mind, has gone from far-fetched speculation to contemporary reality. Research and development started 70 years ago, but it went through winters of low interest. Despite strong enthusiasm beginning with the 1950s, AI ideas could not be transformed into broad applications until recently (Flew, 2021). This has changed dramatically in the last decade thanks to several key enablers:

- Substantial improvement of several technological factors such as the ability to collect, store and aggregate data, computational capacity and the quality of algorithms;
- Exponential growth of funding, due to broader commercial use, as previously AI R&D could not obtain sufficient funding due to the lack of commercial applications;
- Governments' increased interest for deploying AI in the spheres of military, security and surveillance, which are some of the fields where AI has the biggest potential.

Existing AI technology still has important limitations, as it is not yet capable of general-purpose reasoning. Therefore, the potential set



A. Băzăvan, *China's National Innovation System*,
https://doi.org/10.1007/978-981-97-3266-1_8

of applications of each AI system is very narrow and domain-specific, requiring specialised human intervention at every transition to a new application (Kelly, 2017). However, current AI technology revolutionises the way data are processed and transformed into added value, and can be applied to a whole range of industries (Baccala et al., 2018). It acts as a basic enabling technology, similar to the steam engine or electricity in the past (Arenal et al., 2020).

AI is particularly powerful in extracting patterns and generating new insights from complex, multi-dimensional data types such as images, video, audio and speech (Craglia et al., 2018). It can adapt rules learnt independently to new sets of data and produce original answers (Barton et al., 2017). In a way similar to the human mind, AI systems can constantly improve by training, but in contrast to humans, AI has the capacity to process immense amounts of data in considerably less time. Even in smaller sets of data, in the field of image classification and object recognition, the best AI algorithms are already stronger than humans (Chui et al., 2018).

As a result, AI became an economically and strategically important emerging technology, set to change not only our economy and supply chains, but also our society, for the better or for worse (Zeng, 2021). The stakes could not be higher. Previous industrial revolutions reorganised the distribution of power and wealth among nations, providing high benefits to the pioneers. AI can now have a similar effect, in a 'winner-takes-all' and 'first-mover' type of dynamic (Bughin et al., 2018). This led decision makers to increasingly perceive AI as an arena for international competition and, therefore, launch initiatives aimed at securing the broad adoption of AI (Tsinghua University, 2018). At the same time, decision makers must also balance potential benefits against potential risks to their societies (Arenal et al., 2020).

This global trend is largely led by the USA and China, positioned far ahead of other countries, which are followed by the EU, South Korea, India and Japan, as rather minor contenders (Renda, 2019). These realities are reflected in the corporate sector, as the largest internet companies that lead AI development—Google, Amazon, Facebook, Microsoft, Baidu, Alibaba and Tencent—originate from either the USA or China. In the context of comprehensive strategic competition between the USA and China, given the huge economic potential of AI and also the fact that AI applications in the military sector became a major factor of a country's strength, both countries have elevated AI to the level of a top strategic priority (Lundvall & Rikap, 2022).

The USA, the traditional leader in digital technologies and cradle of achievements in chips, algorithms and machine learning software, sees AI as fundamental to maintaining its economic and military edge over China (Bazavan & Huidumac-Petrescu, 2023). It still holds the initiative in computing power, algorithms and essential hardware such as AI-specific semiconductors. Moreover, as far as the complexity of its AI NIS is concerned, the USA still enjoys a significant advantage by the number of AI companies and their global reach, the scale of its VC scene and the available pool of talent.

With increasing funding for R&D and having big tech companies that drive momentum in commercial applications, China has rapidly become the world's second largest hub for AI development in most measures. The country is catching up and even forging ahead in some sectors, thus raising the possibility of overtaking the USA as the leading centre of AI innovation within the next decade. In November 2017, Eric Schmidt, then CEO of Alphabet, raised the alarm in the USA by claiming that "By 2020, they (China) will have caught up. By 2025, they will be better than us. By 2030, they will dominate the industries of AI" (Arenal et al., 2020). Nicolas Chaillan, former Chief Software Officer of the USA Air Force, went one step forward arguing that China's leadership in AI is "already a done deal".[1] The USA National Security Commission on Artificial Intelligence's report in 2021 mentioned that "even large tech firms cannot be expected to compete with the resources of China or make the big investments the U.S. will need to stay ahead. We will need a hybrid approach that combines government and private sector efforts to win the technology competition" (NSCAI, 2021). However, it is important to note that despite strong evolutions, China's AI NIS still has fundamental weakness as regards algorithm development, fundamental theories and top-tier talent. It is also far behind the USA in core hardware technologies, including AI chips, which are fundamental for AI development (Lundvall & Rikap, 2022).

China missed past technological revolutions, which had a long way to catch up (Tsinghua University, 2018). Currently, given the fertile grounds

[1] Katrina Manson, "US has already lost AI fight to China, says ex-Pentagon software chief," Financial Times, October 10, 2021, https://www.ft.com/content/f939db9a-40af-4bd1-b67d-10492535f8e0.

laid by China's massive economic scale and wide range of industries, the power of its technology giants, the growing pool of talent and intense policy prioritisation, China is now set for a head start in the fourth industrial revolution(Allison et al., 2021). Its potential gains are enormous as AI presents an opportunity to address the systemic challenges of an ageing population, sustainable development and continued economic transformation. However, on the other hand, China is also threatened by potential disruptions to the labour market that can be caused by AI.

As a result, in the past few years, China has embarked on a coordinated approach to develop its AI capabilities, including government policy, industrial applications and research (Craglia et al., 2018; Yang & Al-Sayed, 2022). While the goals of this agenda are primarily internal, serving economic development and governance purposes, it also has an external dimension, as China sees AI as an area in which it can gain parity with the USA and explicitly aims to become the world leader in AI by 2030.

In this competitive environment, the mainstream discussion in international academic and policy circles about the emerging role of China in the global AI landscape is frequently based on limited understanding of the constitution and evolution of China's AI NIS. While China understands the evolving AI environment in the 'West', the latter is, on the contrary, little familiar with the key policies, stakeholders and applications in China. Deciphering the implications of China's AI requires a deeper understanding of how AI NIS is configured in China (Arenal et al., 2020).

Therefore, based on an in-depth qualitative study, personal translations of relevant policy documents, a comprehensive media review and a set of interviews with key experts, this chapter examines the strengths and weaknesses of China's emerging AI NIS, highlighting four significant dimensions: the role played by the government; industry financing mechanisms; FDI and internationalisation; and other systemic factors such as market scale, data availability and clusters of innovation. Furthermore, it also outlines how AI development intersects with public perception and social governance. Finally, the paper addresses several misconceptions about China's AI NIS and concludes with a discussion on the main challenges ahead for China to achieve global leadership. Against this background, it offers reflections on the potential implications for global issues such as safety and ethics, national security, economic development and social governance, concluding with several policy recommendations for

Europe. This is more timely given the growing debate at both EU and MS levels regarding AI.

## 1 Government and Policy

The Chinese government has played an important role in the establishment of China's AI NIS and putting it on the path to catch up with competitors. Under the various development plans, it has funded AI R&D in universities and research institutes, pushed for expanding relevant curricula in higher education, invested significantly in telecommunication infrastructure and used government procurement as a supportive tool (Lundvall & Rikap 2022). On the other side of the spectrum, the state has also made intensive use of protectionist policies, excluding foreign competitors from internal markets and thus supporting the emergence of domestic tech champions.

Therefore, AI plays a prominent role in China's agenda to establish its digital infrastructure, strengthen its smart manufacturing and digitise social governance. Since 2015, China has released a series of framework policies aimed at stimulating AI development, among which the most prominent are *Made in China 2015*, *The Guiding Opinions of the State Council on Vigorously Advancing the 'Internet+' Action* and the *Next Generation Artificial Intelligence Development Plan*. Judging by sheer numbers, the search of central policy documents using keywords related to AI returned 244 documents.

The targets set are wide-reaching, encompassing sectors as diverse as smart agriculture, intelligent logistics, military applications and labour market aspects. Policymakers are also concerned about the dependencies on solutions from foreign suppliers. During the first known study session on AI of the Politburo, General Secretary Xi Jinping stated that 'accelerating the development of a new generation of AI is an important strategic handhold for China to gain the initiative in global science and technology competition ... we need to ensure that the core AI technologies are firmly in our own hands'.

Therefore, it is tempting to regard China's approach to AI development as a centralised and coherent grand strategy, driven by geopolitical ambitions (Zeng, 2021). However, it is important to highlight the fact that China's AI policy is not monolithic. Instead, it is formed of a complex network of central and regional, provincial, and municipal policies, at different levels of development and support, connected or dissipated.

While the central government plays an important guiding role, the agenda is bent by powerful private and state stakeholders that sometimes even have competing interests (Ding, 2018).

Most of China's provinces have followed the central government and established their own AI plans, while some of them have even done so before the central government established AI as a national strategy in 2017. In most cases, such strategies are formulated in a top-down approach, aligned with national guideline policies in light of local conditions. At the same time, subnational AI policies also have their own characteristics and priorities, especially as they are, to a certain degree, in a state of competition with each other (Tsinghua University, 2018).

Actually, inconsistencies are not rare, including at the central level. As China follows its AI vision, different institutions and policy stakeholders are competing for authority over that vision. Given the importance of the topic, several institutions and administrative bodies hope to be chosen as leaders in the advancement of this strategic technology. While competition generates ideas, divergent interests and multiple stakeholders also have an adverse effect in limiting the degree to which initiatives can be integrated. Therefore, AI policymaking should not only be seen as a top-down approach, as bottom-up and centrifugal processes are very important as well.

## 2 Funding

There are several estimates in the available literature on the volume of funding for AI development in China, but these vary greatly due to the high difficulty in identifying and measuring relevant data. As previously mentioned, this is partly caused by a lack of consensus regarding what AI actually is and what kind of companies qualify as having AI as a core business.

However, it can be asserted that funding is a central part of China's national AI strategy and therefore the government disburses significant resources (Arenal et al., 2020). China's funding for AI is guided by the *'1+N' funding strategy*, whereas '1' refers to the establishment of the *New Generation Artificial Intelligence Megaproject* and 'N' designates AI-related tasks to be included in other currently-existing national science and technology (STI) projects. The "1+N" Strategy falls under the responsibility of MIIT, through the Inter-Ministerial Joint Council, and aims to create a coordinated and efficient public-private funding support mechanism for supporting AI (Development Solutions Europe Ltd., 2018).

In addition to direct public funding for AI, China also hosts one of the leading VC scenes for AI globally. Vast investments in core AI start-ups are carried by tech giants such as the BAT, private equity (PE) firms and VC funds (Sinovation Ventures, Cash Capital, Legend Star, ZhenFund, GGV Capital and Volcanics Venture among a few), as well as by GGFs funded from public sources.

As shown in Figs. 1 and 2, the USA leads global PE and VC received by AI start-ups with over USD 23.6 billion in funding in 2020, while China occupies an undisputed second place with a volume of USD 9.9 billion (Zhang et al., 2021).

Finally, by any estimate, despite lagging behind the USA in nominal values, AI funding in China is massive. An open question remains to what extent financial resources are used efficiently and are not causing side effects, such as the crowding out of professional investors among others (Arenal et al., 2020). There are many voices who fear the sustainability of the sector and the potential for an AI investment bubble in China.

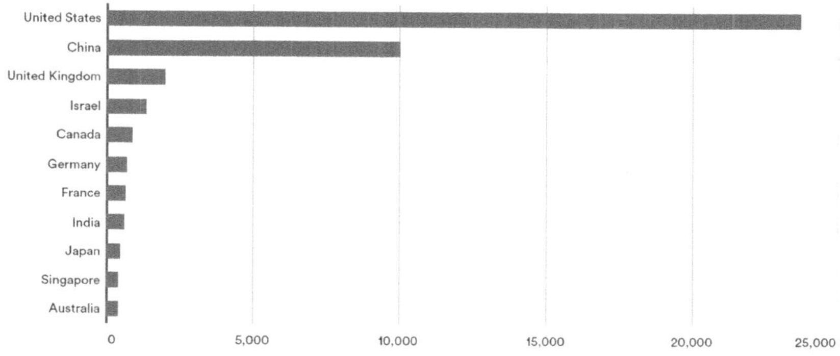


**Fig. 1** Private investment in AI by country, 2020, USD million (*Source* 2021 AI Index Report [Zhang et al.])

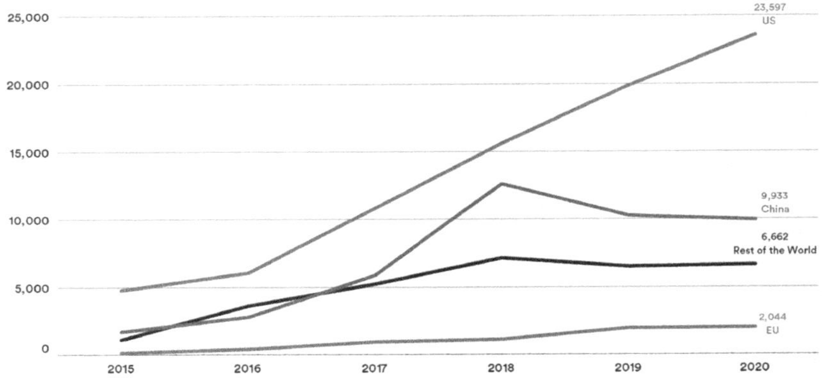


**Fig. 2** Private investment in AI by geographic area, 2015–2020, USD million (*Source* 2021 AI Index Report [Zhang et al.])

## 3 Foreign Direct Investment and Internationalisation

### *3.1 Inbound Investments*

At the policy level, the State Council's *Plan for the Development of the Next Generation of Artificial Intelligence* explicitly encourages international companies and research structures to establish AI R&D facilities in China and to launch cooperation with Chinese domestic actors in AI research. As of January 2021, the *Catalogue of Industries for Encouraging Foreign Investment* also specifically encourages IFDI in the AI sector, at both national and regional levels. Favourable policy takes the form of tariff exemptions, preferential land prices and regulations, tax incentives, etc.

Major international companies such as Apple, Amazon Web Services, Google and Microsoft are increasing their presence in China and partnerships with local partners, to tap into China's large pool of top-notch engineers and scientists, gain access to restricted sectors and receive permission to perform AI experiments. However, there are no large companies from the EU present in China's AI innovation system. Some examples of American AI investments or cooperation projects in China include the following:

(1) Google has an important AI research lab in Beijing (the first in Asia), which is remarkable given that the company's core services are blocked in China. The company also has a joint laboratory with Fudan University and a stake of USD 550 million in Jing Dong, China's second largest e-commerce company.
(2) Microsoft is involved in two joint laboratories established in partnership with the Ministry of Education, at the Harbin Institute of Technology and Shanghai Jiaotong University. The Microsoft Research Asia programme also participates in the National Engineering Laboratory of Brain-like Technology and Application.
(3) Cisco is engaged in several JVs with Chinese companies, including SOEs.
(4) Amazon operates its cloud services through a JV and has an AI research lab in Shanghai.
(5) Ford partnered with Baidu to test self-driving vehicles on Beijing roads. The two companies also cooperate in the development of connected services, artificial intelligence and digital marketing. The USA manufacturer is also a founding member of the Apollo Committee, Baidu's open platform on autonomous driving.
(6) In addition to several investments in China's VC scene, Qualcomm established a JV with Chinese ThunderSoft to form an Internet-of-Things company called Thundercomm Technology with an innovation laboratory in Chongqing. Qualcomm also holds partnerships with Baidu and NetEase, two major Chinese internet companies, for on-device AI applications.

However, overall, foreign tech companies' participation in China's AI NIS remains fairly limited. The COVID-19 pandemic has further decreased the presence of foreign companies in China and even that of foreign professionals. A closed market reduces the technology spillover effects and raises the prospects of a decoupling of digital services.

### *3.2 Outbound Investments*

As mentioned previously, despite benefiting from a huge internal market, China's AI companies do not match the global reach of American companies that have access to more broader, bigger and more diverse markets. Through investment or trade, Chinese AI companies are currently slowly building their CIS beyond China's borders, in an attempt to overcome localised weaknesses by importing solutions or accessing them abroad (Lundvall and Rikap, 2022a). Unlike hardware ICT companies such as Huawei, China's AI and digital services companies have relatively limited success in their internationalisation attempts, as they still remain largely national corporations. ByteDance, the owner of TikTok, created a precedent, becoming the first ever Chinese company to succeed in providing globally digital services, with a strong AI component.

The *Plan for the Development of New Generation Artificial Intelligence*, along with the *'1 + N' funding strategy, supports* domestic companies to invest abroad, especially through a preferential regulatory framework and the provision of facilitated credits. Therefore, despite increased scrutiny in the USA and the EU against Chinese investments in sensitive sectors, Chinese outflows of AI investments to these developed markets exceed the inverse inflows. Some of the most well-known Chinese AI-relevant outbound investments include:

- Lenovo acquired the American IBM PC branch;
- Midea acquired German Kuka Robotics;
- Chinese biotech start-up iCarbonX acquired Israeli vision AI company Imagu;
- Alibaba acquired the German big data start-up Data Artisans and the US start-up MagicLeap specialised in AR/VR technologies;
- Alibaba invested in numerous European start-ups such as Irish Showtime Analytics, Swiss WayRay and Finnish MariaDB Corporation;
- Baidu and JD invested in American ZestFinance;
- Some of Tencent's start-up investments include American ObEN and Atomwise, as well as Canadian Element AI.

In addition to equity investments, another growth strategy for Chinese companies is funding their own research facilities in global innovation hubs overseas, tapping into new knowledge and potential disruptive developments. As in the case of equity investments, with few notable exceptions, most of the research facilities of Chinese companies abroad target the US market. Several examples include:

- Baidu owns two deep learning research centres in Sunnyvale, California;

- Tencent operates a data centre in Silicon Valley and a research centre in Seattle;
- CooTek has an AI research lab in Silicon Valley;
- Ride-sharing unicorn Didi Chuxing owns 'Didi Labs' in Silicon Valley;
- Alibaba invested USD 15 billion to establish the 'Damo Academies' in California, New York, Moscow, Tel Aviv and Singapore. These are R&D laboratories focused on machine intelligence, data computing, robotics and fintech, located close to leading universities;
- China Electronics Technology Group Corporation operates a joint research centre with the University of Sidney;
- TCL Corporation owns a research facility in Warsaw, working on speech recognition and image analysis.

Overall, Chinese AI companies still have a limited degree of internationalisation, which slows innovation and economic potential. This is slowly changing, although at a slower rate than it has with hardware companies. As opposed to hardware (ICT technology, for instance), exporting an AI-powered digital service is usually accompanied by exporting a cultural model of behaviour. Therefore, breaching cultural barriers is a longer cumulative process that China undertakes step by step. And TikTok is the first big step.

## 4 Market Scale and Industrial Output

It is hard to calculate precisely the actual size of China's AI sector and several studies advance various numbers due to methodological differences. As the industry is new and there is not yet an agreed definition for what AI industries are, there is still no authoritative international organisation to propose clear numbers and definitions. However, what is clear and consistent in all studies is that, by any indicator, China's AI industry is, currently the second largest in the world and has grown significantly in both absolute and relative terms over the past few years, powered by an increasingly mature domestic VC scene, as well as by its domestic tech giants.

Despite strong policy support for AI hardware and particularly for AI chips, the AI NIS in China is little focused on basic hardware. On the other hand, the industry is most developed in the areas of image, face and voice recognition, together with the related fields (Craglia et al., 2018).

According to Tsinghua University, Research Centre for Chinese Technology Policies (2018), as of 2018, the segment of computer vision technologies (biometric recognition, image recognition, video recognition) led the AI market in China with a 34.9% share, voice technologies (speech recognition, speech synthesis) were second with 24.8%, followed by natural language processing (machine translation, text mining, emotional analysis) with 21%. The rest 20% are dedicated to other market sectors such as fundamental applications.

## 5 Data Availability

Data are the fundamental input for artificial intelligence, as machine learning systems become more productive as they receive larger and more diverse sets of data.

It is frequently argued in relevant literature that Chinese AI companies would have a data advantage over their global competitors, due to the sheer number of China's pool of digital population, adding to data lax privacy regulations. While the Chinese market does indeed provide unparallel amounts of data, the Chinese market is not sufficient to put domestic companies on a globally advantageous position. Their American competitors are not bound to the USA market alone, as they are truly global companies, dominating across businesses in almost all markets around the world, with the notable exception of China. Therefore, American tech giants have access to a larger pool of data, which is also more diverse. As mentioned in the previous section, the lack of global reach of Chinese AI companies remains a major stumble block to the industry's development.

In addition, the idea that there are fewer obstacles to personal data collection and processing in China due to relatively lax privacy regulations and a young population that would be less concerned about privacy is no longer valid. In recent years, a major debate over data privacy regulation has emerged and the Chinese government took outstanding, some would say disproportionate, actions to limit the reach and power of Chinese tech giants. Recently, two key legislation items were enacted in 2021: *The Data Security Law* and *the Personal Information Protection Law*, which, in certain areas, are stricter than the GDPR of the EU.

## 6 Clusters

Investment in AI is highly concentrated in regional specialised clusters, primarily in the USA, China and Europe. As far as China is concerned, Beijing, Shanghai, Shenzhen and Hangzhou are the clusters with the most dynamic industries, but also the strongest policy support.

Beijing is far ahead of other regions in terms of market scale, number of companies, financing volumes, number of investment transactions, as well as talent and top-ranking universities (Development Solutions Europe Ltd., 2018). The city hosts more than half of the AI-related State Key Laboratories and major research bases, and is also home to the headquarters of tech giant Baidu. More importantly, Beijing benefits from the existence of Zhongguancun District, often referred to as China's Silicon Valley, which hosts some of the nation's brightest universities, research institutions and MNCs headquarters. Not least, the industry in Beijing is also better positioned than in other cities to benefit from government connections, influence policymaking and tap into public procurement.

Shanghai is China's second AI hub, as it hosts some of the nation's major AI research centres such as the Institute of Science and Technology for Brain-inspired Intelligence of Fudan University, alongside several global R&D headquarters of MNCs. Shanghai's AI industry performs best in the sectors of robotics, finance, e-commerce and logistics. Together with Beijing, the city is also a national frontrunner in AI-specific hardware, such as specialised semiconductors.

The Guangdong province, led by Shenzhen, is the third Chinese cluster by number of AI companies and comes second after Beijing in terms of related total investments, hosting the headquarters of important AI companies such as Tencent. Guangdong makes particular progress in deploying AI applications in manufacturing and robots, which are prioritised through a variety of subsidies schemes, preferential access to resources, public procurement and industry-government cooperation.

Zhejiang is another significant AI cluster, led by its provincial capital, Hangzhou. The dynamic ecosystem of the city is dominated by the presence of Alibaba's headquarters, which partners with the company closely with regional authorities, and alongside Zhejiang University and Foxconn, to build an integrated intelligent traffic management system. The city also benefits from powerful PE and venture capital firms, both domestic and foreign, that support start-ups.

## 7 Summary

Based on the national innovation system framework and a detailed qualitative analysis, this chapter highlighted some of the main characteristics of the evolving AI landscape in China, emphasising the synergies but also contradictions between government institutions, public policy, private investment and research. The chapter highlighted some of the strong points but also pertaining limitations for China's AI to accomplish its roadmap to 2030.

China identifies AI as strategic to its internal sustainable economic development and social governance on the one hand, and to its emergence as a confident global power on the other. The industry enjoys a favourable environment in the form of extensive funding and generous capital markets, a vast pool of consumers with appetite for technology and huge volumes of data, strong government support from the central and local authorities as well as a generally positive public opinion. AI-powered applications with a high impact on daily lives of China's citizens are already widely deployed across industries, including in finance, insurance, transportation, retail, security and state surveillance.

The AI industry benefits from a partly coordinated approach to AI, with key policy priorities designed at the top levels of administration and further replicated and adapted in the territory. Both the central government and local authorities have contributed extensively with favourable regulation or even more favourable non-regulation, room for experimentation, funding, access to critical data and, at the same time, blocking foreign competitors. Moreover, in general, there is a significant overall alignment between the interests of private actors and the government. However, at least briefly, this alignment has been challenged starting with 2021.

Nevertheless, China still has many gaps to fill in order to lead global AI development, as its AI industry has not yet met the ambitious targets set by the very confident *Next Generation AI Development Strategy* issued in 2017. One significant obstacle is the fact that China's research capabilities and the corresponding talent are limited in scope and tend towards commercialisation, rather than fundamental theory. The industry also faces challenges in embedding AI into more traditional industries, as well as in preparing, attracting and retaining sufficient top-notch talent in the country. Furthermore, in some core technologies such as AI chips, China is highly reliant on external suppliers. Moreover, its tech giants, despite their power domestically, do not yet have global reach, with the notable exception of ByteDance, which set a precedence with its globally successful application TikTok. Not least, China's policy approach faces difficulties in coordination and implementation, as the authority is rather decentralised between competing institutions and individuals. Finally, in 2021, the government decided to crack down on tech's 'unruly expansion' and adopted new legislation on data and algorithms that exceed the strictness of the EU and the USA which, at least in the short term, further hinders the development of the industry.

From a global perspective, recent years have witnessed the emergence of a highly contested AI competition between the USA and China, with Europe being notably absent on most metrics. The USA aims to maintain its lead over China and, therefore, pursues a strategy of "decoupling" in core sectors such as AI chips. In turn, China is looking to reduce its external dependencies and supply chain bottlenecks, with a view of becoming the global leader in AI by 2030.

However, China and the USA should not be viewed as engaged in a zero-sum competition. Despite political rhetoric, transnational interests between the two play a more important role than one would expect. It is China that has benefited from international collaboration and access to foreign technology, especially those from the United States, but dependencies are currently increasingly bidirectional and multidirectional (Hannas & Chang, 2019; O'Meara, 2019). At the academic level, cooperative works by Chinese and American scientists in the field of AI constitute an important share of relevant global publications. The tech giants on both sides are deeply integrated in the market of each other and remain dependent on the access to knowledge of "the other side". China became a major, or even the first market, for many American AI-related hardware suppliers, data are shared across borders and technology companies on each side own R&D centres in the other country. Therefore, despite setbacks in several years, overall bilateral AI investments have increased significantly during the past decade. It is actually often forgotten that Chinese BAT are multinational public companies, owned in significant portions by foreign capital, sometimes with significant participations from their USA competitors.

Finally, both China and the USA are placing a strategic bet on AI and will both make use of the results, regardless of the evolution of the other. In this environment, the EU is rightfully pushing for rules and principles that could ensure the safe development of AI. However, in comparison with its global peers, the EU severely lags behind in terms of market scale, domestic technology giants, sufficient funding and a coordinated approach. Although the EU should push even harder to promote its values, without also a strong focus on technology development, it will lack the means to actually protect those values.

The EU must act now to shape its own future AI, based on a strong NIS. With a sense of national urgency, the EU should designate AI development as a top policy priority, including in the military sector; adopt a fully integrated approach by pooling MS resources; grant strong public support to AI R&D spending and VC funding; support the increase AI market scale and output, including through public procurement; allow and actively encourage the emergence of domestic tech champions with global reach; design talent retention and attraction programmes, with generous funding; and support private innovation by allowing more experimentation and public-private integration.

Europe is late, but not too late.

## References

Allison, G., et al. (2021). *The Great Tech Rivalry: China vs the U.S.* https://www.belfercenter.org/publication/great-tech-rivalry-china-vs-us. Accessed 2 July 2022.

Arenal, A., et al. (2020). Innovation ecosystems theory revisited: The case of artificial intelligence in China. *Telecommunications Policy, 44*(6). https://doi.org/10.1016/j.telpol.2020.101960

Baccala, M., et al. (2018). *2018 AI predictions: 8 Insights to shape business strategy*. PwC.

Barton, D., Woetzel, L., Seong, J., & Tian, Q. (2017). *Artificial Intelligence: Implications for China*. McKinsey Global Institute.

Bazavan, A., & Huidumac-Petrescu, C. E. (2023). China's drive for technological leadership in artificial intelligence. Key policies and government-industry integration. *Springer Proceedings in Business and Economics*. https://doi.org/10.1007/978-3-031-19886-1_2

Bughin, J., et al. (2018, September). Notes from the AI Frontier: Modeling the impact of AI on the world economy. *Modeling the global economic impact of AI | McKinsey* [Preprint].

Chui, M., et al. (2018). *Notes from the AI frontier insights from hundreds of use cases*. McKinsey Global Institute.

Craglia, M., et al. (2018). *Artificial Intelligence: A European perspective*. European Union. https://doi.org/10.2760/11251

Development Solutions Europe Ltd. (2018). *China's '1+N' funding strategy for Artificial Intelligence*. http://chinainnovationfunding.eu/china-funding-artificial-intelligence/

Ding, J. (2018, March). *Deciphering China's AI dream: The context, components, capabilities, and consequences of China's strategy to lead the world in AI* (pp. 1–44). Future of Humanity Institute, University of Oxford.

Flew, T., Gillett, R., Cole, R. (2021). Platform governance—Power, diversity and accountability. *Journal of Digital Media & Policy, 12*(2).

Hannas, W. C., & Chang, H.-M. (2019). *China's access to foreign AI technology: An assessment*. Center for Security and Emerging Technology. https://cset.georgetown.edu/wp-content/uploads/CSET_China_Access_To_Foreign_AI_Technology.pdf. Accessed 2 July 2022.

Kelly, K. (2017). The Myth of a Superhuman AI. *Wired* [Preprint].

Lundvall, B. Å., & Rikap, C. (2022). China's catching-up in artificial intelligence seen as a co-evolution of corporate and national innovation systems. *Research Policy, 51*(1), 104395. https://doi.org/10.1016/J.RESPOL.2021.104395

National Security Commission on Artificial Intelligence (NSCAI). (2018). *Immigrant founders of the fortune 500*. http://startupsusa.org/fortune500/. Accessed 2 July 2022.

O'Meara, S. (2019). AI researchers in China want to keep the global-sharing culture alive. *Nature*. https://doi.org/10.1038/d41586-019-01681-x

Renda, A. (2019). *Artificial intelligence: Ethics, governance and policy challenges*. CEPS Task Force.

Tsinghua University—Research Centre for Chinese Technology Policies (清华大学中国科技政策研究中心). (2018, July). *China AI Development Report 2018 (中国人工智能发展报告)*.

Yang, J., & Al-Sayed, R. (2022). Barriers to radical innovation in research institutions in China. *International Journal of Innovation Science*. https://doi.org/10.1108/IJIS-04-2021-0075

Zeng, J. (2021). China's artificial intelligence innovation: A top-down national command approach? *Global Policy, 12*(3), 399–409. https://doi.org/10.1111/1758-5899.12914

Zhang, Y. (2021). The regional disparity of influencing factors of technological innovation in china: Evidence from high-tech industry. *Technological and Economic Development of Economy, 27*(4), 811–832. https://doi.org/10.3846/tede.2021.14828

CHAPTER 9

# Global Consequences of China's Rise in S&T and Recommendations for the European Union

## 1 Changes in the System of International Relations

For decades, international cooperation, the globalisation of science and the multilateral trading system brought unprecedented scientific and economic benefits to the world, making significant contributions towards addressing global health, environment, peace and prosperity challenges. However, China's rapid rise and ambitions in foundational technologies such as AI, quantum computing, semiconductors, 5G networks, green energy, the Internet of Things, information science, new materials or biotechnology have also provoked significant concerns about increased competition. Besides their economic and societal relevance, such technologies also bear deep implications for sensitive sectors such as national security. And these concerns go as far as making some actors question the effectiveness and relevance of the rules-based international order system.

This has reinforced a new type of techno-nationalism, dramatic trade policy changes and unilateral actions that undermine the multilateral system and make it increasingly difficult for international organisations, such as the WTO, to fulfil their role. While the outbreak of COVID-19 intensified this crisis, none of the root causes are actually provoked by the pandemic and will not subside with it. This new context threatens to divide the world again into two or more incompatible mediums of technology and knowledge.



A. Băzăvan, *China's National Innovation System*,
https://doi.org/10.1007/978-981-97-3266-1_9

It is especially digital technology that has transitioned from being an economic and trade topic to one seen as deeply integrated in the national security realm. And now many actors see competition in the field as a zero-sum game. In this reality, the world might experience a feudalisation of the internet, having to choose between Chinese and non-Chinese digital products. This would strongly affect the supply chain networks, academic partnerships and business relationships that underpin the globalised world, adding severe costs to everyone.

Currently, the relationships between USA and Chinese markets and people are (still) deep and contribute tremendously to both sides' technology progress. However, since there is a growing consensus on both sides about the need to 'decouple' and ensure self-dependency, the two countries are heading towards increased competition. Competition might not completely severe ties, but might actually do so on a selective basis, with decoupling in certain industries and continuing partnerships in others.

Going forward, countries will need to strike the right balance between the realities of competition and the need to maintain openness and exchanges, which are critical to the progress of everyone. The ongoing rivalry between China and the United States will increasingly constitute an important factor influencing an ever-widening range of fields. For the EU, if this "sense of technological crisis" is defined only as a dual competition between the USA and China, then there is little debate over which of these two countries to partner closer with. However, there is still hope that the EU can change this debate, becoming a strong technology actor itself.

## 2 Policy Recommendations for the European Union

At the Munich Security Conference on 20 February 2022, *High Representative/Vice-President Josep Borrell* declared that "*to Europeans who love to talk about 'the Brussels effect', I say that we will not be a leader on setting technology standards tomorrow if we are not a leader on developing technology today. And we have to be aware of not losing this leadership*".[1]

[1] European External Action Service (EEAS), Munich Security Conference, 20 February 2022—Opening statement by HR/VP Josep Borell https://www.eeas.europa.eu/node/111167_it.

Accordingly, the EU should, and to a limited extend it already does, act firmly to achieve independent innovation and compete with determination for leadership across technology fields, with a strategic mindset. The EU should also increase R&D investment in key and core industries, and be ready to provide substantive subsidies when needed. Below are a set of 10 key policy recommendations for the EU, in a new international environment context.

### 2.1 Build a Truly Integrated European Approach to Research and Innovation

Diversity is EU's strongest resource, but sometimes it also acts as its nemesis. There is a significant lack of congruence between MS with regard to their frontier scientific projects, funding and legislation. As was shown in **Chapter 5. Funding for Innovation**, EU funding for innovation taken as a whole is already limited and smaller than its global peers such as the US and China. But more harmful is the fact that its ability to bring about results is strongly limited by its fragmentation. While there are several EU funding programmes for R&D, such as Horizon Europe, the largest part of funding is separated at the MS level. MS invest in a multitude of small, overlapping projects that cannot bring breakthrough innovation and EU bodies are limited in their power and capacity to set the agenda and to coordinate research funding in a coherent manner.

In response, EU institutions responsible for setting the agenda of technology and research, such as the Directorate General for Research and Innovation (DG RTD), the European Innovation Council (EIC), the European Institute of Innovation and Technology (EIT), the Joint Research Council (JRC) and the European Research Council (ERC), should be further consolidated and empowered with strong policy leverage as well as with meaningful funding that enables them to carry large-scale projects. They should be able to pool MS funding for R&D in a common vision budget, with EU-wide priorities. Just like in trade and the common agricultural policy, in R&D the EU needs to be a unitary actor that acts with a global voice.

### 2.2 Increase R&D and Innovation Spending Significantly

As mentioned, the EU is currently lagging in terms of GERD. The USA and China surpass EU as a whole, in terms of nominal value, share of

GDP allocated, as well as number of companies in top 2500 largest private spenders. In fact, most developed countries around the world, including the OECD average, allocate a larger share of GDP to R&D than the EU. And the gaps are increasing every year.

The EU should increase global R&D spending at both the European and national levels, with a target of 2.5% of the cumulative European GDP. Increased R&D spending should occur in the public sector, in the private sector with public support, as well as and in public–private ventures. Public European, national and regional funds for R&D, especially in frontier technologies such as artificial intelligence, should be greatly strengthened in numbers and volumes. Moreover, the EU and MS should offer powerful subsidies, tax deductions, grants and other favourable policies to companies that perform R&D. Finally, the EU should provide public money to large venture capital funds that are able to feed into a competitive start-up scene on market principles.

### 2.3 Prioritise Key Strategic Domains

The EU is (still) a leader in traditional domains such as aerospace and automotive (traditional combustion engine only, but not a leader anymore in NEVs). These industries are, of course, important and should be further promoted. However, in strategic core technologies such as semiconductors and AI, the EU has very few frontier research activities and capabilities. Actually, it constantly falls behind the USA and Asian countries. Also, even within some industries, the EU is falling behind global trends, as is the case for the automotive industry, where the EU is completely dependent on China for battery technologies.

While in most technologically advanced nations, the leading role of funding R&D belongs to the private sector, there are those strategic sectors where R&D is too expensive, too risky and not economically reasonable to be carried by market forces. Breakthroughs in certain strategic technologies might not even ever produce profits by themselves. However, they can make important contributions to society and the economy in general as public goods. It is there where public funding must assume a leading, powerful role in terms of strategy and funding. And it is especially the case of the EU, which, as opposed to the USA, China, Japan and Korea, lacks private technology giants which can lead expensive fundamental research.

European business R&D is highly, exceptionally, concentrated in automobiles. According to the 2021 EU Industrial R&D Investment Scoreboard, within the top five largest European spenders on R&D, four come from the automobiles sector (among which one is a Chinese-owned company). In this regard, the EU is very similar to Japan. On the other hand, both China and the USA are concentrating their business R&D spending on high-tech industries, especially in ICT. Moreover, as mentioned before, even in the automobile sector, the EU and Japan are resistant to change and are not leading players in the NEV race, in terms of neither automobiles nor essential components such as batteries.

Therefore, adapting the prioritisation of spending to high-tech, strategic sectors is needed both between industries and within industries. The EU should, on the one hand, diversify away from automobiles investment towards strategic sectors where it is lagging behind, such as semiconductors and AI. While within the automobiles sector, it should make sure that it prioritises NEVs and steps out of previous combustion engine path dependency. It might be painful in the short term, as it might imply reconfigurations of supply chains, a process that will also cause many casualties. Nevertheless, continuing to invest in less strategic domains and falling behind in the most relevant ones will cause more pain in the medium and long term.

### 2.4 Nurture Domestic Tech Champions and Technological Independence

The EU lacks global, all-encompassing digital technology giants, such as Microsoft, Google, Meta, Amazon, Tencent and Alibaba. Actually, among the largest 20 internet companies by market capitalisation, there is no company with its headquarters based in the European Union, with each of the companies being based in either the USA or China. As a consequence, the domestic digital services market is almost entirely monopolised by non-European companies (software, operating systems, e-commerce, navigation, social media, search engines, etc.). This not only severely inhibits domestic innovation, but poses significant risks to EU values and security because the vast majority of data provided by EU citizens, companies and governments are managed by foreign companies. Although the EU start-up ecosystem is increasingly vibrant, most emerging companies tend to move to the United States or to be acquired by non-European actors.

As digital technology companies have become the world's largest companies, surpassing banks, energy and manufacturing enterprises, the decline of corporate Europe is truly striking. If in 2000, 41 of the 100 largest companies in the world by market capitalisation were based in Europe (EU 27 + UK and Switzerland), in 2021, this number reduced to 17 (*The Economist*, 2021). On another measure, in 2000, almost 1/3 of the combined value of the 1,000 largest publicly traded companies in the world was in Europe, as well as 1/4 of their profits. By 2020, both figures have fallen by almost half. Europe has long not been present in the top 10 world's largest companies. In part, this decrease in European and Japanese companies can be explained by the rise of China. However, this is not the case for USA companies which have succeeded in reinventing themselves and maintaining the lead of global business.

This is partly caused by the EU economic policy choice favourable to SMEs and competition, discouraging the growth of strong actors that could entail oligopolistic behaviour. However, it is only big firms that have the financial capacity to take big risks and invest in breakthrough innovation. As the Single Market is not isolated from the world, the lack of European tech giants is replaced by non-EU oligopolists. At the same time, the global market is less efficient, dominated by a few Chinese and US giants, thus suffering from the lack of more companies to compete, which could otherwise come from the EU itself.

Therefore, the EU should not limit access to its digital communication and internet market for foreign companies, as this would be unfair, unsustainable and would severely affect domestic competitiveness. However, in the same way as it has been in the case of agriculture and other industries, the EU should realise the importance of ensuring a sufficient level of domestic autonomy that can be relied on against global vulnerabilities. Therefore, the EU should stimulate a domestic self-reliant digital industry, with powerful domestic giants that are competitive on a truly global scale. While keeping in high regards market rules and commercial fairness, the EU should promote the rise of several domestic private tech giants, competitors to Google, Facebook, Amazon, Baidu, Alibaba, Tencent and Yandex. It is only such corporations that can lead meaningful research, face global competition and create an authentic domestic digital ecosystem.

### 2.5 *Promote the Global Reach of Domestic Companies*

As shown above, European tech companies are being steadily pushed out of global markets by American and Asian competitors. Their limited scale does not allow them to engage in investments and acquisitions of technology and talents from foreign markets. In fact, talents and technology from Europe are increasingly acquired by non-European actors. This adds to the high taxation, labour and compliance costs in Europe.

In line with global competitors, the EU should therefore first provide sufficient subsidies, tax-exemptions and other advantages to high-technology companies to prevent their departure and even attract the relocation of foreign ones into the EU.

Furthermore, the EU and MS should find appropriate policy and funding instruments to actively facilitate and enable technology-orientated investments, mergers and acquisitions abroad.

Finally, the EU should support European tech companies to enter foreign markets by the means of specialised consultancy, diplomacy, grants and facilitated access to credit lines.

### 2.6 *Enhance the Talent Pool*

Many of European top-engineers, programmers and researchers choose to work outside Europe for more competitive salaries and research infrastructure. The higher the complexity and cumulative nature of the industry concerned, the scarcest remaining talent in the EU it is, for example, in the AI and semiconductors industries. Current talent attraction programmes in the EU are fragmented and small-scale, with several examples at the MS level. Several EU joint actions, such as the Marie Skłodowska-Curie Actions carried by the European Research Council, are limited in scale and volume as compared to global competitors such China's national talent attraction programmes.

The EU must be able to train, attract and retain top talent, European on non-European. The EU could launch a dedicated programme to attract top scientists in strategic priority areas, to universities or private companies, by providing subsidies for their payment or initial settlement bonuses in their respective institutions, regardless of whether they are public or private. Moreover, the EU should also do more to stimulate and facilitate joint enterprise-university educational programmes in frontier technologies.

Finally, the EU should also take steps to facilitate talent mobility outside the EU and to attend the best universities and institutes around the world. However, this policy should be complemented with irresistible incentives or compulsory provisions to return home at optimal stages in their career. Such mobile researchers have the additional advantage of strengthening cooperation with foreign institutes. Similarly, connections with foreign scholars who return to their origin country after their research programmes in the EU should be nurtured.

## 2.7 *Encourage Experimentation and Public—Industry Cooperation*

The EU is rightfully a standard leader in terms of consumer rights, privacy and data safety. While the EU is strongly concentrating on data protection, privacy and ethical concerns, without independent, autonomous domestic technology, the values and security of European citizens will be impossible to protect against external threats.

However, in the EU, the regulatory framework grants relatively little space for private companies to experiment with novel ideas. Taking the field of AI as an example, China, USA and Japan are developing strategies to use AI for economic development, scientific leadership and national security, allowing the experimentation with novel systems in limited administrative regions, across limited time spans. They also allow the use of critical infrastructure and data by commercial companies under clear control measures. Such actions are less likely in the EU.

Therefore, the EU should not lower its safety and consumer protection standards, but should put all efforts in promoting technological development, experimentation and public–private cooperation, with highest respects to safety and other public concerns. Technology development is not incompatible with safety and should not be hindered by it. Technology development, however, needs access to data and critical infrastructure. Creative ways should be identified in order to leave more room for experimentation and thus support technology development, rather than inhibiting it. Under well-established rules, EU and national governments should entrust domestic selected tech companies to access public infrastructure and data, which would allow these to grow and further prevent the access to data and public infrastructures of non-EU competitors. Moreover, the EU should allow more pilot projecting with new technologies in limited geographical areas.

### 2.8 *Increase University—Industry Cooperation*

The technological scene is naturally more dynamic than the ability of universities to update their curriculum and enhance their capabilities. Moreover, university research is calibrated to produce a high number of academic articles, rather than commercially viable products. Therefore, tech companies became rather distrustful regarding university training and rely extensively on in-house training for their employees. University and companies cooperate to a limited degree and are actually more frequently in a situation to compete for talent and other resources. However, universities maintain significant resources and infrastructures that private companies lack, as well as first-hand access to talent.

Therefore, the EU should work towards supporting the establishment of more joint academic programmes, research infrastructures and common projects that involve universities and tech companies. The EU should also facilitate the access of private companies to existing academic infrastructure under certain conditions. Finally, the EU should enable academic-private research consortiums to compete in public research tenders.

### 2.9 *Power Military Research and Military-Civil Technology Flows*

In big economies such as China and the United States, the army sector is a fundamental driving force for technological development. The military itself conducts frontier research, or commissions it from the market. Military-developed technologies first ensure defence and secondly spillover into the civil sphere. It was this the case for computers, internet, telecommunication, satellite localisation systems, unmanned vehicles and others crucial technologies for everyday life, which have been first developed by or for the military.

However, European military spending is underfunded, fragmented in 27 states, and little connected to civilian industries. Not only that defence in the EU is underfunded, but also R&D accounts for a very small portion of total military expenditure—1.2% in 2020 according to the European Defence Agency. In comparison, the US Department of Defence invests approximately 2% of the total defence budget of the USA in R&D, accounting for USD 14 billion, which is almost 6 times more than the EU's USD 2.5 billion, and only the Defence Advanced Research Projects

Agency (DARPA) alone with USD 3.5 billion dwarfs the EU's defence R&D budget.

The recent drive towards increasing military expenditure and coordination in spending between EU MS shows encouraging signs. But it still encounters resistance and the starting base is really low, as compared to global peers. Therefore, the EU should raise the level of ambition and achieve fast more military spending and centralisation. A significant proportion of this spending should go to R&D. Procurement in high technologies should always prioritise domestic companies. Moreover, the EU should establish a defence agency dedicated to advanced military research projects, similar to DARPA, which could achieve breakthrough innovations.

### 2.10 Build Innovation Clusters

Innovative clusters constitute geographical 'peaks of excellence' with critical innovation links that attract talent, knowledge, research laboratories and manufacturing capabilities. While the EU is promoting balanced development across its territory and regions, it lacks competitive clusters that could achieve breakthrough innovations.

World investment in high technology such as AI is highly concentrated in geographic hubs primarily in the USA (San Francisco Bay Area, Silicon Valley, Boston and New York), secondly in China (Beijing and Shenzhen) and thirdly, but far away—the UK (London). For example, in the top world cities by number of AI companies, London occupies the third place, Paris the 10th and Berlin the 16th.

Therefore, the EU should collectively support a limited number of certain designated hubs for technological development and funding, regardless of national ambitions that usually promote a just and cohesive spread of resources. At the same time, the EU should establish mechanisms for technological spillover flows to other areas. While London used to be the best established centre focal point for frontier technology, the EU is currently lacking any globally competitive hub. Therefore, the EU should support the creation of 3–4 'Silicon Valleys' with intensive funding.

## 3 Summary

The EU still has many technological advantages, such as its approach to IP, a strong pool of talent and a good educational system, the strategic business channels, operational excellence and branding power. The EU sets, indeed, the golden standards for balancing economic, social and environmental objectives. And the EU needs to make sure it continues to uphold the excellence in these fields. But preserving this performance in a fast-changing environment requires taking bold actions, fast. The EU must react to inevitable transformations and show adaptability, strength, creativity and power.

The EU should also pay increasing attention to understanding China's evolutions, as the country is focused on the speed, agility and scalability of innovation. It has an integrated approach and already larger resources that are creating ecosystems at speed. China is also delivering business-useful and consumer-orientated innovation. While the EU should not replicate China's model which does not fit our values and context, there are important ideas that can still be reflected upon.

The present section does not make a case for a state-led economic model, five-year plans, or for a narrowed disproportionate emphasis on national security over other civic and economic priorities. It is instead arguing for an integrated government-business-led approach to strike a better allocation and prioritisation of resources that account for the technologies of tomorrow.

## Reference

*The Economist.* (2021). Europe is now a corporate also-ran. Can it recover its footing? https://www.economist.com/briefing/2021/06/05/once-a-corporate-heavyweight-europe-is-now-an-also-ran-can-it-recover-its-footing. Accessed 2 July 2022.

CHAPTER 10

# Conclusions

The research attempted to showcase how a developing economy that relies on low-end manufacturing can learn, accumulate resources and transform into an innovative, competitive and knowledge-driven one. China is devoting significant financial, political and human resources to enhance its innovation capabilities. Beyond catching up, the country is aspiring to achieve breakthrough innovation and become a global leader in core technologies.

The tectonic plates are already shifting. China's contributions to world economic growth have become indispensable and China's participation in global supply chains is expected to increase only in the following years. Driven by a strong internal market constituted by a young population of hyper-adopters, speed and agility that enable rapid commercialisation of new business models, combined with supportive policies at national and subnational levels, increased R&D investments, and a strong venture capital scene, China's innovation capacities have grown rapidly and succeeded in catching up with the world's most advanced in a number of fields such as AI, while in others have even achieved leading advantages such as in the case of new energy vehicles and vehicle batteries. Overall, the Chinese tech sector benefiting from strong public support is expanding and aims at stepping overseas and set the world standards.



A. Băzăvan, *China's National Innovation System*,
https://doi.org/10.1007/978-981-97-3266-1_10

However, China still has a long way to go towards developing strong domestic capacities in core technologies such as semiconductors, operating systems, algorithms and aerospace, where significant dependencies on external suppliers remain, and China lacks corporate giants that could compete with their foreign counterparts across sectors. Moreover, the country faces significant challenges in achieving radical and breakthrough innovation, which would require allocating larger investments to fundamental research and thus prioritising innovation quality over quantity. Finally, given several inconsistencies between various pro-innovation initiatives, China would benefit from optimising its innovation governance actions to a more coordinated approach.

Based on both documents analysis and interviews with leading industry players, investors, policymakers and researchers that play a role in China's NIS, this research highlighted the underlying dynamics of innovation in China as shaped by government and public policies, funding for innovation, foreign direct investment and internationalisation, as well as other systemic factors such as talent, intellectual property, patents, public perception towards technology adoption and priority industries. To verify the conclusions, the research chose artificial intelligence as the focus of the study case, due to its high priority on the country's agenda, as well as its wide-reaching geostrategic implications. A holistic approach limited the scope of the analysis to reasonable boundaries. However, the study draws attention to the fact that public policies and economic contexts in China differ greatly between regions, as well as between industrial sectors.

Successive Chinese leaderships have prioritised transforming the country from the world's factory of inputs and low value-added products into a creative and innovative environment that produces or designs high-value items. The Chinese government sees innovation as a crucial component of its growth policy and consequently has gradually developed S&T infrastructures and industrial policies since the late 1980s. China's MLP, launched in 2006, committed to strengthening indigenous innovation capabilities and called on China to "join the ranks" of innovative countries by 2020, to "advance to the forefront of innovative countries" by 2030 and become a 'strong' innovation power by 2050. One key target of the MLP was to increase R&D expenditure to the level of 2.5% of GDP by 2020, which, despite good progress, was slightly missed in 2020, when it reached 2.4%. The Twelfth Five-Year Plan (2011–2015) considered scientific and technological progress to be a principal means towards strategic economic restructuring. Technology development and innovation also feature prominently across sectors in the Thirteenth Five-Year Plan (2016–2020), while the Fourteenth Five-Year Plan (2021–2025) places even higher emphasis on innovation, identifying key performance indicators, establishing deadlines for achievements and presenting the accountability of provincial and local governments for these results. Therefore, increasingly more, core policy documents emphasise the need to develop indigenous technology, with a goal to decrease the country's reliance on foreign suppliers.

Alongside the Fourteenth Five-Year Plan, in 2021, China also released multiple sectorial five-year plans, among which an increased emphasis on national security, data protection, "self-reliance" and "autonomous innovation" are common themes. Such themes have gained increasing ground in policy documents and official policy statements during Xi Jinping's tenure. A common view stemming from policy documents and statements is that while in the previous industrial revolution Beijing lost ground, today, as we are in the midst of a new technology revolution, China has the opportunity to start again and be at its forefront. Therefore, under President Xi Jinping's tenure, an increasingly persistent sense of national superiority, trust and optimism in own capacities, alongside an entitlement to global leadership, can be identified. The nation believes that it has learnt the lessons of Japan and Korea, that it can adapt them to "Chinese characteristics" and achieve even better results, on a larger scale. And this is in the spirit of Chinese pragmatic nationalism, which tends to identify a need to learn from, replicate and eventually exceed external competitors, rather than to antagonise them. This socialisation at the policymaking level is further translated from the top down into individual expectations and then systemic independent actions on a scale, further advancing strategic goals without the government's intervention.

There are a series of priority industries where the government intervenes strongly by setting policy goals for subordinated institutions, providing large financial resources and incentives, setting favourable regulatory environment, as well as by imposing protectionist measures, limiting foreign investments and distorting markets in the interest of political goals. The study demonstrates the magnitude of state-led efforts to advance policy goals in strategic technologies such as artificial intelligence, ICT and semiconductors.

However, at the same time, a new style of laissez-faire governance for innovation is increasingly gaining traction. As mentioned, currently, China has a significant number of varied industrial policies, plans and targets that cover almost all sectors and influence national economy across the board. With such a complex agenda, micromanagement is becoming increasingly unfeasible. Therefore, the centre attempts to delegate as much as possible to market forces as well as to local governments, businesses and industry actors, while the central government keeps focus on the overall picture. In other words, as it increases in policy sophistication, the state aims to facilitate a more efficient system for governing innovation and allocating resources, taking the role of a platform creator, facilitator and strategy-setter rather than a strong actor itself across the spectrum.

Although often overlooked in China's S&T studies by other aspects considered more pressing, the state-directed strategy to establish global technological standards will have a lasting impact on global competitiveness. The research also examines China's state-centric approach to standardisation and explores the country's efforts to have a stronger say in relevant international bodies, while highlighting the implications for the EU.

As China is soon to become the largest R&D spender in the world, the study analysed funding mechanisms as a decisive factor in technological innovation. One of the key findings of this research is the fact that contrary to common belief, research funding in China is primarily market-driven, while government participation through direct funding or fiscal incentives is lower than in most other innovative economies. Recently, the paradigm of public funding for innovation has been shifting, as China's government seeks to stimulate innovation by participating as a VC and PE actor. Therefore, a unique public–private approach is emerging in the form of GGFs. Consequently, instead of disbursing funding for innovation to beneficiaries itself, the Chinese government is increasingly channelling massive amounts of public money on the basis of market mechanisms via private-owned VC funds and PE firms. The aim is to leverage market expertise, reassure venture capital markets by bearing risks, act as a multiplier for more private investment, nurture emerging technology companies and eventually strengthen a broader ecosystem of support for high-tech start-ups.

It is important to note that China's business expenditure for R&D is highly atomised in the industrial sectors and the population of companies. This reflects strong incremental innovation action performed by a large number of actors, but is also conducive to the fact that Chinese innovation champions with the capacity to venture into costly basic research eventually leading to radical scientific breakthroughs are still lacking.

Another fundamental factor of China's NIS is foreign technology acquisition and technology spillovers as a result of inbound and outbound FDI, as well as of internationalisation in its broader sense. The analysis reflected upon the ways in which technology transfers from abroad contributed to higher productivity and revenue growth. It also described how different factors influenced the absorption and diffusion of newly introduced foreign technology.

Learning from MNCs acted as a fundamental driver for domestic innovation in China, with foreign companies serving as both sources of knowledge and of mobilising competition. Chinese firms, while lacking financial resources and technology development skills, accomplished to climb reverse product cycles firstly by imitation, process that played a crucial role in technological upgrade. Following processes of variety creation and selection eventually led domestic firms to become competitive innovators themselves. However, technological spillovers have not always been effective, especially as a result of the weak absorptive capacity of Chinese companies of new technologies. Moreover, as previously mentioned, the spillover effect of foreign technologies has not helped alleviate, or potentially has even worsened, regional differences in China, given the fact that technology-intensive inbound FDI has mostly concentrated in the east of the country.

On the other hand, China's policies towards inbound FDI have raised many questions to foreign partners. Forced technology transfers and JV requirements are some of the most pressing complaints in ongoing trade disputes. Such policies complement the four-decades-old 'two markets, two resources' theory, which was complemented in 2020 by the 'dual circulation' economic policy, proposing an asymmetric integration into the global economy, in an attempt to maximise the benefits of globalisation by minimising risks.

Following, the study also explores the positive effects of technology-oriented OFDI on Chinese domestic firms' innovation ability. China's OFDI usually takes the form of M&As, especially in developed economies and sectors with potential for technology acquisition. Chinese OFDI started to rise since the launch of the "Go Global" strategy in 2005, which encouraged Chinese companies, for the first time, to invest abroad. Following, Chinese outflows have increased rapidly, but since 2017, they have suffered several setbacks, due to increased regulatory scrutiny in destination markets against Chinese-led investments, which led to an important number of acquisition deals being cancelled, also adding to stricter regulations and capital controls in China, and finally the emergence of COVID-19. However, even in this unpredictable environment, in 2020 Chinese OFDI flows exceeded those of the USA, leading China to become the world's largest source of investment.

Beyond the sheer numbers of transactions and the volumes of outbound investment, the capacity to actually integrate overseas M&As plays a determinant factor in achieving added-value innovation in the home country. Chinese companies are still limited in their ability to effectively integrate technologies and business models after performing overseas M&A. Integration capacity is especially lower among SOEs and companies that receive government subsidies. Therefore, Chinese enterprises are more likely to succeed in maximising technology spillovers if they choose to invest in sectors with which they have a high degree of complementarity.

In addition to funding and supportive policies, innovation requires human capital. China has made significant investments in its higher education system to close the gap with leading institutions worldwide, and this effort has been relatively successful. Peking University, Tsinghua University and Fudan University are achieving high rankings globally in STEM, exceeding any EU-based university. Consequently, the higher education system has expanded rapidly in terms of both quantity and quality, and based on current trends, it is anticipated that the number of STEM Ph.D. graduates in China will double that of the United States by 2025.

Moreover, giving the demographic situation and the economy's increasing needs, the government has come to realise that foreign non-ethnic Chinese talents, as well as overseas Chinese, are significant resources in addition to domestic talent. Therefore, attracting talented individuals from overseas has become an integral part of China's innovation policy. The central and subnational governments have established, with partial success, multiple programmes aimed at enticing foreign talents, including ethnic Chinese returning from abroad and non-Chinese foreigners who have studied or worked at leading global institutions and have acquired extensive skills and networks.

AI is seen as a top-priority industry, benefiting from ample funding and generous capital markets, a large consumer base with a hunger for technology and vast amounts of data, strong government support from both central and local authorities, and a generally positive public perception. High-impact AI-powered applications are already widely used in various industries, such as finance, insurance, transportation, retail, security and state surveillance, significantly affecting the daily lives of Chinese citizens.

However, China's AI industry still faces significant gaps. Research capabilities are limited and tend towards commercialisation rather than fundamental theory, and embedding AI into traditional industries is challenging. China also relies heavily on external suppliers for core technologies such as AI chips, and its tech giants lack global reach, with the exception of ByteDance. Moreover, recently, the government's crackdown on big tech's expansion hindered the industry development in the short term. Nonetheless, on most metrics, China's AI industry is competing the USA, while Europe is notably absent.

Overall, the experience of China in innovation across the board offers a very interesting case study for emerging countries that aim to climb value chains and transition towards high-quality growth. Although many lessons can be drawn from China's story, policymakers should bear in mind that its model might not and should not be replicated in a different context, given China's economic scale, political establishment, cultural background, market scale and consumers' behaviour. Nevertheless, there is no overarching China recipe. Its policies, achievements and failures, should be only analysed on an industry-to-industry and region-to-region basis.

Finally, the research raises significant concerns about the EU's decreasing competitiveness relative to China and to other global actors in foundational technologies such as AI, quantum computing, semiconductors, 5G networks, green energy, the Internet of Things, information science, new materials and biotechnology. These losses are significant not only in economic and societal terms but also have far-reaching implications for Europe's capacity to preserve its values and security. In this context, the paper advances 10 policy recommendations for the EU which include but are not limited to allocating increasing resources for research while targeting certain strategic industries that exceed the capacity and interest of the private sector, designing innovation-friendly policies and allowing more room for experimentation, promoting technological European autonomy and the emergence of European major technology companies that can dominate global markets, actively stimulating the acquisition of foreign technology as a government objective, improving the capacity to retain existing talent and attract foreign talent, etc. While ultimately innovation is driven by the market, the EU and MS should intensify their efforts to be effective facilitators, platform creators and strategic planners of the innovation system, which includes also allocating significant support resources. The recommendations for the EU put forward at the end of this research are the following Click or tap here to enter text.:

1. Build a truly integrated European approach to research and innovation;
2. Increase significantly R&D spending;
3. Prioritise key strategic domains;
4. Nurture domestic tech champions and technological independence;
5. Promote the global reach of domestic companies;
6. Enhance the talent pool;
7. Encourage experimentation and public-industry cooperation;
8. Increase university-industry cooperation;
9. Power military research and military-civic technology flows;
10. Build innovation clusters.

# Annex I: National Talent Programmes in China

National and regional initiatives for attracting overseas talents aim to recruit the most eminent global researchers, particularly those who have studied or worked at the most prestigious universities overseas and who can demonstrate outstanding research achievements. They have generally focused on highly skilled Chinese nationals living abroad, or foreign citizens with Chinese origins, rather than foreign citizens without Chinese origin. That is possibly because persons of Chinese origin integrate more easily. In addition, historically, China has been an origin for migrants, rather than a destination. Therefore, it might be said that the country lacks the institutional and cultural experience in accommodating non-Chinese citizens, let alone policies for settlement and citizenship. To make sure, most of the programmes are officially equally open to both Chinese returnees and foreigners.

In general, the talent programmes are very supportive to both research and researchers, as they provide a high-level recognition of excellence and generous funding schemes. Awardees receive highly lucrative subsidies, covering research work, living expenses, as well as other forms of assistance. One is allowed and even encouraged to win multiple funding schemes simultaneously, for example, by being awarded both a national and a municipal grant.



A. Băzăvan, *China's National Innovation System*,
https://doi.org/10.1007/978-981-97-3266-1

However, China's talent programmes have a mixed track record. So far the overall number of foreign researchers coming to China is not satisfactory. Nevertheless, retention (if China really aims for that) is relatively low.

This annex briefly reviews the national governmental programmes that target foreign researchers. These are replicated by numerous regional, provincial, city and district level talent attraction programmes that are beyond the scope to mention. Current annex considers foreign researchers to be those non-Chinese citizens who are PhD students, post-doctoral fellows or holders of higher academic titles. They should come to China to work in universities, research institutes or enterprises, being employed specifically for research activities. It is important to note that most talent programmes are mixed, targeting both Chinese and non-Chinese citizens, as well as both researchers and other categories of overseas talents. The following list purposely omits those programmes or branches of the programmes that target entrepreneurs, experts in particular industries and sportsmen, as well as overseas Chinese researchers, unless they specifically target foreign researchers. Therefore, China's talent programmes are more numerous and diverse than the ones mentioned below.

## Thousand Talents Programme ("The Recruitment Programme of Global Experts")

Launched in 2008 with substantial financial backing, the programme has enticed talented scholars to work in China. Relying upon National Key Innovation Projects, National Key Disciplines and National Key Laboratories, various industrial parks (mainly the high-tech development zones), central SOEs and state-owned commercial and financial institutions, the plan calls for scientists and leading talents who can make breakthroughs in key technologies or can enhance China's high-tech industries and emerging disciplines. Unfortunately, there is no official data publicly available on the actual number of foreign talents attracted to date.

The programme's structure has evolved in time but currently there are six subprojects, out of which 5 are targeted towards researchers:

## 1. The Recruitment Programme for Innovative Talents (Long Term)

Targets people under 55 years of age who are willing to work in China on a full-time basis, with full professorships or the equivalent in prestigious foreign universities and R&D institutes, or with senior titles from well-known international companies or financial institutions.[1]

The programme awards a one-off, start-up package of CNY 1 million and further salary based on their previous jobs overseas through negotiation with due living allowances. Spouses receive employment and children are guaranteed admission to schools.

## 2. The Recruitment Programme for Young Professionals (Long Term)

Applicants engaged in scientific researches and below the age of 40, holders of a PhD degree granted by prestigious overseas universities, with formal teaching and researching positions in overseas prestigious universities, institutions or enterprises, able to work full time in China. Outstanding PhD students can also be recruited in exceptional cases.

Awardees will receive a lump sum of CNY 500,000 and research subsidies, varying from RMB 1 million to 3 million, in batches throughout the programme.

## 3. The Innovative Talents Recruitment Programme (Short Term)

The programme calls for researchers that maintain their overseas position but are available to work in China at least 2 months per year for at least 3 consecutive years. They receive a CNY 500,000 allowance. After the completion, researchers might be enrolled in "The Recruitment Programme for Innovative Talents (Long Term)" and be awarded "The National Distinguished Expert".

[1] Ibid.

### 4. The Recruitment Programme for Foreign Experts (Long Term)

Requires talents to work in China for more than 9 months per year during 3 consecutive years. A lump sum of CNY 1 million research subsidies shall be granted to each talent enrolled. A total amount of CNY 3-5 million research subsidies shall be granted to those engaged in basic science research.

### 5. The Recruitment Programme for Top-notch Talents and Teams

Awarded on a case-by-case basis to winners of important international awards, such as the Nobel Prize, the A.M. Turing Award, the Fields Medal, etc., members of academies of sciences or engineering in developed countries, famous scholars from world top universities or R&D institutes and other urgently needed top talents.

## Natural Science Foundation of China

### 1. International Young Scientists Fellowship

The Fund supports foreign young researchers to work for 6 or 12 months in a Chinese university or research institute, recommended by the Chinese host organisation. Candidates should be holders of a PhD, have more than 3 years of basic research or post-doctoral experience and be aged under 35.

This funding covers research expenses only. The host organisation is responsible for covering living costs, insurance, research facilities, etc. and provide CNY 100,000 for 6 months or CNY 200,000 for 1 year.

After completion, grantees are eligible for renewing the fund once. The drawback of this programme is that it has a maximum duration of two years, which means that successful applicants would still not be eligible to apply for another higher-level NSFC grant afterwards (e.g. an international cooperation grant), as these require successful completion of a three-year project.

# Chinese Academy of Science (CAS)

## 1. President's International Fellowship Initiative (PIFI)

The fellowship is awarded to highly qualified international scientists and postgraduate students to work and study in cooperative projects at CAS-affiliated institutions for 1–12 months. The PIFI programme is available to four categories of international researchers: distinguished scientists, visiting scientists, postdoctoral researchers and international PhD students.

It provides a monthly stipend for living expenses, health insurance in China and economy-class round-trip international travel. Full professor or holders of equivalent titles will receive monthly stipends of CNY 40,000, associate professors or equivalent title—CNY 30,000 per month and assistant professors or equivalent title—CNY 20,000, respectively.

The CAS-TWAS President's Fellowship for International PhD students supports 200 international graduates each year, to pursue their PhD degrees at the University of the Chinese Academy of Sciences (UCAS), the University of Science and Technology of China (UST) or CAS institutes around China. In addition to tuition waivers, this programme provides travel support and visa application fees for selected awardee, as well as a monthly allowance to each awardee.

# Chinese Government Scholarships

## 1. Doctoral Scholarships

Currently, usual scholarship packages for international PhD students include tuition fees, accommodation and a monthly stipend of 3500 RMB for social and humanistic sciences and 4000 for natural sciences.

## 2. Postdoctoral Scholarship

Postdoctoral salaries in different institutions range between 10,000 and 20,000 RMB per month, with the addition of annual bonuses. Accommodation and medical insurance (or an accommodation allowance) is also usually included in the employment package.

## The "High-End Foreign Experts Recruitment Plan"

Launched in 2019 by MOST, the plan merges other similar programmes previously managed by the State Administration of Foreign Experts Affairs (SAFEA), which has ceased to exist following its integration within MOST in March 2018.[2] It aims to attract talents in the fields of strategic technology development; industrial technology innovation; social and ecological construction; agriculture and rural revitalisation.

The recruitment of high-end takes into account the following principles:

1. Serve national major strategic needs;
2. Focus on leading, qualified and urgently needed talents;
3. Persistence on project result performance.

## Innovation Talents Promotion Programme

Aims to attract world-class scientists, top-notch technology and engineering leaders, outstanding innovative teams and entrepreneurs, as well as to establishing demonstration bases for the cultivation of new talents.[3] It targets winners of the "Ten Thousand Talents Plan"—category of "exceptional talent"; young and middle-aged scientists working in institutes of higher education, research structures or enterprises; STI entrepreneurs; and innovative teams in key areas.

### 1. **Innovative Teams in Key Fields**

The Innovative Teams in Key Fields category is designed to provide stable and continuous support to teams implementing national-level major research programmes, and key engineering and construction projects.[4]

[2] Development Solutions Europe Ltd. *National High-end Foreign Experts Recruitment Plan (2019 annual call)*. via http://chinainnovationfunding.eu/project/2019-high-end-foreign-experts-recruitment-plan/.

[3] Development Solutions Europe Ltd. Advance EU Access to Financial Incentives for Innovation in China. Seventh Ad hoc study. Analysis of the Bases and Talents Programme. Via http://chinainnovationfunding.eu/wp-content/uploads/2018/10/Analysis-of-the-Bases-and-Talents-Programme-1.pdf.

[4] Ibid.

# References

Ai, Q., & Tan, H. (2020). Uncovering neglected success factors in post-acquisition reverse capability transfer: Evidence from Chinese multinational corporations in Europe. *Journal of World Business, 55*(3). https://doi.org/10.1016/j.jwb.2019.101053

Alarcón, S., & Sánchez, M. (2013). External and internal R&D, capital investment and business performance in the Spanish agri-food industry. *Journal of Agricultural Economics, 64*(3), 654–675. https://doi.org/10.1111/1477-9552.12015

Alberts, B., & Narayanamurti, V. (2019). Two threats to U.S. Science. *Science*. https://doi.org/10.1126/science.aax9846

Alfaro, L. (2017). Gains from foreign direct investment: Macro and micro approaches. *World Bank Economic Review, 30*. https://doi.org/10.1093/wber/lhw007

Alisson, G., & Schmidt, E. (2021, December 7). China will soon lead the U.S. in tech. *Wall Street Journal*. https://www.wsj.com/articles/china-will-soon-lead-the-us-in-tech-global-leader-semiconductors-5g-wireless-green-energy-11638915759. Accessed 2 July 2022.

Allison, G., et al. (2021). *The Great Tech Rivalry: China vs the U.S.* https://www.belfercenter.org/publication/great-tech-rivalry-china-vs-us. Accessed 2 July 2022.

Amankwah-Amoah, J., & Hinson, R. E. (2019). Contextual influences on new technology ventures: A study of domestic firms in Ghana. *Technological Forecasting and Social Change, 143*, 289–296. https://doi.org/10.1016/j.techfore.2019.01.019



A. Băzăvan, *China's National Innovation System*,
https://doi.org/10.1007/978-981-97-3266-1

Amankwah-Amoah, J., Osabutey, E. L. C., & Egbetokun, A. (2018). Contemporary challenges and opportunities of doing business in Africa: The emerging roles and effects of technologies. *Technological Forecasting and Social Change, 131*, 171–174. https://doi.org/10.1016/j.techfore.2018.01.003

Andergassen, R., Nardini, F., & Ricottilli, M. (2018). Innovation, specialization and growth in a model of structural change. *B.E. Journal of Macroeconomics, 18*(2). https://doi.org/10.1515/bejm-2017-0095

Anzola-Román, P., Bayona-Sáez, C., & García-Marco, T. (2018). Organizational innovation, internal R&D and externally sourced innovation practices: Effects on technological innovation outcomes. *Journal of Business Research, 91*, 233–247. https://doi.org/10.1016/J.JBUSRES.2018.06.014

Arenal, A., et al. (2020). Innovation ecosystems theory revisited: The case of artificial intelligence in China. *Telecommunications Policy, 44*(6). https://doi.org/10.1016/j.telpol.2020.101960

Arrow, K. J. (1962). *Economic welfare and the allocation of resources for invention. The rate and direction of inventive activity: Economic and social factors*. Princeton University Press [Preprint]. https://www.nber.org/chapters/c2144.pdf

Atkinson, R. D. (2017). *Testimony of Robert D. Atkinson, President, Information Technology and Innovation Foundation, Before the U.S.-China Economic and Security Review Commission. Hearing on Chinese Investment in the United States: Impacts and issues for policymakers*. Information Technology & Innovation Foundation. https://www.uscc.gov/sites/default/files/Atkinson_USCC%20Hearing%20Testimony012617.pdf

Autor, D. H., Dorn, D., & Hanson, G. H. (2013). The China syndrome: Local labor market effects of import competition in the United States. *American Economic Review, 103*(6). https://doi.org/10.1257/aer.103.6.2121

Baccala, M., et al. (2018). *2018 AI predictions: 8 Insights to shape business strategy*. PwC.

Bai, X., Wang, Y., & Su, X. (2019). R&D subsidies or tax incentives: An empirical analysis of government intervention on enterprise innovation performance and innovation quality. *Science Research Management, 40*(6), 9–18.

Baker McKenzie and Rhodium Group. (2022). *Trends and spotlights of the Chinese investment landscape*. https://www.bakermckenzie.com/-/media/files/insight/publications/2022/02/fdi-china-report-2022-english.pdf?sc_lang=en&hash=054A2FD520CD9CB19224E661D8A777E8. Accessed 1 July 2022.

Barton, D., Woetzel, L., Seong, J., & Tian, Q. (2017). *Artificial Intelligence: Implications for China*. McKinsey Global Institute.

Bazavan, A. (2019a, September). Chinese government's shifting role in the national innovation system. *Technological Forecasting and Social Change, 148*. https://doi.org/10.1016/j.techfore.2019.119738

Bazavan, A. (2019b). How does China innovate? A deconstruction of China's national innovation system. *Hyperion International Journal of Econophysics & New Economy, 12*(1), 99–107.

Bazavan, A. (2020). China's transition to a knowledge economy—Institutional mechanisms, public policies and private investment. In C. R. Pamfilie, V. Dinu, L. Tăchiciu, D. Pleşea, & C. Vasiliu (Eds.), *6th BASIQ international conference on new trends in sustainable business and consumption*. ASE Bucharest.

Bazavan, A., & Huidumac-Petrescu, C. E. (2023). China's drive for technological leadership in artificial intelligence. Key policies and government-industry integration. *Springer Proceedings in Business and Economics*. https://doi.org/10.1007/978-3-031-19886-1_2

Berger, B., & Russel, D. (2021, December 2). *Is China stacking the technology deck by setting international standards?* https://thediplomat.com/2021/12/is-china-stacking-the-technology-deck-by-setting-international-standards/. Accessed 2 July 2022.

Berman, S. J., & Hagan, J. (2006). How technology-driven business strategy can spur innovation and growth. *Strategy and Leadership, 34*(2). https://doi.org/10.1108/10878570610700848

Bertrand, O., & Capron, L. (2015). Productivity enhancement at home via cross-border acquisitions: The roles of learning and contemporaneous domestic investments. *Strategic Management Journal, 36*(5). https://doi.org/10.1002/smj.2256

Bessant, J., Öberg, C., & Trifilova, A. (2014). Framing problems in radical innovation. *Industrial Marketing Management, 43*(8), 1284–1292. https://doi.org/10.1016/J.INDMARMAN.2014.09.003

Bloomberg. (2021a, February 2). *China stockpiles chips, chip-making machines to resist U.S.* https://www.bloomberg.com/news/articles/2021-02-02/china-stockpiles-chips-and-chip-making-machines-to-resist-u-s. Accessed 2 July 2022.

Bloomberg. (2021b, February 5). *One thing China and the U.S. can agree on*. Bloomberg. https://www.bloomberg.com/news/newsletters/2021-02-05/top-china-stories-this-week-ant-overhaul-semiconductor-self-sufficiency. Accessed 2 July 2022.

Boeing, P. (2016). The allocation and effectiveness of China's R&D subsidies—Evidence from listed firms. *Research Policy* [Preprint]. https://doi.org/10.1016/j.respol.2016.05.007

Bogers, M., Foss, N. J., & Lyngsie, J. (2018). The "human side" of open innovation: The role of employee diversity in firm-level openness. *Research Policy, 47*(1). https://doi.org/10.1016/j.respol.2017.10.012

Breslin, S. (2011). China and the crisis: Global power, domestic caution and local initiative. *Contemporary Politics* [Preprint]. https://doi.org/10.1080/13569775.2011.565987

Buckley, P. J., et al. (2018). A retrospective and agenda for future research on Chinese outward foreign direct investment. *Journal of International Business Studies, 49*(1). https://doi.org/10.1057/s41267-017-0129-1

Bughin, J., et al. (2018, September). Notes from the AI Frontier: Modeling the impact of AI on the world economy. *Modeling the global economic impact of AI | McKinsey* [Preprint].

Carraro, C., & Galeotti, M. (1997). Economic growth, international competitiveness and environmental protection: R & D and innovation strategies with the WARM model. *Energy Economics, 19*(1). https://doi.org/10.1016/s0140-9883(96)01005-5

Chandy, R. K., & Tellis, G. J. (2000). The incumbent's curse? Incumbency, size, and radical product innovation. *Journal of Marketing, 64*(3). https://doi.org/10.1509/jmkg.64.3.1.18033

Chen, J., et al. (2018). The distinct signaling effects of R&D subsidy and non-R&D subsidy on IPO performance of IT entrepreneurial firms in China. *Research Policy, 47*(1), 108–120. https://doi.org/10.1016/j.respol.2017.10.004

Chesbrough, H., & Crowther, A. K. (2006). Beyond high tech: Early adopters of open innovation in other industries. *R and D Management, 36*(3). https://doi.org/10.1111/j.1467-9310.2006.00428.x

Chesbrough, H. W. (2003). The era of open innovation. *MIT Sloan Management Review, 44*(3), 35–41.

*China Daily*. (2022). Postgraduate exam more competitive. https://www.chinadaily.com.cn/a/202203/30/WS62439074a310fd2b29e54042.html. Accessed 2 July 2022.

China Policy. (2018). *April: Circuit breaker. Roundup from our portfolios.* https://mailchi.mp/policycn/observer-2746697?e=95d012ca4e

Choi, C., & Yi, M. H. (2017). The Internet, R&D expenditure and economic growth. *Applied Economics Letters, 25*(4), 264–267. https://doi.org/10.1080/13504851.2017.1316819

Christensen, C. M. (2011). *The Innovator's Dilemma*. Vahlen. https://doi.org/10.15358/9783800642816

Chu, C. C., et al. (2021). Uncertainty, venture capital and entrepreneurial enterprise innovation—Evidence from companies listed on China's GEM. *Pacific Basin Finance Journal, 68*(September 2020), 101576. https://doi.org/10.1016/j.pacfin.2021.101576

Chui, M., et al. (2018). *Notes from the AI frontier insights from hundreds of use cases*. McKinsey Global Institute.

Craglia, M., et al. (2018). *Artificial Intelligence: A European perspective*. European Union. https://doi.org/10.2760/11251

Crawford, A. (2020). *The U.S.-China conflict over chips is about to get uglier*. Bloomberg. https://news.bloomberglaw.com/tech-and-telecom-law/the-u-s-china-conflict-over-chips-is-about-to-get-uglier. Accessed 2 July 2022.

Dai, C., & Liu, Y. (2008). Comparative analysis of the impact of tax incentives and financial subsidies on corporate R&D. *Economic Science, 3*, 58–71.

Dazheng, W. (2009). Encourage the introduction of technology or encourage self-innovation. *Science & Technology Progress and Policy* [Preprint].

Degbey, W., & Pelto, E. (2013). Cross-border M&A as a trigger for network change in the Russian bakery industry. *Journal of Business and Industrial Marketing, 28*(3). https://doi.org/10.1108/08858621311302831

Deloitte. (2018). 中国人工智能产业白皮书 [White Paper on China's AI Industry].

Development Solutions Europe Ltd. (2016). *Comparison of the 12th five-year plan for S&T development, and the 13th five-year plan for S&T innovation*.

Development Solutions Europe Ltd. (2017a). *Fifth ad hoc study—Analysis of national high- and new-technology zones*.

Development Solutions Europe Ltd. (2017b). *Technology innovation guiding fund in China*. http://chinainnovationfunding.eu/technology-innovation-guiding-fund/. Accessed 4 December 2018.

Development Solutions Europe Ltd. (2018a). *China's '1+N' funding strategy for Artificial Intelligence*. http://chinainnovationfunding.eu/china-funding-artificial-intelligence/

Development Solutions Europe Ltd. (2018b). *China's funding for innovative start-ups: Three key systemic approaches* (pp. 1–12).

Ding, J. (2018, March). *Deciphering China's AI dream: The context, components, capabilities, and consequences of China's strategy to lead the world in AI* (pp. 1–44). Future of Humanity Institute, University of Oxford.

Dominguez Lacasa, I., et al. (2019). Paths of technology upgrading in the BRICS economies. *Research Policy, 48*(1). https://doi.org/10.1016/j.respol.2018.08.016

Dong, Z., Miao, Z., & Zhang, Y. (2021). The impact of China's outward foreign direct investment on domestic innovation. *Journal of Asian Economics, 75*, 101307. https://doi.org/10.1016/j.asieco.2021.101307

Dosi, G. (1997). Opportunities, incentives and collective patterns of technological change. *Economic Journal* [Preprint]. https://doi.org/10.1111/1468-0297.00239

Eichengreen, B., Park, D., & Shin, K. (2011). When fast growing economies slow down. *NBER Working Paper Series* [Preprint].

Elman, B. A. (2006). *A cultural history of modern science in China*. Harvard University Press. https://doi.org/10.4159/9780674036482

European Commission. (2017). *Survey on researchers outside of Europe—Annex to MORE3 study: Support data collection and analysis concerning mobility patterns and career paths of researchers*. Brussels. https://cdn5.euraxess.org/sites/default/files/policy_library/survey_on_researchers_outside_of_europe_0.pdf. Accessed 1 July 2022.

European Union Chamber of Commerce in China. (2021). *European Business in China Position Paper 2021/2022*. https://europeanchamber.oss-cn-beijing.aliyuncs.com/upload/documents/documents/European_Business_in_China_Position_Paper_2021_2022[964].pdf. Accessed 2 July 2022.

Fagerberg, J., & Sapprasert, K. (2011). National innovation systems: the emergence of a new approach. *Science and Public Policy, 38*(9), 669–679. https://doi.org/10.3152/030234211X13070021633369

Fagerberg, J., & Srholec, M. (2008). National innovation systems, capabilities and economic development. *Research Policy* [Preprint]. https://doi.org/10.1016/j.respol.2008.06.003

Feng, K. (2016). Chinese indigenous innovation in the car sector. In Y. Zhou et al. (Eds.), *China as an innovation nation* (pp. 133–164). https://doi.org/10.1093/acprof:oso/9780198753568.003.0005

Feng, W., & Li, J. (2021). International technology spillovers and innovation quality: Evidence from China. *Economic Analysis and Policy, 72*, 289–308. https://doi.org/10.1016/j.eap.2021.09.003

Filippetti, A., & Archibugi, D. (2011). Innovation in times of crisis: National systems of innovation, structure, and demand. *Research Policy, 40*(2), 179–192. https://doi.org/10.1016/J.RESPOL.2010.09.001

Flew, T., Gillett, R., Cole, R. (2021). Platform governance—Power, diversity and accountability. *Journal of Digital Media & Policy, 12*(2).

Freeman, C. (1987). *Technology and economic performance: Lessons from Japan*. Pinter Publishers.

Freeman, C., & Louçã, F. (2003). The emergence of a new techno-economic paradigm: The age of Information and Communication Technology (ICT). In *As time goes by: From the industrial revolutions to the information revolution* (pp. 301–335). Oxford University Press. https://doi.org/10.1093/0199251053.003.0009

Freeman, C., & Soete, L. (2012). *The economics of industrial innovation* (pp. 1–470). Routledge. https://doi.org/10.4324/9780203357637

Gârleanu, N., Panageas, S., & Yu, J. (2012). Technological growth and asset pricing. *Journal of Finance, 67*(4), 1265–1292. https://doi.org/10.1111/j.1540-6261.2012.01747.x

Geldes, C., et al. (2017). Proximity as determinant of business cooperation for technological and non-technological innovations: A study of an agribusiness cluster. *Journal of Business and Industrial Marketing, 32*(1), 167–178. https://doi.org/10.1108/JBIM-01-2016-0003

Gill, I., & Kharas, H. (2007). *An East Asian renaissance ideas for economic growth*. World Bank.

Godoi, F. C., Prakash, S., & Bhandari, B. R. (2015, February). Final report: National Security Commission on Artificial Intelligence. *Public*, 12–15.

Gong, C. (2021). Government R&D investment, knowledge accumulation, and regional innovation capability: Evidence of a threshold effect model from China. *Complexity*. https://doi.org/10.1155/2021/8963237

Grassano, N., Hernandez Guevara, H., Fako, P., Tübke, A., Amoroso, S., Georgakaki, A., Napolitano, L., Pasimeni, F., Rentocchini, F., Compaño, R., Fatica, S., & Panzica, R. (2021). *The 2021 EU industrial R&D investment scoreboard—Publications Office of the EU*. Luxembourg. https://doi.org/10.2760/559391

Grimes, S., & Sun, Y. (2016). China's evolving role in Apple's global value chain. *Area Development and Policy, 1*(1). https://doi.org/10.1080/23792949.2016.1149434

Grossman, G. M., & Helpman, E. (1994). Endogenous innovation in the theory of growth. *Journal of Economic Perspectives, 8*, 23–44.

Guan, J. C., & Yam, R. C. M. (2015). Effects of government financial incentives on firms' innovation performance in China: Evidences from Beijing in the 1990s. *Research Policy* [Preprint]. https://doi.org/10.1016/j.respol.2014.09.001

Guo, D., Guo, Y., & Jiang, K. (2016). Government-subsidized R&D and firm innovation: Evidence from China. *Research Policy, 45*(6), 1129–1144. https://doi.org/10.1016/j.respol.2016.03.002

Hage, J., & Rogers Hollingsworth, J. (2000). A strategy for the analysis of idea innovation networks and institutions. *Organization Studies* [Preprint]. https://doi.org/10.1177/0170840600215006

Hall, B. H. (2002). The financing of research and development. *Oxford Review of Economic Policy, 18*(1). https://doi.org/10.1093/oxrep/18.1.35

Hall, L. A., & Bagchi-Sen, S. (2002). A study of R&D, innovation, and business performance in the Canadian biotechnology industry. *Technovation, 22*(4). https://doi.org/10.1016/S0166-4972(01)00016-5

Hannas, W. C., & Chang, H.-M. (2019). *China's access to foreign AI technology: An assessment*. Center for Security and Emerging Technology. https://cset.georgetown.edu/wp-content/uploads/CSET_China_Access_To_Foreign_AI_Technology.pdf. Accessed 2 July 2022.

He, S., & Han, W. (2021). *China's big data industry to top $470 billion by 2025*. Caixin Global. https://www.caixinglobal.com/2021-12-01/chinas-big-data-industry-to-top-470-billion-by-2025-101812002.html. Accessed 2 July 2022.

Heilmann, S. (2008). Policy experimentation in China's economic rise. *Studies in Comparative International Development, 43*(1), 1–26. https://doi.org/10.1007/S12116-007-9014-4/FIGURES/2

Heilmann, S. (2018). *Red Swan: How unorthodox policy making facilitated China's rise*. The Chinese University of Hong Kong Press.

Hitt, M. A., Hoskisson, R. E., & Ireland, R. D. (2019). *Strategic management: Competitiveness & globalization: Concepts and cases 12e*. Cengage Learning Asia.

Holmes, T. J., McGrattan, E. R., & Prescott, E. C. (2013). Quid pro quo: Technology capital transfers for market access in China. *Review of Economic Studies, 82*(3). https://doi.org/10.1093/restud/rdv008

Homme, D. P., & Von Zedtwitz, M. (2018). The changing face of innovation in China—Foreign companies must Retool their R&D strategies to keep pace with newly innovative Chinese Entreprises. *MIT Sloan Management Review, 59*(4), 24–32.

Hong, J., et al. (2016). Do government grants promote innovation efficiency in China's high-tech industries? *Technovation, 57–58*(4), 4–13. https://doi.org/10.1016/J.TECHNOVATION.2016.06.001

Hout, T. M., & Ghemawat, P. (2010). China vs the world: Whose technology is it? *Harvard Business Review* [Preprint].

Howell, A. (2017). Picking "winners" in China: Do subsidies matter for indigenous innovation and firm productivity? *China Economic Review, 44*, 154–165. https://doi.org/10.1016/j.chieco.2017.04.005

Hu, A. G. (2001). Ownership, government R&D, private R&D, and productivity in Chinese industry. *Journal of Comparative Economics, 29*(1). https://doi.org/10.1006/jcec.2000.1704

Hu, A. G. Z., Zhang, P., & Zhao, L. (2017). China as number one? Evidence from China's most recent patenting surge. *Journal of Development Economics, 124*, 107–119. https://doi.org/10.1016/j.jdeveco.2016.09.004

Huang, Q., Jiang, M. S., & Miao, J. (2016). Effect of government subsidization on Chinese industrial firms' technological innovation efficiency: A stochastic frontier analysis. *Journal of Business Economics and Management, 17*(2), 187–200. https://doi.org/10.3846/16111699.2015.1061590

IC Insights. (2021). *China forecast to fall far short of its "Made in China 2025" goals for ICs*. https://www.icinsights.com/news/bulletins/China-Forecast-To-Fall-Far-Short-Of-Its-Made-In-China-2025-Goals-For-ICs/. Accessed 2 July 2022.

International Labour Organisation (ILO). (2017). *Attracting skilled international migrants to China: A review and comparison of policies and practices*. https://publications.iom.int/system/files/pdf/attracting_skilled_en_0.pdf

Joia, R. M., & Huidumac, E. (2011). China's geostrategic position—FDI flows and stock analysis. *Hyperion International Journal of Econophysics & New Economy*, 129–140.

Kang, J., & Im, Y. (2021). Competition for TECHNOLOGY HEGEMONY between the U.S., & China from a Geopolitical Point of View. *J-Institute, 6*(1), 20–26. https://doi.org/10.22471/military.2021.6.1.20

Kelly, K. (2017). The Myth of a Superhuman AI. *Wired* [Preprint].

Kim, W.-H., Chen, B., & Hwang, J.-S. (2021). Imitation, technology, and firm performance: The Korean firms case in China. *Journal of Korea Trade, 25*(4), 128–145. https://doi.org/10.35611/jkt.2021.25.4.128

Koc, T., & Ceylan, C. (2007). Factors impacting the innovative capacity in large-scale companies. *Technovation, 27*(3), 105–114. https://doi.org/10.1016/J.TECHNOVATION.2005.10.002

Kuo, T., & Liu, K.-C. (1978). Self-strengthening: The pursuit of Western technology. *The Cambridge History of China*, 491–542. https://doi.org/10.1017/CHOL9780521214476.011

Laursen, K., & Salter, A. (2006). Open for innovation: The role of openness in explaining innovation performance among U.K. manufacturing firms. *Strategic Management Journal, 27*(2). https://doi.org/10.1002/smj.507

Lee, J. (2021). *Mapping China's place in the global semiconductor industry*. https://merics.org/en/short-analysis/mapping-chinas-place-global-semiconductor-industry. Accessed 2 July 2022.

Lee, J., & Lee, K. (2021). Catching-up national innovations systems (NIS) in China and post-catching-up NIS in Korea and Taiwan: Verifying the detour hypothesis and policy implications. *Innovation and Development, 11*(2–3), 387–411. https://doi.org/10.1080/2157930X.2021.1932062

Lee, K. (2014). *Schumpeterian analysis of economic catch-up*. Cambridge University Press. https://doi.org/10.1017/cbo9781107337244

Lee, K., Gao, X., & Li, X. (2016, December). Industrial catch-up in China: A sectoral systems of innovation perspective. *Cambridge Journal of Regions, Economy and Society*, rsw037. https://doi.org/10.1093/cjres/rsw037

Lee, K., & Kim, B. Y. (2009). Both institutions and policies matter but differently for different income groups of countries: Determinants of long-run economic growth revisited. *World Development, 37*(3). https://doi.org/10.1016/j.worlddev.2008.07.004

Lee, L. (2019). *The art of economic catch-up: Barriers, detours and leapfrogging in innovation systems*. https://doi.org/10.1017/9781108588232

Li, D., Chau, P. Y. K., & Lai, F. (2010). Market orientation, ownership type, and E-business assimilation: Evidence from Chinese firms. *Decision Sciences, 41*(1). https://doi.org/10.1111/j.1540-5915.2009.00261.x

Lin, Y. F. (2017). Industrial policy and China's economic development: A perspective of new structural economics. *Journal of Fudan University, 59*(2), 148–153.

Lin, Y., Qin, Y., & Xie, Z. (2021). Does foreign technology transfer spur domestic innovation? Evidence from the high-speed rail sector in China.

*Journal of Comparative Economics, 49*(1), 212–229. https://doi.org/10.1016/j.jce.2020.08.004

Liu, F. C., et al. (2011). China's innovation policies: Evolution, institutional structure, and trajectory. *Research Policy, 40*(7). https://doi.org/10.1016/j.respol.2011.05.005

Liu, J., & Zhao, H. (2021). Privacy lost: Appropriating surveillance technology in China's fight against COVID-19. *Business Horizons, 64*(6), 743–756. https://doi.org/10.1016/j.bushor.2021.07.004

Liu, X., et al. (2017). Beyond catch-up—Can a new innovation policy help China overcome the middle income trap? *Science and Public Policy, 44*(5), 656–669. https://doi.org/10.1093/scipol/scw092

Liu, X., Li, X., & Li, H. (2016). R&D subsidies and business R&D: Evidence from high-tech manufacturing firms in Jiangsu. *China Economic Review* [Preprint]. https://doi.org/10.1016/j.chieco.2016.08.003

Liu, Y. (2008). The construction of pro-science and technology discourse in chinese language textbooks. *Language and Education, 19*(4), 304–321. https://doi.org/10.1080/09500780508668683

Li, W., Li, H., & Li, H. (2016). Innovation incentives or tax shield? A study of the tax preferences of high tech enterprises. *Science Research Management, 37*(11). http://journal26.magtechjournal.com/Jwk3_kygl/EN/abstract/abstract11193.shtml. Accessed 1 July 2022.

Li, W., & Zheng, M. (2016). Is it substantive innovation or strategic innovation?—Impact of macroeconomic policies on micro-enterprises' innovation. *Economic Research Journal, 51*(4), 60–73.

Li, Y. (2017). *Innovation pathways in the Chinese economy* (Doctoral dissertation, Georgia Institute of Technology). http://hdl.handle.net/1853/59127

Lundvall, B. (1992). *National innovation system, toward theory of innovation and interactive learning*. Pinter Publisher.

Lundvall, B. Å., & Rikap, C. (2022). China's catching-up in artificial intelligence seen as a co-evolution of corporate and national innovation systems. *Research Policy, 51*(1), 104395. https://doi.org/10.1016/J.RESPOL.2021.104395

Luong, N., Arnold, Z., & Murphy, B. (2021, March). Understanding Chinese government guidance funds. *Center for Security and …* [Preprint]. https://cset.georgetown.edu/wp-content/uploads/CSET-Understanding-Chinese-Government-Guidance-Funds.pdf

Luo, Y., & Tung, R. L. (2018). A general theory of springboard MNEs. *Journal of International Business Studies*. https://doi.org/10.1057/s41267-017-0114-8

Lu, Q. (2000). *China's leap into the information age: Innovation and organization in the computer industry*. Oxford University Press.

Mansell, R., & Steinmueller, W. E. (2020). *Advanced introduction to platform economics*. Edward Elgar Publishing.

McKinsey\&Company. (2017, December). *Digital China: Powering the economy to global competitiveness*. https://www.mckinsey.com/%7B~%7D/media/McKinsey/Global

MERICS. (2018). *Serve the people: Innovation and IT in China's social development agenda*. MERICS Papers on China [Preprint], (6).

Metcalfe, J. S. (1998). *Evolutionary economics and creative destruction* (1st ed.). Routledge. https://doi.org/10.4324/9780203275146

Ministry of Foreign Affairs of PRC. (2016). *No Title, China's Position Paper on the Implementation of the 2030 Agenda for Sustainable Development*. https://www.fmprc.gov.cn/mfa_eng/topics_665678/xjpdmgjxgsfwbcxlhgcl70znxlfh/t1357701.shtml

Mulloy, P. (2019). Coerced tech transfer: The heart of the China problem. *The American Prospect*. https://prospect.org/world/coerced-tech-transfer-heart-china-problem/. Accessed 1 July 2022.

National Bureau of Statistics of China. (2021). *Communiqué on National Expenditures on Science and Technology in 2020*.

National Development and Reform Commission (NDRC). (2020). *The national development and reform commission answers reporters' questions on the "Guiding Opinions on Expanding Investment in Strategic Emerging Industries and Cultivating Strengthened New Growth Points and Growth Poles"*. http://www.gov.cn/zhengce/2020-09/24/content_5546618.htm. Accessed 2 July 2022.

National Security Commission on Artificial Intelligence (NSCAI). (2018). *Immigrant founders of the fortune 500*. http://startupsusa.org/fortune500/. Accessed 2 July 2022.

National Security Commission on Artificial Intelligence. (2021). *Final Report*. https://www.nscai.gov/wp-content/uploads/2021/03/Full-Report-Digital-1.pdf. Accessed 2 July 2022.

Nelson, R. R. (Ed.). (1993). *National innovation systems: A comparative analysis*. Oxford University Press.

Normile, D. (2018). China narrows U.S. lead in R&D spending. *Science*, *362*(6412), 276–276. https://doi.org/10.1126/science.362.6412.276

OECD. (2019). *Gross domestic spending on R&D (indicator)*. https://doi.org/10.1787/d8b068b4-en

OECD. (2021a). *FDI regulatory restrictiveness index*. www.oecd.org/investment/fdiindex.htm. Accessed 10 May 2018.

OECD. (2021b). *Main science and technology indicators, Volume 2021 Issue 1*. https://doi.org/10.1787/eea67efc-en. Accessed 1 July 2022.

OECD. (2021c, March). *R&D tax incentives: China, 2021* (pp. 1–4). OECD.

OECD/Eurostat. (2005). *Oslo Manual: Guidelines for collecting and interpreting innovation data. The measurement of scientific and technological activities, Oslo Manual*.

Office of the U.S. Trade Representative. (2019). *2019 Report to the congress on China's WTO compliance*.

O'Keeffe, K., Somerville, H., & Yang, J. (2021, November 12). *U.S. companies aid China's bid for chip dominance despite security concerns*. https://www.wsj.com/articles/u-s-firms-aid-chinas-bid-for-chip-dominance-despite-security-concerns-11636718400. Accessed 2 July 2022.

O'Meara, S. (2019). AI researchers in China want to keep the global-sharing culture alive. *Nature*. https://doi.org/10.1038/d41586-019-01681-x

Pereira Cabral, B., Lage de Sousa, F., & Canêdo-Pinheiro, M. (2020). Assessing the impacts of innovation barriers: A qualitative analysis of Brazil's natural resources industry. *Resources Policy, 68*. https://doi.org/10.1016/j.resourpol.2020.101736

Pfeffer, J., & Salancik, G. R. (2003). *The external control of organizations: A resource dependence perspective*. Stanford University Press.

Piperopoulos, P., Wu, J., & Wang, C. (2018). Outward FDI, location choices and innovation performance of emerging market enterprises. *Research Policy, 47*(1). https://doi.org/10.1016/j.respol.2017.11.001

Poo, M. M. (2019). Culture and history of Chinese science. *National Science Review, 6*(4), 607. https://doi.org/10.1093/NSR/NWZ074

Prahalad, C. K., & Mashelkar, R. A. (2010). Innovation's holy grail. *Harvard Business Review, 88*(7–8), 134–141.

Ray, J., et al. (2016, October). China's industrial and military robotics development. *Research Report Prepared on Behalf of the U.S.-China Economic and Security Review Commission* [Preprint].

Renda, A. (2019). *Artificial intelligence: Ethics, governance and policy challenges*. CEPS Task Force.

Reuters. (2021). *China seeks better cross-border control of big data with new plan*. Reuters. https://www.reuters.com/article/china-regulation-data-idCAKBN2IF09S. Accessed 2 July 2022.

Romer, P. M. (1994). The origins of endogenous growth. *Journal of Economic Perspectives, 8*(1), 3–22. https://doi.org/10.1257/JEP.8.1.3

Rothwell, R. (1992). Successful industrial innovation: Critical factors for the 1990s. *R&D Management, 22*(3). https://doi.org/10.1111/j.1467-9310.1992.tb00812.x

Rühlig, T. (2021). *The shape of things to come: The race to control technical standardisation*. Beijing.

Saiidi, U. (2019). *Chinese foreign direct investment to the US falls in 2018: Data, data show*. CNBC. https://www.cnbc.com/2019/01/15/chinese-foreign-direct-investment-to-the-us-falls-in-2018-data.html. Accessed 1 July 2022.

Sapkota, P., & Bastola, U. (2017). Foreign direct investment, income, and environmental pollution in developing countries: Panel data analysis of

Latin America. *Energy Economics, 64*. https://doi.org/10.1016/j.eneco.2017.04.001

Schmidt, E. (2020). *I used to run google. Silicon Valley could lose to China. We can't win the technology wars without the federal government's help*. https://www.nytimes.com/2020/02/27/opinion/eric-schmidt-ai-china.html. Accessed 1 July 2022.

Schneider, J. (2021a). *China's chip industry: Running faster but still falling behind*. https://rhg.com/research/china-chips/. Accessed 1 July 2022.

Schneider, J. (2021b). *DiDi's troubles, Tweets of the week (Corruption, Waluigi+Mao, Fish Hugging, Which Ministry Works the Hardest?)*. China Talk. https://chinatalk.substack.com/p/didis-troubles-tweets-of-the-week. Accessed 2 July 2022.

Schneider, J. (2021c). *Labs over fabs: Support the future, not the past*. https://chinatalk.substack.com/p/labs-over-fabs-support-the-future?s=r. Accessed 2 July 2022.

Schneider, J. (2021d). *Will China hit back on chips?* China Talk. https://chinatalk.substack.com/p/will-china-hit-back-on-chips?s=r. Accessed 2 July 2022.

Schniederjans, D. G. (2017). Adoption of 3D-printing technologies in manufacturing: A survey analysis. *International Journal of Production Economics, 183*, 287–298. https://doi.org/10.1016/j.ijpe.2016.11.008

Schumpeter, J. (1934). The theory of economic development—An inquiry into profits, capital, credit, interest, and the business cycle. *Regional Studies*.

Schumpeter, J. A. (1942). Creative destruction from capitalism, socialism and democracy (1942). *Democracy* [Preprint].

Select USA. (2017). *Foreign Direct Investment (FDI): China*. International Markets Fact Sheets. https://www.selectusa.gov/servlet/servlet.FileDownload?file=015t0000000LKM1

Shelton, R. D. (2008). Relations between national research investment and publication output: Application to an American Paradox. *Scientometrics* [Preprint]. https://doi.org/10.1007/s11192-008-0212-2

Sheng, J., Amankwah-Amoah, J., & Wang, X. (2019). Technology in the 21st century: New challenges and opportunities. *Technological Forecasting and Social Change, 143*, 321–335. https://doi.org/10.1016/j.techfore.2018.06.009

Smith, N., & Thomas, E. (2017). Regional conditions and innovation in Russia: The impact of foreign direct investment and absorptive capacity. *Regional Studies, 51*(9), 1412–1428. https://doi.org/10.1080/00343404.2016.1164307

Solow, R. M. (1957). Technical change and the aggregate production function. *The Review of Economics and Statistics, 39*(3), 312. https://doi.org/10.2307/1926047

State Council of the People's Republic of China. (2006). *The national medium- and long-term program for science and technology development (2006–2020)—An Outline*.

State Council of the People's Republic of China and The Central Committee of Communist Party of China (CPC). (2016). 国家创新驱动发展战略纲要 *(National Strategy of Innovation-Driven Development)*.

Steiber, A. (2018). *Management in the digital age: Will China surpass Silicon Valley?* SpringerBriefs in Business Management. https://doi.org/10.1007/978-3-319-67489-6

Sun, Y., & Cao, C. (2020). The dynamics of the studies of China's science, technology and innovation (STI): A bibliometric analysis of an emerging field. *Scientometrics, 124*, 1335–1365. https://doi.org/10.1007/s11192-020-03500-x

Sykes, A. O. (2021). The law and economics of 'forced' technology transfer and its implications for trade and investment policy (and the U.S.-China Trade War). *Journal of Legal Analysis*. https://doi.org/10.1093/jla/laaa007

Szczygielski, K., et al. (2017). Does government support for private innovation matter? Firm-level evidence from two catching-up countries. *Research Policy, 46*(1), 219–237. https://doi.org/10.1016/j.respol.2016.10.009

Szopik-Depczynska, K., Cheba, K., & Wiśniewska, J. (2020). Innovation, R&D and user-driven innovation activity in R&D Departments in Poland. The multi-criteria analysis. *Procedia Computer Science, 176*, 2705–2713. https://doi.org/10.1016/j.procs.2020.09.290

Tambosi, S. S. V., Gomes, G., & Amal, M. (2019). Organisational learning capability and innovation: Study on companies located in regional cluster. *International Journal of Innovation Management, 24*(6). https://doi.org/10.1142/S1363919620500577

Teixeira, A. A. C. (2014). Evolution, roots and influence of the literature on national systems of innovation: A bibliometric account. *Cambridge Journal of Economics, 38*(1), 181–214. https://doi.org/10.1093/cje/bet022

*The Economist*. (2021). Europe is now a corporate also-ran. Can it recover its footing? https://www.economist.com/briefing/2021/06/05/once-a-corporate-heavyweight-europe-is-now-an-also-ran-can-it-recover-its-footing. Accessed 2 July 2022.

The Ministry of Commerce, the National Bureau of Statistics and the State Administration of Foreign Exchange. (2021). *Statistical Bulletin of China's Outbound Direct Investment in 2020 (2020年度中国对外直接投资统计公报)*.

Tsinghua University—Research Centre for Chinese Technology Policies (清华大学中国科技政策研究中心). (2018, July). *China AI Development Report 2018 (中国人工智能发展报告)*.

UNCTAD. (2021). World investment report 2021|UNCTAD. *United Nations Conference on Trade and Development* [Preprint].

U.S.-China Economic and Security Review Commission. (2020). *2020 Report to Congress of the US-China Economic and Security Review Commission*. https://www.uscc.gov/sites/default/files/2020-12/2020_Annual_Report_to_Congress.pdf. Accessed 1 July 2022.

Varas, B. A., et al. (2020, September). *Government incentives and US competitiveness in semiconductor manufacturing* (pp. 1–32). Semiconductor Industry Association.

Wang, F., & Zhu, D. (2021). The influence of industrial policy on innovation in startup enterprises: An empirical study based on China's GEM listed companies. *Complexity*. https://doi.org/10.1155/2021/9650741

Wang, H., & Miao, L. (2016). *China goes global: How China's overseas investment is transforming its business enterprises*. Palgrave Macmillan.

Wang, Y., et al. (2014). Foreign direct investment spillovers and the geography of innovation in Chinese regions: The role of regional industrial specialization and diversity. *Regional Studies, 50*(5), 805–822. https://doi.org/10.1080/00343404.2014.933800

Webster, G., Creemers, R., Triolo, P., & Kania, E. (2017). *Full translation: China's "New Generation Artificial Intelligence Development Plan"*. https://www.newamerica.org/cybersecurity-initiative/digichina/blog/full-translation-chinas-new-generation-artificial-intelligence-development-plan-2017/

Wei, S.-J., Xie, Z., & Zhang, X. (2016). From "Made in China" to "Innovated in China": Necessity, prospect, and challenges. *Journal of Economic Perspectives*. https://doi.org/10.3386/w22854

Wilhelm, M., & Dolfsma, W. (2018). Managing knowledge boundaries for open innovation—Lessons from the automotive industry. *International Journal of Operations and Production Management, 38*(1), 230–248. https://doi.org/10.1108/IJOPM-06-2015-0337

WIPO. (2021). *Global Innovation Index 2021: Tracking innovation through the COVID-19 crisis*. Geneva. https://www.wipo.int/edocs/pubdocs/en/wipo_pub_gii_2021.pdf

World Bank. (2022). *Eurostat-OECD PPP programme, World Development Indicators database*. https://data.worldbank.org/indicator/NY.GDP.MKTP.PP.CD?locations=CN. Accessed 1 July 2022.

World Intellectual Property Organisation (WIPO). (2022). *World Intellectual Property Report 2022*. https://www.wipo.int/publications/en/details.jsp?id=4594&plang=EN. Accessed 2 July 2022.

Wu, J., Ma, Z., & Zhuo, S. (2017). Enhancing national innovative capacity: The impact of high-tech international trade and inward foreign direct investment. *International Business Review, 26*(3), 502–514. https://doi.org/10.1016/j.ibusrev.2016.11.001

Wyne, A. (2020). How to think about potentially decoupling from China. *Washington Quarterly, 43*(1). https://doi.org/10.1080/0163660X.2020.1735854

Xia, L., & Zhao, L. Y. (2012). "市场换技术"方针的历史演变 [Historical evolution of the "Trade Market for Technology" strategy]. 当代中国史研究 *[Contemporary China History Studies], 19*(2), 27–36.

Xin, K., et al. (2019). R&D intensity, free cash flow, and technological innovation: evidence from high-tech manufacturing firms in China. *Asian Journal of Technology Innovation, 27*(2), 214–238. https://doi.org/10.1080/19761597.2019.1635894

Yakob, R., Nakamura, H. R., & Ström, P. (2018). Chinese foreign acquisitions aimed for strategic asset-creation and innovation upgrading: The case of Geely and Volvo Cars. *Technovation*, 70–71. https://doi.org/10.1016/j.technovation.2018.02.011

Yang, J., & Al-Sayed, R. (2022). Barriers to radical innovation in research institutions in China. *International Journal of Innovation Science*. https://doi.org/10.1108/IJIS-04-2021-0075

Yano, G., & Shiraishi, M. (2022). Innovation spillovers between domestic firms in China. *Emerging Markets Finance and Trade, 58*(4), 1042–1060. https://doi.org/10.1080/1540496X.2021.1926978

Yip, G. S., & McKern, B. (2016). China's next strategic advantage: From imitation to innovation. *Asian Pacific Economic Literature*. https://doi.org/10.1142/S1363919616800025

Yu, F. (2013). Government R&D subsidies, political relations and technological SMEs innovation transformation. *iBusiness, 05*(03). https://doi.org/10.4236/ib.2013.53b022

Yu, Y., Yu, J., & Pan, X. (2017). Governance and the China innovation economy. *Asia-Pacific Journal of Regional Science, 1*(1), 63–84. https://doi.org/10.1007/s41685-017-0013-9

Zeng, J. (2021). China's artificial intelligence innovation: A top-down national command approach? *Global Policy, 12*(3), 399–409. https://doi.org/10.1111/1758-5899.12914

Zenglein, M. J., & Holzmann, A. (2019). *Evolving Made in China 2025: China's industrial policy in the quest for global tech leadership*, *Merics*.

Zeng, S., & Zhou, Y. (2021). Foreign direct investment's impact on china's economic growth, technological innovation and pollution. *International Journal of Environmental Research and Public Health, 18*(6), 1–25. https://doi.org/10.3390/ijerph18062839

Zero2IPO. (2019). *Report China's Government Guidance Funds in 2019, From 'Large Scale Blossom' to 'Intensive Cultivation'* [2019年我国政府引导基金由"遍地开花"到"精耕细作"].

Zero2IPO. (2020). *Report on performance evaluation of Chinese government guidance funds 2020* [2020年中国政府引导基金绩效评价研究报告].

Zhang, D., et al. (2021). *2021 AI Index Report* (pp. 1–222). https://aiindex.stanford.edu/report/

Zhang, H., & Shi, J. (2011). On the technical efficiency of new product in Chinese provincial industry. *Economic Research Journal, 1*, 83–96.

Zhang, W., et al. (2022). Experimentalist governance in China: The National Innovation System, 2003–2018. *Journal of Chinese Governance, 7*(1), 1–26. https://doi.org/10.1080/23812346.2021.1934328

Zhang, X., & Daly, K. (2011). The determinants of China's outward foreign direct investment. *Emerging Markets Review, 12*(4), 389–398. https://doi.org/10.1016/j.ememar.2011.06.001

Zhang, Y. (2021). The regional disparity of influencing factors of technological innovation in china: Evidence from high-tech industry. *Technological and Economic Development of Economy, 27*(4), 811–832. https://doi.org/10.3846/tede.2021.14828

Zhang, Y., & Zhou, Y. (2015). *The source of innovation in China: Highly innovative systems*. Palgrave Macmillan.

Zhou, W., & Fang, M. M. (2021). Subsidizing technology competition: China's evolving practices and international trade regulation. *Washington International Law Journal, 30*(3), 470–544.

Zhou, X., et al. (2021, February). Technological innovation and structural change for economic development in China as an emerging market. *Technological Forecasting and Social Change, 167*, 120671. https://doi.org/10.1016/j.techfore.2021.120671

Zhu, H. (Susan), et al. (2019). Home country institutions behind cross-border acquisition performance. *Journal of Management, 45*(4). https://doi.org/10.1177/0149206317699520

Zou, L., Cao, X. Z., & Zhu, Y. W. (2021). Research on regional high-tech innovation efficiency and influence factors: Evidence from Yangtze River Economic Belt in China. *Complexity*. https://doi.org/10.1155/2021/9946098

# Index


**A**

advanced economies, 18, 92
aerospace, 6, 46, 130, 140
Africa, 45, 82
Alibaba, 47, 64, 69, 100, 101, 104, 118, 119, 121, 131
Alipay, 22, 45
Alphabet, 50, 111
Amazon, 110, 117, 131, 132
Ant Financial, 81
Apple, 116
applied research, viii, 17, 61, 62, 67, 69
artificial intelligence (AI), viii, 4, 7, 11, 12, 41, 47, 49, 52, 67, 81, 92, 95, 109, 110, 117, 120–124, 127, 130, 131, 133, 134, 136, 139–141, 144, 145
Asia, 45, 82, 90, 93, 117
automobiles, 67, 76, 77, 95, 131
autonomy, vii, 42, 49, 53, 54, 132, 145

**B**

Baidu, 47, 64, 81, 117, 118, 121
Baidu, Alibaba and Tencent (BAT), 67, 77, 80, 101, 103, 110, 115, 123, 132
basic research, 9, 17, 60–62, 67, 142, 150
Beijing, 36, 37, 49, 52, 117, 121, 136, 141
Biden, Joe, 48, 93
big data, 41, 100, 102, 118
breakthrough innovation, 11, 24, 69, 129, 132, 136, 139, 140
Business Expenditure on Research and Development (BERD), 62–66, 69, 142
business R&D, 64, 131
ByteDance, 64, 118, 123, 145

**C**

catching-up, ix, 11, 18
catch-up, 12, 18, 88, 113
central government, viii, 8, 9, 40–44, 68, 114, 122, 142




A. Băzăvan, *China's National Innovation System*, https://doi.org/10.1007/978-981-97-3266-1

Chinese government, viii, 3, 8, 10, 11, 41, 43, 46, 47, 50, 53, 54, 59, 62, 64, 76–78, 83, 84, 98, 113, 120, 140, 142
chip design software (EDA), 96, 97, 99
chips, 46, 99, 100, 111, 119, 122, 123, 145
core technologies, 3, 5, 6, 8, 12, 41, 47, 122, 130, 139, 140, 145
Corporate innovation system (CIS), 21, 117
COVID-19, 11, 100, 127, 144
culture, 20, 94

D

Daimler, 76, 81
decentralisation, 8, 43
decentralised approach, 9
defence, 6, 48, 135, 136
Deng Xiaoping, 2, 39, 74
developed economies, 1, 2, 80, 143
developing countries, 2, 18, 22, 23
developing economies, ix
Didi Chuxing, 81, 104, 119
diffusion, 16, 19, 20, 43, 143
domestic companies, 4, 6, 23, 47, 54, 73, 75, 77, 83, 92, 96, 118, 120, 133, 136, 146

E

e-commerce, 21, 22, 103, 117, 121, 131
economic growth, vii, 1–3, 7, 10, 18, 19, 22, 26, 60, 92, 95, 139
education, 19–22, 87, 88, 91, 105, 113, 144, 152
emerging economies, 18, 21, 22, 26
energy, 3, 80, 127, 132, 145
entrepreneurship, 7, 16, 45
environmental, 3, 91, 137
Europe, 1, 2, 22, 79, 82, 94, 100, 113, 121, 123, 124, 129, 132, 133, 145
European Union (EU), vii–x, 5, 7, 9, 11, 12, 37, 47, 51, 53, 59, 60, 62, 65, 66, 69, 75, 84, 88, 90, 93, 96, 104, 110, 113, 116, 118, 120, 123, 124, 128–137, 142, 145, 146
experimental development, viii, 61, 62, 69
experimentalism, 8
experimentalist governance, 41, 43
experimentation, viii, ix, 8, 40, 42, 43, 45, 122, 124, 134, 145, 146

F

Facebook, 50, 110, 132
fintech, 21, 22, 119
fiscal, 9, 41, 62, 64, 142
foreign companies, viii, 3, 10, 35, 50, 73, 77, 78, 83, 84, 92, 117, 131, 132, 143
foreign direct investment (FDI), ix, 7, 10, 11, 18, 22, 35, 73, 76, 78, 79, 81, 82, 112
foreign investment(s), 36, 44, 77, 79, 141
foreign suppliers, 8, 41, 47, 96, 113, 141
foreign technology, vii, 10, 22, 39, 49, 53, 123, 143, 145
Freeman, C., 16, 19–21
Fudan University, 88, 117, 121, 144
Fujian, 43
fundamental R&D, 3
funds-of-funds (FOF), 68

G

5G, 41, 52, 83, 102, 127, 145
Geely, 65, 81

Genworth Financial, 81
Go Global, 79, 83, 143
Google, 6, 110, 116, 117, 131, 132
government direct funding, 50, 62, 63, 69
government funding, 10, 24, 25, 64
government guidance funds (GGFs), 67, 68, 115, 142
grants, 124, 130, 133, 134, 147, 150
Gross Domestic Product (GDP), 2, 3, 5, 9, 44, 60–64, 69, 100, 103, 130, 140
Gross Expenditure on Research and Development (GERD), 46, 50, 59–63, 65, 69, 129
Guangdong, 43, 121
Guangzhou, 36, 37

H

Hage, J., 17
Hangzhou, 36, 121
high-speed rail (HSR), 49, 76, 83
high-speed railways, 4
high-speed trains, 47
high-tech, 4, 41, 44–46, 48, 49, 69, 80, 92, 105, 131, 142
Hong Kong, 5, 37, 44, 79, 82
Huawei, 44, 48, 64–66, 69, 75, 81, 83, 92, 96, 97, 118

I

imitation, ix, 10, 21, 22, 74, 83, 143
inbound FDI (IFDI), ix, 10, 11, 73, 78, 143
India, 2, 5, 110
industrial output, 46, 50, 51, 119
industrial policy(ies), vii, 1, 10, 19, 39, 41, 47, 52, 68, 140, 141
industrial revolution, 39, 110, 112, 141
industrial system, 4, 10, 19, 73, 75, 83
information and communication technology (ICT), 4, 11, 21, 47–49, 52, 65, 66, 69, 77, 94, 95, 100–102, 106, 118, 119, 131, 141
information technology, 20, 46, 101, 102
innovation governance, 41–43, 140
innovation outputs, 4, 23, 69
integrated circuit, 46, 96, 97
intellectual property (IP), 11, 87, 91, 92, 105, 137, 140
intellectual property rights (IPR), viii, 48, 77, 78, 91, 92, 105
internationalisation, 22, 73, 87, 90, 112, 118, 119, 140, 143
international relations, 6, 7, 11
international system, 12
international trade, 4, 10
Internet of Things (IoT), 41, 127, 145
investment funds, 41, 59

J

Japan, 1, 2, 5, 20, 47, 60, 62, 65, 78, 88, 90, 96, 110, 130, 131, 134, 141
joint ventures (JVs), 10, 74, 76, 78, 79, 117, 143

K

Korea, 2, 5, 62, 69, 78, 88, 96, 130, 141

L

leapfrogging, 21, 22, 26
Learning Models, 21, 22, 26
Li, Keqiang, 60, 61

local authorities, 42, 122, 144
local governments, 36, 42, 43, 68, 141, 142

M
Made in China 2025, 4, 41, 46, 49, 52, 96
manufacturing, ix, 1, 3, 4, 21, 44, 46, 49, 73, 74, 77, 96, 99, 102, 105, 113, 121, 132, 136, 139
Mao Zedong, 39
mergers and acquisitions (M&As), ix, 81, 82, 84, 143, 144
Metcalfe, J.S., 21
microchips, 96
microprocessors, 49
Microsoft, 110, 116, 117, 131
middle-income trap, 1, 3, 19
military, 6, 48, 95, 109–111, 113, 124, 135, 136, 146
Ministry of Industry and Information Technology (MIIT), 100–102, 114
Ministry of Science and Technology (MOST), 47, 59
MLP, 46, 140
multinational companies (MNCs), 10, 23, 44, 62, 74–76, 78, 83, 92, 105, 121, 143

N
national innovation system (NIS), vii, viii, 1, 2, 6–8, 11, 12, 15, 19–22, 24, 26, 35, 36, 38, 40–42, 62, 73, 84, 87, 91, 94, 105, 111–113, 117, 119, 122, 124, 140, 143
new energy vehicles (NEV), 4, 46, 131, 139
new materials, 46, 127, 145

O
Obama, Barack, 48, 97
open door policy, 3
opening-up, 2, 3, 10, 39, 40, 45
outbound FDI (OFDI), 10, 11, 23, 37, 73, 77–80, 82, 84, 143, 144
outbound foreign investment, viii, 82
outbound investments, 7, 11, 23, 79, 83, 84, 118, 144

P
party, 36, 50, 53
patent(s), viii, 4, 11, 24, 44, 65, 87, 93, 94, 105, 140
pilot project, 43
pilot projecting, viii, ix, 43, 134
private equity (PE), 115, 121, 142
productivity, ix, 18, 19, 23, 45, 100, 101, 143
protectionist, 8, 54, 84, 113, 141
publications, 4, 35, 123
public funding, 9, 10, 24, 96, 115, 130, 142
public opinion, 42, 79, 82, 122
public perception towards technology, viii, 7, 11, 87, 94, 105, 140
public policies, viii, 7, 15, 26, 35, 42, 95, 122, 140

R
R&D expenditure, 9, 23, 36, 37, 46, 59, 61, 62, 64–67, 69, 140
R&D funding, 9, 46, 62, 69
R&D funding intensity, 5
R&D intensity, 9, 23, 60, 61
R&D investment, 9, 23–25, 129, 139
R&D spending, ix, 60–62, 65, 124, 130, 131, 146
radical innovation, ix, 10, 17, 23, 74

regions, viii, ix, 2, 8, 9, 18, 35, 40, 43, 51, 54, 66, 93, 95, 121, 134, 136, 140, 145

S

Schumpeterian economics, 19
Schumpeter, Joseph, 15, 16, 18, 36
security, 1, 6, 11, 40, 48, 49, 52, 76, 77, 82, 95, 96, 102, 104, 109, 112, 122, 127, 128, 131, 134, 137, 141, 145
semiconductor(s), ix, 6, 11, 47–49, 95–100, 106, 111, 121, 127, 130, 131, 133, 140, 141, 145
semiconductors manufacturing equipment (SME), 96, 97, 99
Shanghai, 36, 37, 44, 117, 121
Shenzhen, 36, 37, 44, 45, 121, 136
Singapore, 44, 81, 90, 119
special administrative regions (SARs), 42, 43
Special Economic Zones (SEZs), 43, 45
standardisation, 51–53, 142
standards, 51, 52, 77, 83, 134, 137, 139, 142
standards developing organizations (SDOs), 52, 53
start-up ecosystem, 9, 68, 69, 131
start-up scene, 67, 130
State Council, 3, 46, 52, 101, 103, 116
state-owned enterprises (SOEs), 24, 25, 50, 52, 64, 74, 104, 117, 144, 148
Stock Market, 37
structured uncertainty, viii, 8, 43
subnational administrations, 41
subnational authorities, viii, 7–9, 41–43, 47
subnational governments, 42, 89, 102, 144
subsidies, viii, 8, 10, 25, 48, 50, 59, 63, 67, 78, 98, 121, 129, 130, 133, 144, 147, 149, 150
supply chains, vii, 5, 10, 11, 19, 47, 49, 67, 87, 95, 97, 105, 110, 123, 128, 131, 139
surveillance, 48, 109, 122, 145
sustainable development, 2, 15, 112

T

Taiwan, 79, 95, 96, 98
Taiwan Semiconductor Manufacturing Company (TSMC), 95, 97
talent, ix, 5, 6, 11, 12, 23, 44, 53, 73, 75, 78, 83, 84, 87, 89–91, 105, 111, 112, 121, 122, 124, 133–137, 140, 144–150, 152
tax deductions, 130
tax incentives, 25, 41, 59, 62–64, 69, 116
technical standards, 51–53
technological independence, 49, 131, 146
technological self-sufficiency, 47
technology independence, ix, 54
technology independency, 47
technology spillover(s), ix, 10, 22, 75, 117, 143, 144
technology transfer(s), 10, 48, 76–78, 92, 143
telecommunication(s), 46, 83, 92, 94, 113, 135
Tencent, 47, 64, 81, 82, 100, 101, 104, 118, 119, 121, 131
TikTok, 118, 119, 123
Torch Programme, 45
trade policy, 6, 47, 127
trade tensions, 5, 47, 49, 98
trade war, 48
Trump, Donald, 43, 77, 97
Tsinghua University, 88, 110, 111, 114, 120, 144

## U

United Kingdom of Great Britain and Northern Ireland (UK), 20, 132, 136

United States of America (USA), vii, ix, 1, 2, 5, 6, 8, 9, 11, 20, 22, 37, 47–49, 51, 59, 60, 62, 65, 66, 69, 75, 77, 79–82, 84, 88–90, 93–101, 104, 105, 110–112, 115, 117, 118, 120, 121, 123, 128–132, 134–136, 144, 145

universities, 5, 6, 16, 37, 88, 90, 105, 113, 119, 121, 133–135, 144, 147–150

## V

VC funds, 37, 67, 80, 115, 130, 142
venture capital (VC), 3, 37, 67–69, 81, 111, 115, 117, 119, 121, 124, 139, 142
Volkswagen, 76
Volvo, 81

## W

WeChat, 22, 104

## X

Xi Jinping, 40, 47, 49, 89, 113, 141

## Z

ZTE, 44, 48, 64, 75, 97

# GPSR Compliance

*The European Union's (EU) General Product Safety Regulation (GPSR) is a set of rules that requires consumer products to be safe and our obligations to ensure this.*

*If you have any concerns about our products, you can contact us on ProductSafety@springernature.com*

In case Publisher is established outside the EU, the EU authorized representative is:

Springer Nature Customer Service Center GmbH
Europaplatz 3
69115 Heidelberg, Germany

The manufacturer's authorised representative in the EU is Springer Nature Customer Service Centre GmbH, Europaplatz 3, 69115 Heidelberg, Germany. If you have any concerns regarding our products, please contact ProductSafety@springernature.com

Printed and bound by CPI Group (UK) Ltd, Croydon, CR0 4YY

01/10/2026

02225924-0001